Supply Chain Excellence

Third Edition

Supply Chain Excellence

A Handbook for Dramatic Improvement Using the SCOR Model

Third Edition

**Peter Bolstorff
and Robert Rosenbaum**

⁂AMACOM

American Management Association

New York • Atlanta • Brussels • Chicago • Mexico City
San Francisco • Shanghai • Tokyo • Toronto • Washington, D.C.

This publication is designed to provide accurate and authoritative information in regard to the subject matter covered. It is sold with the understanding that the publisher is not engaged in rendering legal, accounting, or other professional service. If legal advice or other expert assistance is required, the services of a competent professional person should be sought.

Various names used by companies to distinguish their software and other products can be claimed as trademarks. AMACOM uses such names throughout this book for editorial purposes only, with no intention of trademark violation. Individual companies should be contacted for complete information regarding trademarks and registration.

SAP, AcceleratedSAP, and R/3 are the trademark(s) or registered trademark(s) of SAP AG in Germany and in several other countries; SCOR is a registered trademark in the United States and Europe; DCOR and CCOR are trademarks of the Supply Chain Council; ProcessWizard is a trademark of Xelocity Limited; Microsoft, Excel, Access, Office Communicator, and Lync are registered trademarks of the Microsoft group of companies; Minitab is a registered trademark of Minitab, Inc.; GoToMeeting is a registered trademark of Citrix Online, LLC; and Cisco is a registered trademark of Cisco Systems, Inc.

Library of Congress Cataloging-in-Publication Data

Bolstorff, Peter.
    Supply chain excellence : a handbook for dramatic improvement using the SCOR model / Peter Bolstorff and Robert Rosenbaum.—3rd ed.
        p.   cm.
    Includes bibliographical references and index.
    ISBN 978-0-8144-1771-3 (HC : alk. paper)
    ISBN 978-0-8144-3753-7 (PB : alk. paper)   1. Business logistics—Management.   I. Rosenbaum, Robert (Robert G.)   II. Title.
HD38.5.B64   2012
658.7—dc23

                                    2011026467

About AMA
American Management Association (www.amanet.org) is a world leader in talent development, advancing the skills of individuals to drive business success. Our mission is to support the goals of individuals and organizations through a complete range of products and services, including classroom and virtual seminars, webcasts, webinars, podcasts, conferences, corporate and government solutions, business books, and research. AMA's approach to improving performance combines experiential learning—learning through doing—with opportunities for ongoing professional growth at every step of one's career journey.

Printing number

10   9   8   7   6   5   4   3   2   1

Dedications

Peter:

To my wife, Cary, with whom
I have spent 25 amazing years!

Bob:

To my wife, Barb, a source of partnership,
support, and so much more.

Contents

Preface

Using experience gained from 35 supply chain improvement projects, the first edition of *Supply Chain Excellence* (AMACOM, 2003) was an instruction manual for anybody who sought a rigorous and proven methodology for systematic improvement in supply chain performance, using a cross-industry reference called the Supply Chain Operations Reference (SCOR®) model.

The second edition (AMACOM, 2007) updated the method and approach based on an additional 30 engagements with companies that completed multiple projects and integrated deliverables and analytical concepts in continuous improvement methods using Six Sigma and Lean. The second edition also expanded the process scope to encompass the entire value chain—including product design and customer sales processes. This was done with addition of two new frameworks: the Design Chain Operations Reference (DCOR) and Customer Chain Operations Reference (CCOR) models.

The third edition (AMACOM, 2012) updates the tips and techniques based on experience with 30 more projects—a majority of which were completed by companies that have not only used the approach multiple times but also extended its application in three areas: global alignment, small business schedule, and utilization of SAP® software. As with previous editions, updated and expanded key concepts, steps, tasks, outcomes and behaviors are illustrated in the context of a composite case: Fowlers Inc. Specific additions for this third edition include:

- A refined, more efficient project timeline conducive to global and small business use
- Simplified deliverables that better utilize resources and sharpen focus on performance
- Integration of SAP functionality and system implementation processes into the Fowlers examples
- A section on effective global supply chain strategy
- SCOR Level 4 examples of sales and operations planning and master scheduling
- Updating to SCOR 10.0

Acknowledgments

We would like to acknowledge those companies and individuals who have directly (and indirectly) contributed to this book. First and foremost, we would recognize Ralph Maltese. Ralph has been a colleague on past projects, a subject matter expert for SAP functionality and implementation methodology and business practices in general, and a great friend. Without his insight, contributions, and energy, this edition would have been nearly impossible. Second, we would recognize our supply chain colleagues at Amway, the United States Air Force, the Diverse Manufacturing Supply Chain Alliance (DMSCA), Kohler Co., McCormick and Co., and Nortech Systems, who again committed themselves to the approach—bringing ideas and suggestions that challenged us to make *Supply Chain Excellence* easier, more effective, and more relevant. This third edition is another tribute to them. Specific thanks are in order to George Calvert and his team, as well as to Gerry Phillips, Jane McCarthy, Jeff Akers, David Burton, Jim Radin, Denise Layfield, Mike Degen, Pete Kucera, Davor Grgic, Joe Hnilicka, Gerrard Gallenberger, Oliver Kaestner, and the Supply Chain Operating System (SCOS) team.

Third, we would like to recognize Xelocity, eKNOWtion, and SCE Africa, who as partners have adopted the approach, added their expertise and regional perspectives, and successfully delivered project after project—including the application of the ProcessWizard tool—

to all but one continent on the planet. Specific thanks go to Ikhlag Kashkari, Michael Diver, Douglas Kent, and Jolanda Pretorius.

Fourth, we would thank the Supply Chain Council. Its dedication to improving SCOR (introducing 10.0) and to introducing new tools, like DCOR 2.0, CCOR 1.0, the SCORmark survey, and a SCOR People section, has provided the platform from which all of us experiment. Thanks are in order for the Council's permission to use the process models in this project and for its commitment to education through the SCOR Implementation Workshop. We would particularly like to recognize Joe Francis and Caspar Hunsche.

Fifth, we would acknowledge those who have translated *Supply Chain Excellence* into Korean (collaborated work by Northeast Asia Logistics Innovation Cluster, Bumhan Publishing, 2007); German (Dr. Rolf Poluha, Springer Verlag Berlin Heidelberg, 2007); and Japanese (Japan Business Create Co., Ltd., Japan Institute of Plant Maintenance).

Supply Chain Excellence

Third Edition

Introduction

During dinner at a recent supply chain conference, a senior executive asked me about the latest thinking on how to improve global supply chain performance. Without hesitation I whispered, "Have you tried the sardine strategy yet?" Anticipating the puzzled look, I continued: "For schooling fish, staying together is a way of life. Fish in a school move together as one."

Photo by Ihoko Saito/Toshiyuki Tajima/Dex Image/Getty Images.

For schooling fish, the "move as one" trait is innate. Separation means likely death. For global supply chains, misalignment—failure to move as one—means poor service, high inventory, unexpected costs, constrained growth and profits, and loss of market share.

The purpose of this book is not to convince anyone of the importance of supply chain management (SCM). That case has been well made many times in many industries since the first edition of *Supply Chain Excellence* was published in 2003. Even then, only the first two paragraphs of the book's introduction argued the "why" of SCM. The rest was about the "how."

While using the methodology of this book on roughly 100 supply chain projects around the world, "how" has been further refined into a series of processes to achieve the highest levels of supply chain alignment: moving as one.

Here are the 15 most common contributors to supply chain misalignment. Which ones are relevant to you?

Fifteen Common Causes of Misalignment

1. Lack of a Technology Investment Plan

A chief information officer deflected pressure to install the latest and greatest advanced planning system—making the case that simply having state-of-the-art tools was not a good enough reason to put her entire company into the kind of upheaval that such implementations create. As she watched the rapid evolution of web-based applications, event management tools, and demand-driven advanced planning systems, she found herself without a clear technology investment plan that supported the company's business strategy.

2. Little or No Return on Investment (ROI)

A company bought its Enterprise Resource Planning (ERP) package during the vendor's end-of-quarter push to meet sales goals. The deal included all the latest add-ons—things like customer relationship management, transactional processing, advanced supply chain planning, event management, and web portals providing self-service for customers and suppliers. Now the executive team is looking for an answer to a deceptively difficult question: When will a return on investment start to show up in the earnings statement?

3. Isolated Supply Chain Strategies

Three executive vice presidents—for sales, marketing, and operations—assembled their own well-articulated strategies for developing supply chain competence within their departments. Then they invested in application technology, manufacturing processes, and product development—all with measurable success. Now what's missing is a comprehensive blueprint that combines their individual efforts to drive profit and performance across the entire company.

4. Competing Supply Chain Improvements

A company's top executive for SCM assembled a dozen of his brightest managers for a structured brainstorming process—resulting in a list of 45 high-priority projects. But when the managers began implementation, the results were not encouraging. General managers were being asked to support multiple initiatives that used many of the same financial, human, and technical resources. Goals seemed in conflict. They needed to align their objectives and prioritize projects to make good use of the available resources.

5. Faulty Sales and Operations Planning

The vice president of operations for one of the companies had serious cash-to-cash problems and declining customer satisfaction—all resulting from raw materials shortages, mismatched capacity, poor forecasting, and inventory buildup. The challenge was to address the planning and forecasting issues and put the balance sheet back in shape.

6. Failure to Meet Financial Commitments

A company's CEO promised the board of directors that he would improve earnings per share. An analysis of competitors' balance sheets and income statements indicated that the company's direct and indirect costs were out of line, and that its cash-to-cash cycle was too long. The leadership was charged with identifying the right mix of improvements to obtain a predictable result that would satisfy shareholders. The CEO's credibility then was at stake.

7. Lack of Support and Specialized Expertise

The director of a new supply chain solutions team needed a proven method for evaluating and implementing projects. That meant being able to show documented examples of its use, and evidence that it was both scalable and repeatable. Then she would have to sell the method throughout the organization—which would require executive references and easy, low-cost access to the method itself. Finally, she would have to develop a team that could use the model to deliver early successes.

8. Mismatch Between Corporate Culture and ERP

As the ERP implementation wore on and business processes were increasingly automated at one of the organizations, things suddenly started to go wrong. The project leader had a pretty good idea why: The company was organized in rigid, vertical functions that directed AS IS practices. But the ERP system was essentially horizontal, organized by transaction flow for purchase orders, sales orders, forecasts, master data, and so on. How could the corporate culture shift from functional management to process management?

9. Underutilization of Existing Technology

A vice president of administration was being pressured by her colleagues to replace a two-year-old transactional system with a new, name-brand system offering advanced supply chain planning. But the ROI analysis just wasn't adding up. A more detailed investigation revealed that not all of the business leaders were complaining. In fact, the vice president found a direct correlation between a business leader's satisfaction and the effort he or she had exerted to learn the system. Those who were least satisfied didn't handle implementation very well and as a consequence were utilizing few of the available modules. The challenge was to motivate business leaders to use existing functionality better.

10. Vaguely Defined Goals

The executive team achieved consensus that it would differentiate the company through a strategy of operational excellence. The other choices had been customer intimacy and product innovation. Now that the decision was made, the team had to define—at more tactical levels—the characteristics of an operationally excellent supply chain.

11. Impact of Mergers and Acquisitions

The executive teams from companies that had been acquired or were purchasing others needed the acquisition to go smoothly and yield short-term synergies. The challenge was how to leverage efficiencies in material flow, technology platforms, work and information flow, and capacity in the due diligence, integration, and stabilization stages of the merger.

12. Mismanagement and Poor Standardization of Business Processes

Five years after a "successful" ERP implementation, a company found pieces of chaos at different levels of its organization. Fifteen plants opted to turn off select pieces of the system functionality in the name of continuous improvement and leaning out their processes. Three business units independently opted to redefine how date fields were used by customer service to promise-date orders for their customers. Corporate logistics added a transportation optimization tool that subordinated the promised ship date to efficient truck load. And finally, business rules to manage planning master data were changed, ignored, or forgotten by new employees, who did not have the benefit of the original training.

The net result was poor delivery performance, extended order cycle times, and seemingly routine feast-or-famine capacity mismatches to demand. After a disastrous performance review by the company's largest retail account, the executive team members finally realized that they needed to get a handle on defining and managing supply chain process performance . . . at their level.

13. Extension from Supply Chain to the Value Chain

One company's operating committee issued the difficult directive to simultaneously improve quality and reduce cost in manufacturing. It challenged the supply chain executive with some equally difficult improvement pairings: support the increased pace of new-product rollouts while making material acquisition more efficient; support increased sales productivity while making presale and postsale customer service more effective; make global distribution more flexible while increasing the efficiency of warehouse and transportation costs; and implement planning for customer supply chains while improving internal planning efficiency. The challenge with competitive global manufacturing and sophisticated information exchange is that the improvement pairings move beyond the four walls of the company and include more than just supply chain processes. Executives need to define the concept of "value chain" processes and figure out how to improve them.

14. Running Out of Ideas for New Improvement Projects

After five years of using the annual "brainstorming" technique, a company's Lean Sigma executive steering team concluded that corporate impact on operating income had peaked. With all efforts seemingly aimed at inventory, many project scopes were competing for the same resources and had conflicting metric impact (supply chain cost versus service level improvement). Projects were moving further and further away from having legitimate strategic impact, and the proximity of the projects still seemed to be manufacturing. The steering team's challenge was to more effectively and efficiently identify and scope projects to solve more than just manufacturing issues.

15. An Organization That Defies Effective and Efficient Supply Chain

"We've got five business units, six high-level profit and loss statements, two headquarters, four global regions, 26 regional distribution centers, 18 plants, the requirement to implement collaborative planning, forecasting, and replenishment with our largest accounts, and about 5,000 active suppliers. We need a buildup to one unit forecast that supports the corporate financial plan *and* a set of supply chain plans to support the regional service levels and cost commitments. How do we staff this thing?" There is no more to be said about the challenge here.

Why Supply Chain Excellence?

Ultimately, one or more of these performance issues will inflict enough pain that the enterprise takes action. The question is how to do that without disrupting other areas where things are going well—how to move globally as one. Put another way, how to act like a school of sardines.

The content of the third edition of *Supply Chain Excellence* is refined by 30 additional project experiences (now more than 90 in total). It also has been enriched with more practices that have helped global supply chains move as one, with special emphasis on processes and practices in the SAP environment, including:

- Effective integration with global supply chain strategy
- Techniques for global organizational supply chain design
- Effective cross-references with software tools
- Project implementation case studies
- Quick assessments focused solely on smaller-scale performance analysis

As with the first and second editions, this book follows the progress of one company, Fowlers Inc., toward supply chain excellence. It is intended as a working handbook for using SCOR (the Supply Chain Operations Reference model) as a tool to help leaders at every step as they undertake supply chain initiatives. It is structured on a week-by-week project timetable, providing achievable action plans to navigate through the steps of a SCOR project.

Specifically, each chapter focuses on a week's worth of work conducted in face-to-face, remote, or classroom meetings with follow-up assignments (or "homework," which many clients have learned to love). Included are sample deliverables, summaries of tasks, tables, and figures to illustrate the step-by-step processes. An important note about Fowlers Inc.: It is not a real company, and the Fowlers employees are not real people. Fowlers is a compilation of circumstances found in a variety of projects. The purpose was to provide a textbook case study that addresses the broadest range of issues, while maintaining continuity to help readers follow the logic of the SCOR approach from beginning to end.

CHAPTER 1

The Supply Chain Operations Reference Model

> **The Cross-Industry Standard for Supply Chain**

Peter Bolstorff was introduced to the Supply Chain Operations Reference (SCOR) model in the fall of 1996 when he became part of a newly formed corporate "internal consulting" team for Imation, which had just been spun off from 3M. He's been using the SCOR model in supply chain improvement project work ever since. He was a delegate at the first conference of the Supply Chain Council, and has remained active in the Council, involved in the process of improving SCOR and teaching others how to use it. In fact, the Supply Chain Council adopted *Supply Chain Excellence* as the core text for its SCOR Project implementation workshops globally.

So he's heard all the questions. Among those most frequently asked are these: What is the Supply Chain Council? What is SCOR? How do I use SCOR? What is the value to my organization? How do I learn more about SCOR?

The Supply Chain Council

The Supply Chain Council (www.supply-chain.org) is an independent not-for-profit corporation formed in 1996 as a grassroots initiative to develop a supply chain process model. Among those involved at the start were individuals from such organizations as Bayer; Compaq; Procter & Gamble; Lockheed Martin; Nortel; Rockwell Semiconductor; Texas Instruments; 3M; Cargill; Pittiglio, Rabin, Todd & McGrath (PRTM); and AMR Research, Inc. In all, 69 of the world's leading companies participated in the council's founding. Its mission today is to perpetuate use of the SCOR model through technical development, research, education, and conference events. By the end of 2010, the council's technical community had released nine subsequent versions of SCOR, providing updates to process elements, metrics, practices, and tools. SCOR 10.0 also incorporates a "People" standard for describing skills required to perform tasks and manage processes.

The council has about 1,000 corporate members worldwide, with chapters in Australia/New Zealand, Latin America, Greater China, Europe, Japan, Southeast Asia, and South Africa. Membership is open to any organization interested in applying and advancing principles of supply chain management. In 2010 there were four tiers of membership: global, standard, small business, and nonprofit.

The SCOR Framework

SCOR combines elements of business process engineering, metrics, benchmarking, leading practices, and people skills into a single framework. Under SCOR, supply chain management is defined as the integrated processes of PLAN, SOURCE, MAKE, DELIVER, and RETURN—from the supplier's supplier to the customer's customer (Figure 1-1). The Supply Chain Council Web site, www .supply-chain.org, has an online overview of the model that can be viewed both by members and nonmembers.

Here's what's included in each of the SCOR process elements:

> **PLAN:** Assess supply resources; aggregate and prioritize demand re-
> quirements; plan inventory for distribution, production, and ma-

Figure 1-1. The SCOR Framework.

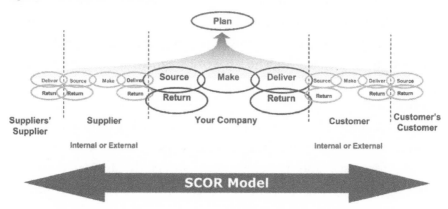

terial requirements; and plan rough-cut capacity for all products and all channels.

SOURCE: Obtain, receive, inspect, hold, issue, and authorize payment for raw materials and purchased finished goods.

MAKE: Request and receive material; manufacture and test product; package, hold, and/or release product.

DELIVER: Execute order management processes; generate quotations; configure product; create and maintain customer database; maintain product/price database; manage accounts receivable, credits, collections, and invoicing; execute warehouse processes including pick, pack, and configure; create customer-specific packaging/labeling; consolidate orders; ship products; manage transportation processes and import/export; and verify performance.

RETURN: Defective, warranty, and excess return processing, including authorization, scheduling, inspection, transfer, warranty administration, receiving and verifying defective products, disposition, and replacement.

In addition, SCOR includes a series of ENABLE elements for each of the processes. These processes focus on management around performance, information, policy, inventory strategy, capital assets, transportation, physical logistic network, regulatory, and other management processes to enable the planning and execution of supply chain activities.

SCOR spans all customer, product, and market interactions surrounding sales orders, purchase orders, work orders, return authorizations, forecasts, and replenishment orders. It also encompasses material movements of raw material, work-in-process, finished goods, and return goods.

The SCOR model includes three levels of process detail. In practice, *Level 1* defines the number of supply chains, how their performance is measured, and necessary competitive requirements. *Level 2* defines the configuration of planning and execution strategies in material flow, using standard categories such as make-to-stock, make-to-order, and engineer-to-order. *Level 3* defines the business processes and system functionality used to transact sales orders, purchase orders, work orders, return authorizations, replenishment orders, and forecasts. *Level 4* process detail is not contained in SCOR but must be defined to implement improvements and manage processes. Advanced users of the framework have defined process detail as far as *Level 5*, software configuration detail.

Value Chain Processes

In 2004, the Supply Chain Council introduced two new frameworks that help piece together more of the detailed mosaic of enterprise value chains (Figure 1-2). The Customer Chain Operations Reference (CCOR 1.0) model defines the customer part of the value chain as the integration of PLAN, RELATE, SELL, CONTRACT, SERVICE, and ENABLE processes.

The Design Chain Operations Reference (DCOR 2.0) model

Figure 1-2. Value Chain frameworks.

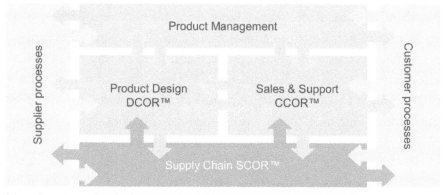

defines the design part of the Value Chain as the integration of PLAN, RESEARCH, DESIGN, INTEGRATE, AMEND, and ENABLE processes.

Chapter 19 will discuss how these process models can be used with SCOR to drive overall value chain performance improvement.

Using SCOR to Drive Supply Chain Improvement

For all its power and flexibility, the SCOR model is still essentially a series of definitions for processes, metrics, and leading practices. Simply having the "dictionary" doesn't do any good for a business. To use SCOR, it is necessary to add effective change management, problem-solving techniques, project management discipline, and business-process engineering techniques. *Supply Chain Excellence* is a handbook on how to use SCOR with a refined five-step formula that has been tested and proven in the course of more than 100 projects on six continents, in ten languages and with six enterprise software systems, incorporating Lean and Six Sigma, growing sales and profits, improving inventory turns, increasing productivity, and making customers happier.

The phases of the *Supply Chain Excellence* approach, as detailed in this third edition of the book, have been refined to support global projects in which units operate more like small business. The refinements have helped reduce the resource and time requirements to develop a project list by 50 percent and have eliminated non–value-added analysis by shifting material, work, and information flow analysis to implementation. We use the same analytical tools but focus only on the scope of each project. The refined steps are as follows:

1. Build organizational support
2. Define project scope
3. Analyze performance
4. Develop project portfolio
5. Implement projects

Build Organizational Support

Chapter 2 examines how to build organizational support for a SCOR project. The chapter explores four important roles: the "evangelist," the person in the company who has the passion, experience, and talent to lead a supply chain project; the "active executive," the individual who is accountable as sponsor of a supply chain project through modeling, influence, and leadership; the "core steering team," which has the champion role to review and approve recommendations and ultimately lead the implementation efforts; and the "design team," which analyzes the supply chain from end to end and assembles recommendations for change.

Define Project Scope

Chapter 3 helps to define and prioritize the organization's supply chains using a combination of data and strategic assessment. One of the primary outcomes from the discovery step is a Project Charter, which helps define a project's scope, approach, objectives, schedule, milestones, deliverables, budget, organization, measures of successes, and communication plan.

Analyze Performance

The analysis stage (Chapters 4 through 7) is where the metrics are defined, data are collected, defects are analyzed, benchmarks are tallied, and performance gaps are calculated. Frequently used SCOR metrics include cash-to-cash cycle time, inventory days of supply, perfect order fulfillment, order fulfillment cycle time, total supply chain management cost, and upside supply chain flexibility. This phase also helps the team to prioritize and balance customer metrics with internal-facing metrics: delivery, reliability, flexibility/responsiveness, cost, and assets.

Develop Project Portfolio

Chapters 8 through 10 describe the analytical steps required to identify a company's preliminary project list. Tasks in this phase include further analysis of metric defects; conducting a brainstorming session; using problem-solving tools such as fishbone diagrams, run charts, and affinity grouping; and working with finance to validate both financial and customer-service improvement commitments.

Implement Projects

Chapters 11 through 18 describe the thirteen steps necessary to implement a project identified in the portfolio. Analytic techniques for this phase include process and geographic mapping, transactional data analysis, leading practice assessment, "staple yourself to an order" interviews, storyboarding, design and test solutions, and the final rollout to the enterprise. This section also discusses effective supply chain strategy as a means to sustain gains and build momentum for future years.

Extend to the Greater Value Chain

Chapter 19 introduces a Value Chain Excellence project roadmap that can be used with any combination of DCOR, CCOR, and/or SCOR process frameworks. Although every project follows the same five steps, the deliverables have been tweaked to accommodate the broader scope of value chain issues, such as product development, sales, postsale service, or engineering changes and product life cycle management.

The Value of a SCOR Initiative

The *Supply Chain Excellence* approach is reliable and predictable with respect to project duration, cost, and benefits. Implementation results across the 100-plus projects for which this approach has been used are consistent:

♦ Operating income improvement, from cost reduction and service improvements in the initial SCOR project portfolio, averaging 3 percent of total sales; depending on how your company compares with benchmark data, it could be as high as 4.5 percent or as low as 1.5 percent. Return on investment of two to six times within twelve months—often with cost-neutral quick-hit projects under way on a six-month timeframe.

♦ Full leverage of capital investment in systems, improving return on assets for fixed-asset technology investments.

♦ Reduced information technology operating expenses through reduced need for customization and improved use of standard system functions.

♦ Ongoing profit improvement of 0.5 percent to 1 percent per year, using continuous supply chain improvement.

CHAPTER 2

Phase 0: Build Organizational Support for Supply Chain Improvement

▶ **Finding the Tipping Point for Change**

Brian Dowell called out of the blue after getting my name from a Google search; his keywords included SCOR, Supply Chain, Metrics, Operational Excellence, and Value Chain. He was looking for some direction for his company, Fowlers Inc., and had enough motivation within the company to justify a visit.

We showed up a week later, and Brian, the company's chief operating officer, gave us a warm greeting. His introductory overview demonstrated Fowlers to be a well-run worldwide manufacturing conglomerate with the seeds of supply chain improvement already in place. "In fact," he said proudly, "we are six months past our SAP® go-live and have closed the books on time each month." But more on that later.

The supply chain action plan had been developed at the division level by David Able, vice president of operations in the technology products group—one of the four operating units. He had pieced it together with just a little background in supply chain management and a whole lot of operating pain at the global level. His efforts had been encouraged by his boss, the division president, who had brought the concept of more integrated global supply chain improvement to the attention of other executives in the company. His last comment in most conversations on the subject went something like, "Not all of the company is on an SAP platform and most of the regions outside North America are *not* figuring out how to improve."

They had become a self-selected "gang" whose common feeling was that although David's ideas would solve some short-term issues, there had to be a way to solve the company's global supply chain problems to move as one at a more strategic level. Figure 2-1 is Fowlers' current organizational chart.

We began the formal meeting in the company's boardroom, with several executives present and a few others in teleconference from around the world. It didn't take much prodding to get this gang to start sharing their thoughts.

"Our products are good for a week, maybe ten days, in the

Figure 2-1. Fowlers' executive-level organizational chart.

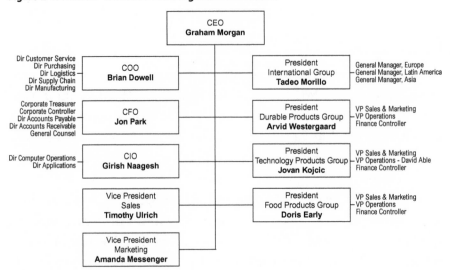

store," said Doris Early, president of the food products group. "We've got to move a lot of product around with a lot of speed. And if regulators were to bring in the label from something we processed six months ago, we need to be able to identify the plant, the line, the day, and the names of everyone on the shift who produced it."

"Our shelf life is short, but not that short," added Jovan Kojcic, David's boss and the president of the technology products group, from an office in Warsaw. "We also have some other things in common with the food group; we buy a lot of commodities. The prices we pay change daily, but our customers won't let us be so flexible. There's seasonality in our sales, and many new products that are harder to forecast—all of which makes it difficult to maintain consistent margins." He added, "We've been challenged to be more flexible in shorter time with less cost and minimal inventory. The experts are telling us that we need to think about how to respond to consumer demand—that is to say, point of sale—more effectively."

Arvid Westergaard, president of the durable products group, spoke up from Sweden: "Our issues are about the rate of improvement. We have tried to address the performance issues in our group through our continuous improvement program. Four years ago, we invested in a Lean Six Sigma program that has trained hundreds of black, green, and yellow belts. We have been disciplined as an executive team managing the project list. We started out quickly with most of the work directed at our manufacturing plants. In the past year, it seems we started to run out of steam; most of our projects now seem to be smaller and smaller in scope. They are smaller in payback too. But we still believe there are big issues to address. So how do we identify a more strategic list? How do we integrate supply chain improvement with Lean Six Sigma?"

Last, Graham Morgan, the chief executive officer, added, "In our strategic planning session cycle in January we—the business presidents and I—asked ourselves, 'How good is our supply chain strategy? What do we need to address as an executive team and what should we delegate to the business units? It seems that our corporate supply chain–related roles are always complaining about the business and vice versa.' It raised the question: How should we organize ourselves for the future and prepare a clear strategic roadmap for supply chain improvement?"

The last conversation was about the SAP implementation. Girish Naagesh, the chief information officer, started off by saying that Fowlers' initial SAP scope was North America. This was to be followed by regional implementations in Europe, Asia Pacific, and everywhere else. He also stated that he and his consulting partners followed the basic AcceleratedSAP (ASAP) Roadmap for implementation (Figure 2-2).

This was the longest discussion of the day; it generally filtered into three streams of dialogue. The first had to do with *getting information* out of the system. Admittedly, there was a gross underinvestment in reporting capability. That, in combination with leadership's stubborn demands about wanting to see the SAP report "exactly like

Figure 2-2. AcceleratedSAP Roadmap for implementation.

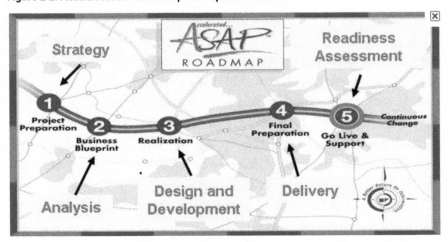

their current legacy reports," left data analysts creating custom Z reports as opposed to developing data warehouse capability. The second stream was the frustration that some of the plants were having around *capacity planning*. The unverified feedback was that the SAP system was adding days of work on the backs of an already stressed team. Lines were either too loaded or not loaded enough, or material was not showing up at the right time to run the schedule, causing unnecessary changeovers. In fact, manufacturing variances were going up. The third stream was concern for a general *increase in inventory* and *decline in customer service*. The embarrassing fact was customers were calling to tell their reps about the late orders, as opposed to the reps calling them.

It all came together as they spoke: products that have short shelf life and short life cycles; disconnected supply chain and product development; price-sensitive customers sold through varied and sophisticated channels with volatility on both ends—demand and supply; a continuous improvement program that needed to be rejuvenated; poor assimilation to SAP processes; and an organization that needed the right focus and alignment.

The executives described how a chosen leader, David Able, had outlined an improvement plan and its main components. They then assigned the plan to their direct reports in other divisions to execute.

Brian wasn't quite ready to admit this at our first meeting, but it was clear what happened: The business-unit leaders at the next level down thought they'd just been briefed on the latest program-of-the-month and, still frustrated with the new system, did very little with the strategy. To placate the executives, they did take some small steps: they identified a few projects, assigned some green belts, and improved a metric here or there—generally at the expense of others. But after three months, Brian pushed Arvid, Jovan, and Doris to join him in looking for an outside perspective. "We can't be the only ones with this dilemma," he said.

Without realizing it, Brian had already taken a few important steps to ensure a successful approach. Selling supply chain management to an organization is tough. It's an educational sell to everyone involved. Not only is the reality of an integrated supply chain complex; everyone has his or her own preexisting ideas of what supply chains are all about, how they fit in with operational strategy, and what to do to fix them.

SCOR, as an industry standard, makes the sell easier because it has gained credibility from a long list of successful case studies, but the model can't sell itself, and it can't teach people who aren't ready to learn. That's why any SCOR project will depend on four key roles in the education process. These are the evangelist, an active executive sponsor, the core members of an executive steering team, and the analytical design team. Without these, you can't hope for a project's success.

The Evangelist

As is the case with any successful SCOR application, the people who brought SCOR to Fowlers started by educating the organization to support the effort. Their first step was to develop an evangelist. This is the person who is best able to learn the SCOR model; who can sell it to upper management; who has the experience to pilot a project and gain early results; and who can become the executive-level project manager, charged with spreading the model throughout the business. If nobody steps up to this role, then a SCOR-based project probably cannot succeed.

The evangelist, who may be self-selected or appointed from above, typically acts as project manager of the first SCOR project.

At Fowlers, David Able, vice president of operations in the technology products group, placed himself into the role of evangelist based on his interest in supply chain integration, his diverse background, and his reputation as an effective, influential leader. He was readily confirmed by Brian Dowell, the company's chief operating officer and the man who would quickly assume the important role of executive sponsor.

The Evangelist's Resume

As the appointed evangelist, David Able had a portfolio of experiences that would help create general understanding of the relationship between financial performance and the central factors of organization, process, people, and technology. Over the course of 15 years at the company, he had demonstrated knowledge of "how things work" and had built a strong foundation of leadership roles. He had participated in a large-scale reengineering effort a few years before, and so had seen the way an enterprise project works. Those who worked for him also confirmed such important qualities as the ability to teach, communicate, resolve conflict, and add humor at just the right time.

Experience

The right evangelist candidate will have the following experience on his or her resume:

Financial Responsibility and Accountability. The former means understanding the details of how cost, revenue, and assets are assembled on a profit and loss statement and balance sheet—and all the financial impacts in real time. The latter means being able to tell the business story behind the numbers. Accountability also means defending executive critique, explaining bad news with confidence, preparing for operations reviews, and having the ability to focus and effectively motivate an entire organization to "hit" a common set of financial goals and objectives.

Aligning Business Goals with Appropriate Strategy. Cascading goals is the art of organizing objectives in such a way that every employee understands the higher levels of success and how day-to-day goals support that success.

Setting the Organizational Learning Pace. This means developing an atmosphere that supports team learning and fosters dialogue among individuals, teams, and departments. In managing the performance of individuals and departments, evangelists understand the day-to-day effort that is required to achieve success.

Multiple Worker Roles. The evangelist will have firsthand experience in a variety of business functions that map to the SCOR Level 1 elements of PLAN, SOURCE, MAKE, DELIVER, and RE-TURN. Leading practices in PLAN—such as sales and operations planning, materials requirements planning, and promotional event forecasting—can come from experiences as a demand planner, forecast analyst, supply planner, and inventory analyst. Leading practices in SOURCE and MAKE—such as Kanban, vendor-managed inventory, rapid replenishment, cellular manufacturing, Six Sigma, total quality management, ISO 9002, to name a few—can come from experiences as a buyer, production superintendent, master production scheduler, and engineer. Leading practices in DELIVER and RETURN—such as available-to-promise, cross-docking, cellular kitting and packaging, and so on—can come from experiences as a customer service representative, transportation analyst, and supervisor for shipping and receiving.

As vice president of operations for one of the operating divisions at Fowlers, David Able had experience with a number of these areas. In addition, his previous participation in a well-run reengineering effort had exposed him to disciplines in four important areas necessary to a supply chain improvement: process mapping, recommendations, justification, and project management.

Natural Talent. The right evangelist candidate will demonstrate the following five talents in his or her daily work:

1. *A Talent for Teaching.* This is part skill and part art. The skill is showing employees how to perform a task, modeling the appropriate skill, guiding them to understanding, and finally letting them try it on their own. The art is a sixth sense that seems to monitor everyone's level of understanding and automatically adjusts the lesson for each individual involved in a project. The ability to generate examples or anecdotes in the context of each individual's understanding can separate the great teachers from the average ones. Good evangelists are effective storytellers.

2. *A Talent for Listening.* It's important to know when to ask clarifying questions and when not to interrupt, further building an understanding of the speaker's point of view. For a successful evangelist, listening and clarifying are more valuable than preaching.

3. *A Talent for Communicating with Executives and Peers.* There are four prerequisites for effective executive communication. The evangelist must:

   ♦ Have earned personal and professional credibility with members of the executive team.

   ♦ Be a subject matter expert.

   ♦ Be able to assemble effective executive presentations.

   ♦ Balance formal group communications (presentations, proposals, meetings) with informal one-on-one communications (lunch, golf, hallway, in private).

4. *A Talent for Using Humor Appropriately.* Every good evangelist has a great sense of humor and can introduce comic relief at just the right moment—whether planned or unplanned. The evangelist doesn't have to be the funniest person in the room;

on a team of 15 people, there will be at least two or three others who can be counted on to help at any time.

5. *A Talent for Conflict Management Among Groups and Peers.* The constraint to successful supply chain projects does not always lie in the technical challenges of material flow and application architecture; it's often in the conflicts that occur between people. Successful evangelists can handle large-group conflicts and individual conflicts—not by quashing them, but by constructively helping one side or both to move toward common ground.

The Active Executive Sponsor

The active executive sponsor represents the leaders in the organization who will sign off on resources needed to make the changes happen. This person has the most to gain or lose based on the success of the project and therefore takes on responsibility to review and approve recommended changes as proposed by the project design team. Behind the scenes, the executive sponsor needs to sell the changes up to the chiefs and down to their managers, eliminate barriers to progress, take ownership of the financial opportunity that comes through improvement, and prepare the organization for implementation.

As with the evangelist, picking the right person is critical. At Fowlers, the obvious choice was Brian Dowell, the chief operating officer and the executive with supervisory responsibility over the directors of planning (PLAN), purchasing (SOURCE), manufacturing (MAKE), logistics (DELIVER and RETURN), and customer service. Organizational role is just one factor.

One gauge of the right executive sponsor uses the scale of "more savings faster" (MF) versus "less savings later" (LL). The choice of MF sounds intuitive, but there are a lot of LL executives in the world; they behave in a manner that slows the rate of improvement and lengthens timeframes. The nature of a project life cycle demands different behaviors at different times from the active executive sponsor. In all cases, the sponsor will be better served by MF behaviors.

Educate-for-Support Behaviors of the Active Executive Sponsor

MF executives can look at their organizations from a process perspective as opposed to seeing them as a collection of individuals grouped by a functional silo. They have experienced the power of process improvement and understand key roles in process management. MF executives have invested personal time learning about the strategic value of supply chain in their respective marketplace. That's why they are comfortable learning new things in a public forum regardless of rank—sometimes setting the capacity for change of the entire organization.

MF executives accelerate the educate-for-support step of a project (often from six months to one year) by encouraging the progress of the evangelist as a SCOR subject matter expert and by facilitating core team buy-in.

LL executives, when in public, seem to know everything—whether they do or not. They depend on individual heroics to make things better. Thus, LL executives need to be sold on the merits of supply chain improvement.

Planning and Organizing Behaviors of the Active Executive Sponsor

In this second step of the project life cycle, the focus is on three essential areas: an understanding of how organizational change occurs, a respect for supply chain complexity, and an effective integration of business resources. The critical output of this step is a project charter that defines project scope, objectives, organization, benefits, and approach. MF executives understand their sponsor role and can articulate a burning platform for change. They learn to look at supply chain performance needs from various perspectives such as organization, process, people, technology, and strategy. MF executives can accelerate the discovery stage by effectively involving business leaders and participating directly in early steps of the project design.

LL executives, on the other hand, short-circuit the discovery work by directing efforts to focus on one or two prescribed metrics, rather than actively engaging business teams to define scope and opportunity. LLs delegate learning about SCOR to subordinates rather than understanding the basic steps of the SCOR Project Roadmap and associated deliverables themselves.

Measures and Strategy Behaviors of the Active Executive Sponsor

At this stage of the project life cycle, important behaviors are respect for the schedule and fueling the fire on the platform for change.

MF executives commit themselves, their evangelists, and their design teams to the detailed, 17-week analyze-and-design process. This process involves two days per week for 17 weeks plus homework for design team members and half a day two times per month plus homework for executive members of the steering team. The project manager will work on the effort full time, and the MF executive sponsor will spend part of each week in oversight and review.

MF executives spend time understanding how actual, benchmark, and other comparative data were gathered, and they accept the completed analysis at face value as a defined opportunity. MF executives begin laying the groundwork for organizational change by initiating regular communication regarding the relative opportunity, the expected changes, and the approximate timing of the project.

LLs skip design team sessions, miss some executive sponsor reviews, and don't put in any personal time. They discount the validity of the data because they don't understand how they were gathered, and they view the analysis as the end of the project—not the beginning.

Design Solutions Behaviors of the Active Executive Sponsor

At this stage of the project life cycle, the focus is on understanding the integrated nature of material, work, and information flow; sparring with the difficulties of designing improvement; and prioritizing change.

To this end, an MF executive sponsor will spend time each week with the design team learning about the basic steps of producing desired material, work, and information and then leverage this knowledge to educate his or her other C-level peers and prepare them for anticipated supply chain changes.

MF executives constructively challenge the design team on assumptions and results, and invest time to understand the scope and sequence of recommended changes. LL executives are only concerned with the "what," not with how key milestone deliverables were built. LLs use a shotgun approach to savings by initiating all projects at the same time and letting the strong survive.

Establishing Core Team Buy-In

Once Brian Dowell was established as the active executive sponsor, he recruited Jovan Kojcic as the business unit sponsor; together they affirmed David Able as the evangelist and project leader, and the three became solely responsible for picking the rest of the people for the steering team.

This group would bear responsibility to review and approve the project as it progressed. The challenge was to build the right mix of leaders who ultimately will determine the supply chain changes that happen.

It's a reality in any corporation that an executive steering team will contain some members who are not going to be helpful and forward thinking. That's why it was so important for Brian, David, and Jovan to hand-select the core of this team—an elite group who would actively power the steering team to provide constructive oversight and help keep the project moving. Leveraging momentum and knowledge gained in David's earlier supply chain strategy discussions, David, Jovan, and Brian picked the steering team to include Tadeo Morillo, president of the international group, and Amanda Messenger, vice president of marketing and a long-time proponent of organizational alignment. They also included Timothy Ulrich, vice president of sales; Girish Naagesh, CIO; Jon Park, CFO; and two executives from the technology products group, the vice president of sales and marketing and the finance controller.

There are four important criteria for the evangelist and executive sponsor(s) to consider as they begin assembling this core group: collective experience, attitude, effective communication skills, and ability to cope well in chaos.

Collective Experience

Experience is measured individually and as a team. In either case, important considerations when forming this group include the following:

Level of Authority. Effective steering teams have members at similar levels of authority within the organization who are willing to assign resources from their own teams to the project design effort and have earned confidence from the senior executive team.

Cross-Functional Relationships. An effective steering team member has built relationships over time instead of leaving a trail of "my way or the highway" casualties. The best contributors have a sense of how the whole business works and have developed cooperative relationships with other functional leaders.

Knowledge Contribution. Depth of historical perspective is important—not only of the business process evolution but also of the organizational response to change. This perspective can be both good and bad; the right steering team members can balance their application of knowledge with the occasionally unavoidable attitude of "we've tried that before."

Attitude

Steering team members don't have to go through a battery of psychological tests to determine whether they have the right attitude, but they should pass three simple ones. First, they should be immune to the "not invented here" syndrome. Second, they should have a controlled and adaptable style of communication. Third, they should be effective learners.

Effective Communication Skills

An effective steering team sets the learning pace of a SCOR project by dictating the effectiveness of the learning environment. It is deliberate about expectations and spells out exactly the type and frequency of feedback it needs to help keep the project moving. The most valued feedback can be categorized as critique, opinion, or clarifying dialogue (team learning). Effective critique assumes that the steering team members understand the material under review, have assembled a list of checking questions for the design team, and are comfortable exploring the logic to check the integrity of the work. Opinion is reserved for forks in the road at which decisions must be made to go forward with the project. Opinion is rendered only after initial dialogue and critique. Clarifying dialogue is as simple as asking questions and discussing work both spontaneously and at planned reviews. The objective is simply to understand the design team's point of view with an open mind.

Ability to Cope Well in Chaos

Many leaders in industry suggest that the closer an organization can get to the edge of chaos without going over, the more it will thrive in today's business environment. Let's not kid ourselves; moving toward the edge of chaos is stressful, so steering team members need an intuitive feel for how close is too close. Process thinking helps set the appropriate distance from the edge. Process thinkers look at performance as the result of the interaction of process steps. They look at an organization from a systems point of view. They can articulate the basic relationships between the supplier inputs (capital, human resources, raw materials), the organization (business processes and functions), the customer (who buys products and services), the competitors (who compete for supplies and customers), and other factors that touch the system. The alternative to a process thinker is a functional thinker who stakes out some territory, builds a big wall, and shuts out the rest of the world. This silo behavior is, at some level, an attempt to avoid chaos, and it is one of the first big changes to be addressed in a SCOR project.

The Fowlers core team rounded out the short list for an executive steering team to include Jon Park, chief financial officer; Tim Ulrich, vice president of sales; and Girish Naagesh, chief information officer.

Picking the Project Design Team

Once the steering team was in place, its first official duty was to pick the right project design team, the group of people who would ultimately spend time analyzing supply chain issues and assembling recommendations for change. As is the case with every other significant initiative, the obvious guideline was to pick "the best and brightest." Experience has proven that four additional factors equally contribute to the quality of project output: problem-solving experience, personality factors, dedication/discipline to task, and access to data.

Problem-Solving Experience

Design teams that have at least one black belt or green belt take the analysis deeper and faster at each project phase than do those without such training. Real experience with certain Lean Six Sigma disciplines will help the team pinpoint root causes of problems, identify effective solutions, and more accurately predict the value of and confidence in improvement recommendations. Particularly useful disciplines include value stream analysis and eliminating the eight areas of waste; Kano, voice of the customer, and force field analyses; calculating cost of poor quality; putting together data collection plans; calculating process sigma levels; using data analysis tools such as Pareto and run charts, histograms, and scatter plots; and using process analysis tools such as SIPOC (suppliers-inputs-process-outputs-customers), value stream, and cross-functional maps.

Personality Factors

There seem to be four personality factors to consider when picking individuals for the project design team. The first scale contrasts *facts* and *feelings*. The *facts* side of the scale describes people who prefer to look just at the numbers and let the data do the "talking," whereas the *feelings* side describes people who look only at the human factors of change. The second scale contrasts *details* and *vision*. The *details* side of the scale describes people who look at situations from the "ground up"; they come to conclusions by putting the pieces together. The *vision* people look at the whole, the big picture, and come to their conclusions by looking at the trends. The third scale contrasts *introvert* and *extrovert*. The *introvert* side of the scale describes people who "think inside" and stereotypically are the quiet ones in groups. The *extrovert* side of the scale describes people who "think out loud" and, right or wrong, will refine their hypotheses in public and can sway a group through verbal skills. *Introverts* gain energy with individual down time, whereas *extroverts* gain energy in the group. The fourth scale is focused on degree of *organization*. This scale contrasts the unorganized on the one side with the highly organized on the other.

Although these personality factors may seem trivial, considering the right mix of people on the team can help avoid two common pitfalls. The first we'll call the Loud Lead. Characterized by *feelings*, *vision*, *extroverts*, and low *organization*, this team talks a good game but will likely not have the details to stand up to executive scrutiny at the end. We'll call the second pitfall Analysis Paralysis. Characterized by *facts*, *details*, *introverts*, and high *organization*, this team always needs more data and often freezes when confronted with executive teams who want a recommendation or decision.

Dedication: Discipline to Tasks

There was a sign that hung in a colleague's office that read, "The reward for good work is more work." As you will come to appreciate, each deliverable in a *Supply Chain Excellence* project helps make a decision; each decision then becomes a part of the next deliverable and so on until the end. It's like learning algebra (I can hear you groaning): You need to understand multiplying and dividing fractions before you can begin to simplify algebraic expressions; if you don't do your homework, it's difficult to move ahead. Likewise, if the team doesn't complete its project homework, it will be ill prepared to make the next decision.

Access to Data

The last thing to consider in selecting your team is access to data. Although this one is fairly self-descriptive, there are several nuances to consider. The first nuance is in regard to data. During each phase of the project, different "cubes" or "tables" will be queried from your information system in an attempt to extract data. This may be in the form of extracts from the production system, a data warehouse, or standard reports. The second nuance is in regard to access. Team members who have access directly or indirectly to the data versus having to submit a data request generally progress faster and more reliably. The third nuance is in regard to analysis. Team members who have knowledge and skill with applications such as Microsoft Excel and Access and Minitab, which allow them to summarize, segment, and otherwise study data, progress faster and more effectively than team members who don't.

Considering each of the four factors, Fowlers assembled the project design team. It consisted of the following:

- Director, Logistics
- Director, Customer Service
- Director, Manufacturing
- Director, Purchasing
- Director, Planning
- Vice President of Sales and Marketing—Food Products Group
- Corporate Controller
- Director, Applications
- David Able—Project Manager
- SCOR Coach

Phase 1: Define Project Scope

> **Planning and Organizing a Supply Chain Excellence Initiative**

Understanding the business reasons for a project and then properly defining its scope are critical steps to a successful launch. The Fowlers executive team had already provided the "go" decision during an on-site briefing on March 11; now the members wanted to know who, what, when, how, and, of course, how much. During the on-site visit the SCOR coach, Brian, Jovan, and David organized web-based conference calls for the week of April 18, which would be used to review Phase 1 deliverables in preparation for the targeted April 25 project kickoff. There are three primary deliverables for Phase 1: (1) the business context summary, (2) a supply chain definition matrix, and (3) an approved project charter. A fourth deliverable in the first week of active project planning is to assemble a complete presentation of information to be used in the project kickoff meeting.

The Business Context Summary

This deliverable is not raw research. It merely collates existing information into a simple reference source for the duration of the project. Most often, the project leader can assemble this in a few hours. To make it easy, start with a checklist of information that needs to be reviewed and summarized to gain a full understanding of (and appreciation for) the business context for supply chain improvement. This information sets the strategic backdrop for supply chain focus and ultimate project scope.

Just as important, though, are the soft benefits of working through the checklist. Involving the business leaders in this process allows them to help set the agenda for the company's supply chain. Getting these important people engaged in the earliest stages of a project has untold value in the change management challenge that all companies face. Understanding their problems, asking for their point of view, and acknowledging their good work goes a long way toward positioning the supply chain as "our thing" versus "a corporate thing."

Assembling the business context summary involves several techniques, including interviewing key stakeholders; scouring the company's Web site and 10K earnings reports; reviewing existing business plans as found in the annual report or any other big-picture document; locating and reviewing competitive analyses that have been conducted internally or by any external entity; and checking out the reviews of financial analysts readily available on such Web sites as hoovers.com, forbes.com, marketguide.com, and reuters.com.

Why all the emphasis on public documents and financial statements? Because the important step you're taking is to create the often-overlooked connection between the company's operations and the real-world business goals as defined by the people who hold the purse strings. There's always a temptation to dismiss investors and bean counters as being out of touch and unrealistic in their demands, but by understanding their goals and creating a bridge to operations, you can establish the basis for high performance at all levels over the long term.

There are four categories of information that make up a business context summary: (1) strategic background, (2) financial performance, (3) internal profile, and (4) external profile.

Strategic Background

Strategic background summarizes the business and its supply chain performance status in a competitive environment relative to competitors.

A *business description* is the first component of the strategic background. It describes the enterprise, its businesses, and a high-level view of the competitive landscape. It's the kind of information that managers should be able to develop off the top of their heads, or by drawing from the dozens of such descriptions that probably reside in brochures, memos, and written documents throughout the organization.

A strengths/weaknesses/opportunities/threats (SWOT) analysis is another source of information that describes the relationship between the enterprise and its marketplace. First, it outlines where the company surpasses direct competitors and where it falls short. Then it projects ways in which it might grow and ways in which it is most likely to be overtaken by competition. On its surface, the SWOT analysis is a simple, four-point document, but for large or diversified organizations, this can become an intricate document with information on each major product or served market.

Another piece of the strategic background is a *value proposition statement*, which describes the competitive value of a business from the customer's point of view. Inherent in a good value proposition is an intimate understanding of the business requirements of each major customer or customer segment.

For example, a company such as Procter & Gamble—with a broad range of consumer products sold primarily through large retailers—might view its relationship with Wal-Mart as deserving its own value proposition, owing to Wal-Mart's particular requirements of suppliers. At another level, it might include Wal-Mart in a "large retailer" value proposition while developing a separate value proposition for its network of distributors that serve grocery chains and small retailers.

Common requirements in a value proposition statement are price, product quality, technical innovation, customized packaging, delivery reliability, order lead time, strategic relationship, and value-added services such as inventory management. Customer value propositions are commonly found directly or indirectly in contracts or service-level agreements.

The last important components of the strategic background document are critical success factors and critical business issues.

Critical success factors describe three to five variables most central to an organization's success. Success is defined as thriving—not merely surviving.

Supply Chain Operations Reference defines the following as critical success factors in supply chain performance: delivery reliability, flexibility and responsiveness, supply chain cost, and effective asset management.

Critical business issues describe how well an organization stacks up against the competition for each of these factors. In each category, the comparative performance level will be rated as disadvantage, parity, advantage, or superior. Sources for these perspectives are not standardized. Good places to look for ratings include annual business plans, quarterly business reviews, annual reports, analyst web casts, 10K reports, and regular company communications.

Fowlers Inc. Strategic Background

Here are highlights of the strategic background for Fowlers from the business context summary developed by the core team.

Business Description

Fowlers Inc. is a billion-dollar conglomerate with worldwide leadership in three businesses: food processing (food products group), optical technology products (technology products group), and business services (durable products group).

Fowlers' food products group is a leading North American supplier of premium fresh and frozen meat products and management services to the food service, retail, online retail, and government sectors. Customers include SuperValu, Wal-Mart, Aramark, Simon Delivers, and thousands of independent grocers and specialty restaurants.

Fowlers' technology products group is one of the world's largest independent suppliers of optical storage products and services such as CD-ROM replication, CD-read and CD-write media, title fulfillment and distribution services, and optical drives. Customers include retail leaders such as Wal-Mart and Target, and category leaders such as Best Buy and Office Depot. Fowlers is also a major supplier to original equipment manufacturers (OEMs) for the personal computer market. Customers include HP, Dell, and Apple.

Fowlers' durable products group was formed by acquiring one of the fastest-growing suppliers of business services, providing personalized apparel, office supplies, and promotional products to more than 14,000 companies and a million individual wearers. By using a dealer franchise as the route delivery mechanism, Fowlers' durable products group has gained a competitive edge by being both knowledgeable and responsive to individual customers in the markets it serves.

SWOT Analysis

Strengths

◆ Superior product quality in the food products group and technology products group.

◆ Low-cost manufacturer status in the technology products group existed before outsourcing several key items in the product line.

◆ The durable products group is perceived as the most responsive in its chosen geographic markets, often delivering products and services on the same day as ordered.

◆ The food products group has a reputation for superior delivery performance, mitigating criticism of its premium prices in a commodity marketplace.

◆ The company's growth in durable goods exceeded expectations.

Weaknesses

◆ Lack of organization-wide assimilation of SAP functionalities.

◆ Delivery performance is inconsistent, especially in the technology products group. Customer complaints in this market are especially high. Because the market visibility is so high, Fowlers is developing a reputation in customers' eyes as being tough to do business with (hard to place an order with, incomplete and incorrect product shipments, inaccurate pricing, poor order status capability, and so on). This is negatively affecting overall satisfaction ratings.

◆ Operating income of the food and technical product groups is eroding because of price pressure and a too-flat cost-reduction slope.

◆ High indirect purchasing costs, despite lower cost of sales.

- The rate of cost increase for customer service is significantly higher than the rate of sales growth.

- Despite sales growth, Fowlers' stock price has taken a hit because of five quarters of poor profit-after-taxes and a bloating cash-to-cash cycle. Analyst criticism focuses on the inability to effectively manage return on assets and integrate profit potential of the business services acquisition.

Opportunities

- Leverage commodity buys across all product groups to improve gross profit.

- Increase effectiveness and efficiency of order fulfillment to improve customer satisfaction and reduce rate of spending on indirect goods and services (those that don't add value to the product being produced).

- Develop more advanced knowledge management capability to add financial value to customers beyond simple price cutting.

- Accelerate market share in the durable products group by introducing an online catalogue for its end customers.

- Leverage cost-to-manufacture leadership in the technology products group to increase profits.

- Improve the efficiency and effectiveness of SAP utilization.

Threats

- Key competitors in the food products group are buying their way into the marketplace with a "lowest list price" strategy.

- Although the overall market for the technology products group has been in a period of decline, the group's market share is declining even faster; customer satisfaction scores put this group in the lowest quartile of performance.

- Price point in the technology products group is getting too low to meet profit targets with the current cost structure.

- Established catalogue apparel companies are potential competitors to the online sales channel being introduced this quarter.

Value Proposition

- The Fowlers Inc. corporate value proposition is summarized by profitable growth as the preferred supplier of customers in targeted markets, driven by exceeding customer requirements.

Critical Success Factors

- Maintaining revenue contribution by increasing the share of the food products group in existing markets.

♦ Driving revenue growth by introducing durable products in the direct-to-consumer market and capturing targeted share.

♦ Achieving overall revenue growth for current year, targeted at 10 percent, and achieving targeted after-tax profit of 7 percent.

♦ Maintaining an image as technical leader in the technology products and food products groups, while improving overall return on assets and aggressively driving cost out of operations.

♦ Improving overall cash-to-cash position.

♦ Optimizing the utilization of SAP modules.

♦ Effectively integrating assets of the new durable products acquisition.

Critical Business Issues

♦ Customer satisfaction from all channels in the technology products group is negatively affecting sales.

♦ Profits are disappearing from the technology and food products groups because of higher direct and indirect costs.

♦ Revenue is targeted to grow to $1.02 billion, but actual projection after nine months is $1 billion.

♦ The durable products group integration of online capability is behind schedule.

♦ Inventory and receivables are expanding, seemingly uncontrollably.

♦ Key customers in the food products group are leaving on the basis of price-only criteria.

Financial Performance

Finding information about a publicly traded company's financial health is as easy as knowing the stock symbol and logging on to hoovers.com. There you can find all the ratio statistics, share price analyses, profit reports, and cash flow data necessary to paint the relative financial picture of a company.

To complete a current-state summary, you'll need information about income and cash position. The income statement contains revenue, cost, and profit data. The balance sheet looks at the right-now cash position by documenting assets and liabilities, including inventory.

In the *business context document*, profit is considered three ways, and each will eventually have its place in planning a supply chain project.

1. *Gross Margin.* Revenue less the cost of goods sold. This picture of profit is usually stated as a percent of total revenue.

2. *Operating Margin* (also referred to as operating income). Gross margin less the costs of sales and administration. In effect, it's the gross margin with all indirect costs removed. It, too, is usually represented as a percent of total revenue.

3. *Economic Profit.* Operating margin less taxes and interest expense. The interest expense is affected by the amount of cash tied up in the business through inventory, receivables, and payables.

By using these industry standards for developing your profit picture, you'll gain a better understanding of how your business fits into its competitive environment—an important piece of the business context summary.

Internal Profile

The internal profile summarizes the physical aspects of the company as well as other performance measures that influence results. The first physical aspect is the *organization chart*. In a publicly held company, you can find this at the top level—usually down to the management of operating units or divisions—in the executive profile section of a corporate-reporting Web site such as hoovers.com. Many companies also share this information, including names, titles, and brief biographies, on their own Web sites. Good starting places for this hunt are the "investor relations" or "about the company" sections of the Web site.

The second physical aspect of the internal profile is *identification of all locations* where the company has operations, including manufacturing sites, warehouses, call centers, technical service centers, return locations, headquarters, and all contract locations, in cases in which these functions are outsourced. This usually takes some work to collect; good sources for this information are the human resources department, the information technology department, the purchasing department, and accounting.

The third physical aspect of the internal business context is a *picture of how the organization is set up* to plan, manage, and execute key performance measures or indicators. For example, Fowlers' organization chart in Chapter 2 (Figure 2-1) reflects that sales, operations, and finance are controlled at both the corporate level and the business unit level. Note that the chief operating officer is at the same hierarchical level as the product group presidents, and that corporate directors have potential for conflict with the vice presidents of operations in each product group.

Most companies have such intricacies built into their reporting structures, and it can lead to overly complicated supply chains and delays in making improvements, as politics of control get in the way.

Fowlers' physical locations contain similar quirks. Each product group manages its own manufacturing locations, but the distribution locations are a mix—some are managed by a product group, and others are managed at the corporate level, demonstrating previous efforts to manage efficiency.

A final element of the internal profile is *how success is measured.* At Fowlers, the project team discovered five key performance indicators that were on the business team's dashboard:

1. Unit Cost
2. Line Item Fill Rate
3. Operating Income
4. Revenue
5. Backorders

External Profile

The external profile lists customers and suppliers in the context of groups that have significant impact on your supply chain. To keep it simple, a customer group is most easily defined by revenue reporting groups. Often these revenue categories are established by business model (i.e., direct-to-consumer, retail, distributor, and OEM).

Likewise, a supplier group is often defined by a major commodity type, such as packaging; tooling; process materials; maintenance, repair, and operations; value-added service; and so on. In both cases, use the 80/20 rule to list the largest customers and suppliers within each group—the 20 percent who get 80 percent of your revenue and material spend.

In Fowlers' case, the customer profile summary yielded seven market/customer channels across all of the product groups:

1. Retail markets, including mass merchant and category killer
2. Distributor/wholesaler markets
3. Direct-to-consumer markets
4. OEM/key account customers
5. U.S. government
6. Home delivery/route sales markets
7. International markets

Fowlers' key supplier profile included raw material commodity types of resins, packaging, electronic components, live produce, hard goods, and apparel. In addition, the supply base included several contract manufacturers that supply apparel, optical media, precooked food, and computer hardware.

The Supply Chain Definition Matrix

Up to this point in the discovery process, the emphasis has been on gathering background pieces of contextual information. Now is the time when the team needs to develop a consensus on how the company's supply chains are defined—a key to defining the project's scope.

In most cases, a supply chain is defined by a combination of product, customer, and geography. It can also include financial reporting and other factors. To create its definition, the team must take into account all points of view and prioritize the importance of each.

Using a supply chain definition matrix can help. (See Table 3-1 for an example of Fowlers' supply chain definition matrix.) The *financial reporting hierarchy* can help identify "major" geographies of the world. For example, if a company has profit-and-loss reports for Europe, Latin America, the Far East, North America, and Japan, then start with five matrices. To start, choose the geography that either has the most sales or serves as the location of the corporate headquarters.

The columns of each matrix represent demand including markets, customers, and/or channels. To build the columns on your first matrix, look at how sales regions are tracked, market channels are organized, and/or customers are segmented. Adding the revenue in each column should yield total revenue for geography represented

Table 3-1. Fowlers' supply chain definition matrix.

Fowlers North America	Customer/Market Channels						
	Retail Markets	Distributor Markets	Direct-to-Consumer Markets	OEM and Key Accounts	Government	Home Delivery	International
Food Products	X	X			X		
Technology Products	X	X	Developing	X	X		X
Durable Products			X			X	X

in the matrix. The lowest level of detail in a column can be an "invoiceable" customer ship-to address.

The rows in the matrix focus on supply, including business lines or products; indirectly the rows address locations (manufacturing and distribution) and suppliers. To build the rows, start with the highest level of business lines or product families or groups. The lowest level of detail in a row is a stock keeping unit (SKU); the rows should total your costs. There may be disconnects between how financial costs are aggregated versus how product families are aggregated. This has been a challenge in nearly every project; the use of more sophisticated data warehouse applications has started to make data more accessible.

Most companies are in the habit of defining their supply chains from a product cost perspective—solely by product and financial definitions, regardless of the customer. They worry about how the product is made, what suppliers are involved, and where the revenues and earnings are credited, but they often don't view a supply chain from the customer point of view. This can potentially derail a project's success. First, customer requirements are key factors that drive supply chain performance; although the gross margin may look good, the net profit might suffer because of high indirect costs to serve. Second, manufacturers are often indiscriminate about what items of the total product line should be available to a particular customer segment. Third, with a product-only view, supply chain costs can evolve to support the delivery requirements of the most aggressive customers—meaning the manufacturer provides superior delivery performance even where it is not needed or valued.

At Fowlers, the number of supply chains could be viewed in more than one way. If defined by product, the company would have three supply chains: food, technology, and durable products. If defined by market or customer channel, there would be seven supply chains: retail/mass merchant, distributor/wholesaler, direct-to-consumer, OEM, U.S. government, home delivery/route sales, and international. Fowlers could also define supply chain by geography, in which case there would be two: international and North America. Last, and the preferred view, Fowlers could say there are eleven mature supply chains as defined by customer and product (count the X's in Table 3-1) with one developing supply chain.

The next step is to collect data for each supply chain in order to help the team determine a project scope. The mantra *Think big, act small, and scale fast* works here. The idea is to pick supply chains for the analytical scope that would be representative of the rest. It is important to understand supply chain performance at a detailed level; knowing more about less and then applying knowledge to the broad implementation scenarios is a good rule of thumb.

Common data elements include revenue (units and $), profit ($ and % margin), inventory (units and $), number of SKUs, and strategic importance. Between the business context document, critical success factors, critical business issues, the definition matrix, and the data, a project scope generally is readily apparent. If not, the project sponsor and steering team become the ultimate decision-makers on scope. By using its data and some good sparring, the Fowlers core team narrowed the scope for its supply chain project to six supply chains as defined by the U.S. sales of technology products and food products:

Food Products

- ♦ U.S. Retail Markets
- ♦ U.S. Distributor Markets
- ♦ U.S. Direct-to-Consumer Markets
- ♦ U.S. Government

Technology Products

- ♦ U.S. Retail Markets
- ♦ U.S. OEM—Key Accounts

Now, with the four basic components of a business context summary complete—strategic background, financial performance, internal profile, and external profile—the team was able to move ahead to the project charter.

The Project Charter

The project charter is created during this phase to establish a complete understanding of the project's scope and objectives. The document helps to align assumptions and expectations among executive sponsors, stakeholders, and team members. The page most project members jump to first is the *schedule*.

On the schedule, there are three project delivery formats.

Format 1. Two days of classroom each week, focused on specific deliverables to be completed as "homework" before the next session.

Format 2. This completes the same deliverables in the same elapsed time, but the classroom sessions are organized by phase rather than week. Figure 3-1 illustrates an alternative Fowlers schedule using the "by phase" approach. This utilizes three days of classroom work followed by two weeks of time to complete the deliverables. This approach makes more productive use of teams with members who must travel (domestically) as part of the project. Until 2009, this was the most frequently used schedule and still is the one recommended for larger and more complex companies.

Format 3 (which was used to outline this third edition of *Supply Chain Excellence*). This is for global business units in smaller regions and for small businesses. It utilizes a remote meeting schedule—with such teleconferencing platforms as GoToMeeting, Cisco, or Microsoft Office Communicator or Lync—to collect data, followed by a week on-site to develop the project portfolio, with implementation to proceed as normal (Figure 3-2). This option reduces the resource

Figure 3-1. Project schedule by phase.

Schedule by Phase	Deliverable	Classroom Dates
	February 1 to May 1, 2011	
Phase 0 **Build Organizational Support**	Supply Chain Excellence Overview with wide audience	February 7, 2011
	SCOR Framework Workshop	February 21, 2011
	SCOR Implementation Workshop	March 21, 2011
	Organizational Briefings	As Needed
	Executive Briefing - GO/NO GO	April 11, 2011
	May 1 to June 7, 2011	
Phase 1 **Define Project Scope**	Business Context Summary	
	Supply Chain Definition Matrix (with data)	
	Project Charter	
	Metric Definitions and Data Collection Plan	
Phase 2 **Analyze Performance**	Defect Data Collection Plan	May 2, 3, and 4, 2011 May 23, 24, 25, 2011
	Defect Analysis	
	Industry Comparison	
	Competitive Requirements	
	Benchmark Data	
	Preliminary Scorecard	
	Scorecard Gap Analysis	
	June 7 to July 22, 2011	
Phase 3 **Develop Project Portfolio**	Staple Yourself to an Order Interviews	June 13, 14, and 15, 2011 July 5, 6, and 7, 2011
	AS IS Process Diagram	
	Defect Analysis Part 2	
	Brainstorm Event and Documentation	
	Preliminary Project Portfolio	
	Opportunity Analysis	
	Assemble and Approve Implementation Project Charters	
	September 1, 2011, to August 31, 2012	
Phase 4 **Implement Projects**	Kickoff Projects	August 15, 16, and 17, 2011
	Develop Performance Baselines for Metrics	
	Conduct Level 3 and 4 Process Gap Analysis	September 1, 2011, to August 31, 2012
	Conduct Leading Practice Assessment	
	Develop TO BE Process Blueprint	
	Assemble Solution Storyboard	
	Approve Solution Design	
	Build and Test Solution	
	Pilot and Verify Solution - Twice	
	Define Process Control Measures	
	Rollout to Project Scope	
	Rollout to Enterprise	

Figure 3-2. Project schedule for global, remote, and/or small business units.

Schedule for Global and Small Business Applications	Deliverable	Classroom Dates
	February 1 to May 1, 2011	
Phase 0 **Build Organizational Support**	Supply Chain Excellence Overview with wide audience	February 7, 2011
	SCOR Framework Workshop	Opportunity
	SCOR Implementation Workshop	Opportunity
	Organizational Briefings	As needed
	Executive Briefing--GO/NO GO	March 11, 2011
	May 1 to July 1, 2011	
Phase 1 **Define Project Scope**	Business Context Summary	
	Supply Chain Definition Matrix (with data)	
	Project Charter	Remote Web-Based Meetings
Phase 2 **Analyze Performance**	Kickoff	April 18
	Metric Definitions and Data Collection Plan	April 25 May 2
	Defect Data Collection Plan	May 9
	Defect Analysis	May 16
	Industry Comparison	May 23
	Competitive Requirements	May 30 June 6
	Benchmark Data	
	Preliminary Scorecard	
	Scorecard Gap Analysis	
	IDEALLY DEDICATED ON-SITE Staple Yourself to an Order Interviews	On-Site
	IDEALLY DEDICATED ON-SITE AS IS Process Diagram	June 13 to 17, 2011
	July 11 to August 1, 2011	
Phase 3 **Develop Project Portfolio**	OPTIONAL AS IS Process Diagram	
	Defect Analysis Part 2	
	Brainstorm Event and Documentation	On-Site
	Preliminary Project Portfolio	July 11 to 15, 2011
	Opportunity Analysis	
	Assemble and Approve Implementation Project Charters	
	Prioritize Implementation Projects	
	August 1, 2011, to July 31, 2012	
Phase 4 **Implement Projects**	Kickoff Projects	
	Develop Performance Baselines for Metrics	
	Conduct Level 3 and 4 Process Gap Analysis	
	Conduct Leading Practice Assessment	Combination On-Site and Remote Management
	Develop TO BE Process Blueprint	
	Assemble Solution Storyboard	August 1, 2011, to July 31, 2012
	Approve Solution Design	
	Build and Test Solution	
	Pilot and Verify Solution--Twice	
	Define Process Control Measures	
	Rollout to Project Scope	
	Rollout to Enterprise	

requirements by about 50 percent through to portfolio development, but increases difficulty building broad awareness and support
for the initiative. In both formats 2 and 3, the majority of material,
work, and information flow analyses have moved to implementation
so that only those processes scoped in the projects are analyzed. The
exception is the staple-yourself interviews needed to assemble the
SCOR AS IS process diagram. In Format 3, there are two options
to document the AS IS. The first dedicates a week in advance of the
brainstorm event; this allows for more thorough understanding of
the process and truly walks the path of the transaction. The second
option is to spend a day going through the build of the SCOR AS
IS process diagram during the brainstorm week. Essentially, all par-
ties are brought into a conference room and the diagram is created
interactively.

The second-most popular page that people turn to in the charter
is the one defining *roles and responsibilities*. Other important components of the project charter are scope; business and project objectives; methodology; deliverables; risks and dependencies; budget;
organization chart; stakeholder expectations; benchmarks; benefit
analysis; critical success factors; and communication plan. Fowlers'
entire project charter is included as the Appendix.

CHAPTER 4

Phase 2: Analyze Performance

▶ **April 18 and 25: Project Kickoff and SCOR Metrics**

The theme for this phase is *analysis*. The candidate list includes the SCOR metrics, performance defects, benchmarks, and "staple yourself to an order" interviews. The key outputs are a scorecard, a set of competitive requirements prioritized by market, and the AS IS SCOR Level 3 process diagram. To kick things off, we start with a kickoff! For the Fowlers team, the kickoff would be a combination of an on-site at the world headquarters in North America and a video conference for international team members congregating at their regional offices. The time zone was the biggest challenge, as team members included Europe, Asia, and North America. The team decided that two kickoff meetings were necessary because Europe was seven hours ahead of central standard time and China was fourteen hours ahead.

The Project Kickoff

There are two ingredients for a great kickoff. First, all the right people have to be a part of it. The audience should include all resources participating on the project, including the steering team, active executive sponsor, project manager, design team, and extended team. If in doubt about a particular person or group, extend the invitation. Providing the big picture to anyone who might participate in the project makes his or her support in gathering details more productive.

At Fowlers Inc., executive sponsors Brian Dowell and Jovan Kojcic invited the seven-member steering team and ten-member design team as identified on the project charter. They also invited extended team resources from information technology, finance, and site operations. In all, 36 people were on the list.

The second ingredient to a great kickoff is having the right materials presented by the right people. The most popular and effective agenda organizes the content into three basic chunks:

1. Setting the strategic context for supply chain improvement, delivered by the executive sponsor(s);

2. Providing a high-level overview of how Supply Chain Operations Reference (SCOR) works, delivered by the coach;

3. Summarizing critical elements of the project charter, delivered by the project manager.

To prepare for the kickoff, Brian Dowell and Jovan Kojcic prepared "state of the business" summaries highlighting the issues related to both Fowlers' and its technology products group's supply chain improvement. Their presentations summarized business plans, strategy, critical success factors, critical business issues, and expectations with regard to supply chain improvement.

The coach prepared the SCOR overview presentation. It provided the big picture of the SCOR Framework, highlighted the *Supply Chain Excellence* project roadmap, and gave examples of the deliverables that individuals across the design and extended teams would be asked to produce in the coming weeks.

Finally, David Able prepared key points from the approved project charter, emphasizing the thing most people were interested in—the schedule. He allowed time for everyone to synchronize their own calendars to the rhythm of the project as outlined in the project charter. There was a big sigh of relief that not all weeks were travel weeks and that the meetings would be rotated among geographic locations. A side benefit of this approach would be to help the team understand regional supply chain challenges and develop more effective relationships. In addition to the schedule, the kickoff provided the opportunity to set remaining stakeholder interviews left over from Phase 1. These would be incorporated into a revised project charter, in the stakeholder expectations section.

Mixing the three ingredients—the business context for supply chain improvement, the SCOR education, and key points of the project charter—built a powerful shared vision of the pace of the project. It aligned expectations for deliverables and outlined the effort required for the various project roles.

Picking a Balanced Set of Supply Chain Metrics

With the kickoff meetings complete during the week of April 18, the real work begins. Typically, the only people online or in the room for the next session are the project manager, coach, and design team; 10 p.m. central standard time seemed to be the best slot for this first design team meeting. The team agreed that one of the three geographies would be inconvenienced each week and that the burden would be rotated. The team selected an online web-conference platform for remote meetings, allowing all to share content from the computer, see a presenter's material, and use Voice over IP (VoIP) to minimize phone bills. The primary order of business is to select the appropriate metrics from the SCOR 10.0 Level 1 Strategic Metric list (Figure 4-1).

Figure 4-1. SCOR Level 1 Strategic Metrics.

Performance Attribute	Performance Attribute Definition	Level 1 Strategic Metric
Supply Chain Reliability	The performance of the supply chain in delivering: the correct product, to the correct place, at the correct time, in the correct condition and packaging, in the correct quantity, with the correct documentation, to the correct customer.	Perfect Order Fulfillment (RL.1.1)
Supply Chain Responsiveness	The speed at which a supply chain provides products to the customer.	Order Fulfillment Cycle Time (RS.1.1)
Supply Chain Agility	The agility of a supply chain in responding to marketplace changes to gain or maintain competitive advantage.	Upside Supply Chain Flexibility (AG.1.1)
		Upside Supply Chain Adaptability (AG.1.2)
		Downside Supply Chain Adaptability (AG.1.3)
		Overall Value At Risk (AG.1.4)
Supply Chain Costs	The costs associated with operating the supply chain.	Supply Chain Management Cost (CO.1.1)
		Cost of Goods Sold (CO.1.2)
Supply Chain Asset Management	The effectiveness of an organization in managing assets to support demand satisfaction. This includes the management of all assets: fixed and working capital.	Cash-to-Cash Cycle Time (AM.1.1)
		Return on Supply Chain Fixed Assets (AM.1.2)
		Return on Working Capital (AM.1.3)

There are three common approaches to selecting the right mix of metrics. The first is to educate the team on the pure SCOR definition, calculation, and collection requirements using Section 2 of the SCOR 10.0 manual. The team can then contrast the SCOR ideal with its current metrics and ultimately achieve consensus on inclusion, exclusion, or modification.

A second approach is to use the generic (non-Fowlers) guides provided by Tables 4-1 through 4-9, where the SCOR 10.0 definitions are compared to practical calculation components built from multiple project experiences.

Table 4-1. Perfect Line Fulfillment. Also called Line Item On Time and In Full.

Perfect Line Fulfillment	Perfect Line Fulfillment is not an official SCOR 10.0 metric. In practice this measure mimics the definition of Perfect Order Fulfillment but judges good or bad at the line level. In a 10-line order where 5 are delivered perfectly and 5 are not, the Perfect Order Fulfillment would be 0% and the Perfect Line Fulfillment would be 50%. This metric has evolved on mixed orders for which products have different commit dates and lead times. Most ERP packages operate at the line level.			
Measurement Component	**Score**	**Data**	**Calculation Component**	**Query Assumptions**
Line On Time and In Full to Customer Request	**68.4%**	10000	Total Number of Customer Lines	Self-explanatory. This is the base for Request, Commit, and Perfect Order. In this case the 100 orders averaged 100 line items.
		7100	Total Number of Lines Delivered On Time to Customer Request Date	Request date is the first request date from the customer at the line level. This includes agreed-to lead times by SKU that may ultimately be part of the customer's master data settings. This also helps differentiate MTO and MTS items that are on the same order.
		6900	Total Number of Lines Delivered In Full	Request quantity is the first request quantity prior to application of Available To Promise (ATP) checks at the line level.
		6840	Total Number of Lines Delivered On Time and In Full to Customer Request Date	Many applications have a difficult time with both on-time and in-full, even by line. Each line needs to be evaluated and considered good if quantity and date are met. As with the order, many companies do not store original request data and, hence, do not calculate this component.
Line On Time and In Full to Customer Commit	**72.0%**	7456	Total Number of Lines Delivered On Time to Customer Commit Date	Commit date is the original confirmation date first given the customer after the first ATP check at the line level. Ideally this is a committed delivery date to the customer. Many companies are not getting receipt data from their carriers and measure to the committed ship date.
		7209	Total Number of Lines Delivered In Full	Commit quantity is the first confirmation quantity after the application of ATP checks at the line level.

(continues)

Table 4-1. (Continued)

Measurement Component	Score	Data	Calculation Component	Query Assumptions
		7199	Total Number of Lines Delivered On Time and In Full to Customer Commit Date	Many applications have a difficult time with both on-time and in-full even by line. Each line needs to be evaluated against original commit and is considered good if quantity and date are met. Many companies do not store original commit data and, hence, always measure against the latest commit, making the metric look like 100%.
Perfect Line Fulfillment	**49.0%**	4899	Total Number of Lines On Time and Complete Meeting 3-Way Match Criteria	This is the most difficult measure to get. The best method is to evaluate your three-way match percentage at the line level via your customers' purchasing or payables systems. Many companies try to measure this metric using the On-Time and In-Full to Commit as a base and then subtract order invoices that have some deduction associated with it.

A third approach is to rely on the SCORmark benchmark that is offered with membership in the Supply Chain Council. It has calculation components, is based on SCOR definitions, and helps assemble necessary benchmark data.

Whether you use the SCOR manual, SCORmark, and/or the reference tables, a good general rule is to *pick at least one metric from each performance attribute.* By day's end, the Fowlers design team had identified metrics for its balanced supply chain scorecard, created a blank scorecard template (Table 4-10 on page 71), and downloaded a SCORmark survey.

Here are the metrics the Fowlers design team identified, which happen to be the most frequently used metrics:

♦ Perfect Order Fulfillment

♦ Order Fulfillment Cycle Time

♦ Upside Supply Chain Flexibility

(*Text continues on page 63*)

Table 4-2. Perfect order fulfillment.

Perfect Order Fulfillment	The percentage of orders meeting delivery performance with complete and accurate documentation and no delivery damage. Components include all items and quantities on-time (using the customer's definition of on-time), and documentation—packing slips, bills of lading, invoices, etc., SCOR 10.0, page 2.1.1. While this definition comes straight out of the book, the calculations below have been adapted through the course of experience.			
Measurement Component	**Score**	**Data**	**Calculation Component**	**Query Assumptions**
Order On Time and In Full to Customer Request	**38.0%**	100	Total Number of Customer Orders	Self-explanatory. This is the base for Request, Commit, and Perfect Order.
		47	Total Number of Orders Delivered On Time to Customer Request Date	Request date is the first request date from the customer. This includes agreed-to lead times by SKU that may ultimately be part of the customer's master data settings.
		50	Total Number of Orders Delivered In Full	Request quantity is the first request quantity prior to application of Available To Promise (ATP) checks.
		38	Total Number of Orders Delivered On Time and In Full to Customer Request Date	Many applications have a difficult time with both on-time and in-full by order. Each line needs to be evaluated; if all of the lines are on-time and in-full to original request, then the order is considered good. Many companies do not store original request data and, hence, do not calculate this component.
Order On Time and In Full to Customer Commit	**40.0%**	47	Total Number of Orders Delivered On Time to Customer Commit Date	Commit date is the original confirmation date first given the customer after the first ATP check. Ideally this is a committed delivery date to the customer. Many companies are not getting receipt data from their carriers and measure to the committed ship date.
		50	Total Number of Orders Delivered In Full	Commit quantity is the first confirmation quantity after the application of ATP checks.
		40	Total Number of Orders Delivered On Time and In Full to Customer Commit Date	Many applications have a difficult time with both on-time and in-full by order. Each line needs to be evaluated; if all of the lines are on-time and in-full to original commit, then the order is considered good. Many companies do not store original commit data and, hence, always measure against the latest commit, making the metric look like 100%.

(continues)

Table 4-2. (Continued)

Measurement Component	Score	Data	Calculation Component	Query Assumptions
Perfect Order Fulfillment	**24.0%**	24	Total Number of Orders On Time and Complete Meeting 3-Way Match Criteria	This is the most difficult measure to get. The best method is to evaluate your three-way match percentage at the order level via your customers' purchasing or payables systems. Many companies attempt to measure this metric using the On Time and In Full to Commit as a base and then subtract order invoices that have some deduction associated with it.

Table 4-3. Order fulfillment cycle time for make-to-stock (MTS).

Order Fulfillment Cycle Time (MTS)	The average actual cycle time consistently achieved to fulfill customer orders. For each individual order, this cycle time starts from the order receipt and ends with customer acceptance of the order, SCOR 10.0, page 2.2.1. The calculations below are adapted for MTS.		
Score	**Data**	**Calculation Component**	**Query Assumptions**
12.0	4	Customer Authorization to Order Entry Complete	In practice, this is the time from initial receipt of the customer order Purchase Order (PO) until the order entry is complete. For EDI transmissions, the clock starts with the system receipt day and time.
	5	Order Entry Complete to Order Received at Warehouse	This is normally from the time of order-entry-complete until the order delivery is created at the warehouse. This is also where future dated orders sit (dwell time).
	1	Order Received at Warehouse to Order Shipped to Customer	This is the time from delivery creation in the warehouse until the order is shipped to the customer.
	1	Order Shipped to Customer to Customer Receipt of Order	This is often referred to as "in transit" time.
	1	Order Received at Customer to Installation Complete	This category is reserved for those having an installation component, and is calculated from receipt of first good until installation complete.

Table 4-4. Order fulfillment cycle time for make-to-order (MTO) and engineer-to-order (ETO).

Order Fulfillment Cycle Time (MTO ETO)	SCOR 10.0 does not have distinct calculations for MTS, MTO, and ETO. This spreadsheet adds two segments to account for manufacturing time. The calculations below are adapted based on project experience.		
Score	**Data**	**Calculation Component**	**Query Assumptions**
39.0	1	Customer Authorization to Order Entry Complete	In practice, this is the time from initial receipt of the customer order Purchase Order (PO) until the order entry is complete. For EDI transmissions, the clock starts with the system receipt day and time.
	5	Order Entry Complete to Start Manufacture	This is normally from the time of order-entry-complete until the production order is created in manufacturing. This is also where future dated orders sit (dwell time).
	21	Start Manufacture to Manufacturing Ship	This is the time from production-order-create to ship to the warehouse or customer.
	2	Manufacturing Ship to Order Received at Warehouse	This is often referred to as "in transit" time.
	1	Order Received at Warehouse to Order Shipped to Customer	This is the time from delivery creation in the warehouse until the order is shipped to the customer.
	4	Order Shipped to Customer to Customer Receipt of Order	This is often referred to as "in transit" time.
	5	Order Received at Customer to Installation Complete	This category is reserved for those having an installation component and is calculated from receipt of first good until installation complete.

⧫ Cost of Goods

⧫ Supply Chain Management Cost

⧫ Inventory Days of Supply—a subset of Cash-to–Cash Cycle Time

Building on the momentum of the kickoff, and knowing that relationships were critical to executing the schedule, Brian and Jovan sponsored a social event to finish up a day that all agreed was one of the best project launches anyone at the company could recall.

Table 4-5. Upside supply chain flexibility.

Upside Supply Chain Flexibility	The number of days required to achieve an unplanned sustainable 20% increase in quantities delivered. Note: 20% is a number provided for benchmarking purposes. For some industries and organizations a different percentage may be appropriate. The new operating level needs to be achieved without a significant increase of cost per unit, SCOR 10.0, page 2.3.1. The calculation below is a practical adaptation using master data. Essentially, it is the stacked lead time of MRP refresh period plus longest sourced component, plus manufacturing schedule wheel plus delivery lead time.		
Score	**Data**	**Calculation Component**	**Query Assumptions**
113.0	30	Re-Plan Planned Lead Time	Often associated with frequency of MRP update.
	33	Source Planned Lead Time	This is the longest component planned lead time for a SKU's bill of materials.
	45	Make Planned Lead Time	This is frequently associated with a SKU's manufacturing scheduling cycle, i.e., weekly, monthly, quarterly, etc., or it can be part of the "replenishment lead time" found in item setup screens for ATP.
	5	Deliver Planned Lead Time	This is also associated with the "replenishment lead time" and refers to the planned time from order entry to ship.

Data Collection and Benchmarks

The next step is the process of assembling a data collection plan. There are generally five important elements to a data collection plan. First and most important is a *definition of the metric*; as stated previously, we recommend using the SCOR definitions as a baseline.

Second, it's necessary to assemble a *segmentation strategy* that will allow for aggregation and desegregation. Examples of segmentation options are by location, customer, item, country, forecast planning family, or commodity. The third requirement is a *data extract query* (taking into account the segmentation strategy) that includes specific data tables and fields from either the live system or data warehouse. The fourth consideration is the *sample size* of the data. Collecting customer order data for perfect order fulfillment and order fulfillment cycle time may use a sample size of the last three months, whereas total supply chain management cost may use a sample size

Table 4-6. Supply chain management cost.

Supply Chain Management Cost	The sum of the costs associated with the SCOR Level 2 processes to Plan, Source, Deliver, and Return, SCOR 10.0, page 2.4.1. This metric was redefined in the 7.0 release. Aside from SCORmark, much of the benchmark data is based on the definition in version 6.1. This worksheet still uses the 6.1 calculation components but is easily mapped to SCOR 10.0.		

Score	% of Revenue	Raw Data (000s)	Calculation Component	Query Assumptions
		$1,000,000	**Revenue**	
	9.8%	$98,011	**Order Management Cost**	
	3.5%	$35,098	Customer Service Cost	Cost centers that have to do with entering customer orders, reserving inventory, performing credit checks, consolidating orders, processing inquiries and quotes.
	2.4%	$23,908	Finished Goods Warehouse Cost	Cost centers that have to do with the storage, receiving, picking, and shipment of finished goods products.
	2.1%	$21,098	Outbound Transportation Cost	Cost centers that have to do with the transportation (all modes, including export) of finished goods products.
21.9%	0.9%	$9,000	Contract and Program Management Cost	Cost centers that have to do with the initiation and ongoing management of customer contracts, including master agreements, compliance to volume-based incentives, and other special incentives.
	0.0%	$0	Installation Planning and Execution Costs	Cost centers that have to do with the planning and execution of product installation at customer-designated locations.
	0.9%	$8,907	Accounts Receivable Cost	Cost centers that have to do with the processing and closure of customer invoices, including collection.
	6.2%	**$61,638**	**Material (Product) Acquisition Cost**	
	1.9%	$18,997	Purchasing Cost	Cost centers associated with the strategic as well as the tactical parts of the purchasing process.
	0.6%	$5,987	Raw Material Warehouse Cost	Cost centers associated with receiving, storage, and transfer of raw material product.
	0.1%	$1,099	Supplier Quality Cost	Cost centers associated with supplier qualification, product verification, and ongoing quality systems for raw materials.

(continues)

Table 4-6. (Continued)

Score	% of Revenue	Raw Data (000s)	Calculation Component	Query Assumptions
	0.3%	$2,987	Component Engineering and Tooling Cost	Cost centers associated with engineering (design and specification) and tooling costs for raw materials, i.e., packaging.
	2.5%	$24,678	Inbound Transportation Cost	Cost centers that have to do with transportation (all modes including import) of raw material and/or purchased finished goods products.
	0.8%	$7,890	Accounts Payable Cost	Cost centers that have to do with processing and closure of supplier invoices, including credit and disputes.
	0.8%	**$8,092**	**Planning and Finance Cost**	
	0.2%	$2,349	Demand Planning Cost	Cost centers allocated to unit forecasting and overall demand management.
	0.5%	$4,509	Supply Planning Cost	Cost centers allocated to supply planning, including overall supply planning, distribution requirements planning, master production planning, and production scheduling.
	0.1%	$1,234	Supply Chain Finance Control Cost	Cost centers in finance allocated to reconcile unit plans with financial plans, account for and control supply chain cost centers, and report financial performance of the supply chain Scorecard.
	3.1%	**$30,806**	**Inventory Carrying Cost**	
	2.6%	$25,609	Opportunity Cost	The value of inventory multiplied by the cost of money for your company.
	0.3%	$3,452	Obsolescence Cost	Additional cost of obsolescence in the form of accruals and/or write-offs.
	0.1%	$1,245	Shrinkage Cost	Additional cost of shrinkage in the form of accruals and/or write-offs.
	0.1%	$500	Taxes and Insurance Cost	Cost centers allocated to the payment of taxes and insurance for inventory assets.
	2.0%	**$20,000**	**IT Cost for Supply Chain**	

(continues)

Table 4-6. (Continued)

Score	% of Revenue	Raw Data (000s)	Calculation Component	Query Assumptions
	1.0%	$10,000	Supply Chain Application Cost	Cost centers summarizing the fixed costs associated with supply IT application costs to PLAN, SOURCE, MAKE, DELIVER, and RETURN.
	1.0%	$10,000	IT Operational Cost for Supply Chain	Cost centers summarizing the ongoing expenses associated with maintenance, upgrade, and development of IT costs to support PLAN, SOURCE, MAKE, DELIVER, and RETURN.

of the last fiscal year. The fifth element in the data collection plan is to identify a *data collection team*. This team will follow the collection all the way through defect analysis.

As part of the effort to benchmark performance, it's important to consider the level of detail necessary, comfort level of divulging company data, and effort required to get the data back. With this in mind, there are two types of sources for benchmark data. First, there are subscription sources, which generally require a fee to access the data. Subscription data are evolving in the level of detail, require no company data, and can be acquired with little or no effort. Second, there are survey sources, which require a company to complete a survey of supply chain metrics and submit them as contribution to a larger sample. Although the effort is greater (up to 40 hours), this type of resource provides a higher level of detail. The appendix provides some frequently used benchmark sources. In any case, the goal is to get multiple sources of benchmark data for each selected metric.

With the data collection plans in place, the second part of the day focuses on planning how to assemble an industry comparison spreadsheet using information available at www.hoovers.com (Table 4-11 on page 72). This spreadsheet template illustrates actual and benchmark data for profitability, returns, and share performance. The industry comparison list should contain at least 25 companies for statistical reasons; using fewer is considered more of a point-to-point comparison.

Table 4-7. Returns management–warranty costs.

Returns Management–Warranty Costs		Cost to Return Defective Product—the sum of the costs associated with returning a defective product to the supplier. (Processes: sSR1, sDR1.) Cost to Return Excess Product—the sum of the costs associated with returning excess product to the supplier, SCOR 10.0, page 2.4.8. This metric was redefined in the 7.0 release and was no longer considered a stand-alone metric. Aside from SCORmark, much of the benchmark data is based on 6.1. This worksheet still uses the 6.1 calculation components. Returns Management–Warranty Costs is a discrete measure that attempts to segment the cost centers associated with defective product returns, planned and unplanned returns of maintenance, repair and overhaul products (MRO), and returns associated with excess customer inventory. Total Returns Management–Warranty Cost is additive to Supply Chain Management Cost.		

Score	% of Revenue	Raw Data (000s)	Calculation Component	Query Assumptions
		$1,000,000	Revenue	
0.5%	0.01%	$134	Returns Authorization Processing Costs	Cost centers that have to do with entering return authorizations, scheduling receipts, and processing replacements or credit.
	0.22%	$2,222	Returned Product Facility Cost	Cost centers that have to do with labor and space for receipt and storage of returned products.
	0.02%	$222	Returned Product Transportation Costs	Cost centers that have to do with the transportation cost of returned products.
	0.10%	$1,000	Repair Costs	Cost centers that have to do with the material, labor, and repair of damaged products.
	0.10%	$1,000	Warranty Costs	Cost centers that have to do with the material, labor, and problem diagnosis for verification and disposition of returned products.

At Fowlers, the finance controller from technology products group, the corporate directors of logistics, and customer service divided up the metric data collection because those people had the easiest access to the financial and customer order information and also had extended team resources who could help collect the data. The vice president of sales and marketing in the technology products group and David Able—in his capacity as vice president of operations for the technology products group—took responsibility for assembling their industry comparison spreadsheet. Because the team

Table 4-8. Cost of goods sold.

Cost of Goods		The cost associated with buying raw materials and producing finished goods. This cost includes direct costs (labor, materials) and indirect costs (overhead). This is not intended to be additive to Total Supply Chain Management Cost, SCOR 10.0, page 2.4.2.		
Score	**% of Revenue**	**Raw Data (000s)**	**Calculation Component**	**Query Assumptions**
		$1,000,000	Revenue	
76.5%	55.6%	$556,000	Material Cost	Cost centers that include all materials directly incorporated into the cost of the finished good product.
	13.4%	$134,000	Direct Labor	Cost centers that include all labor that directly impacts the manufacturing–assembly of the finished good product.
	7.5%	$75,000	Indirect Labor	Cost centers that include indirect labor and overhead supporting the manufacturing–assembly of the finished good product.

members knew that Fowlers' own data were listed in its industry profile on Hoovers.com, they requested that food and computer industries be added to the list for more specific comparisons with the operating groups. Meanwhile, the director of applications was putting together a short list of analysts for the extended team who could help with data queries and segmentation capability.

Table 4-9. Cash-to-cash cycle time.

Cash to Cash Cycle Time		The time it takes for an investment to flow back into a company after it has been spent for raw materials. For services, this represents the time from the point at which a company pays for the resources consumed in the performance of a service to the time that the company receives payment from the customer for those services, SCOR 10.0 page 2.5.1. The calculation components below are based on project experience. Inventory Days of Supply is the most utilized sub-measure for this performance attribute.	
Score	**Raw Data (000s)**	**Calculation Component**	**Query Assumptions**
117.4	$556,000	**Material Cost**	
	$765,000	**COGS**	
	$1,000,000	**Revenue**	
	95.4	**Inventory Days of Supply**	Total Inventory $ / (COGS / 365); Inventory Turns is calculated by COGS / Total Inventory $
	$200,000	Total Inventory	As defined on your balance sheet.
	$100,000	Finished Goods Inventory	Includes manufactured and purchased FG.
	$25,000	Work In Process Inventory	
	$75,000	Raw Material Inventory	
	54.8	**Days Sales Outstanding**	Total Receivables $ / (Revenue / 365)
	$150,000	Total Receivables	As defined on your balance sheet.
	32.8	**Days Payables Outstanding**	Total Payables $ / (Material Cost / 365)
	$50,000	Total Payables	As defined on your balance sheet.

Table 4-10. Fowlers' scorecard template.

Fowlers, Inc.			Benchmark Data				
7-Feb-11	Level 1 Performance Metrics	2010 Act	Parity 50th Percentile	Advantage 70th Percentile	Superior 90th Percentile	Gap	Source
Performance Attribute or Category							
Supply Chain Delivery Reliability	Perfect Order Fulfillment						
Supply Chain Responsiveness	Order Fulfillment Cycle Time						
Supply Chain Flexibility	Upside Supply Chain Flexibility						
Supply Chain Cost	Cost of Goods						
	Supply Chain Management Cost						
Supply Chain Asset Management Efficiency	Inventory Days of Supply						

External / Internal

Table 4-11. Summary of actual and benchmark data for profitability, returns, and share performance at the enterprise level.

Industry Comparison—Computer Network Industry—Hoovers.com	Revenue MM	SG&A	Cost of Goods	Cash-to-Cash Cycle Time	Inventory Days of Supply	Asset Turns	Gross Margin	Operating Income	Net Operating Income	Return on Assets
YOUR COMPANY	$176.1	40.9%	47.2%	158.6	98.3	0.7	52.8%	11.9%	6.8%	7.8%
Network Appliance, Inc.	$1,006.0	29.0%	40.0%	58.28	20.4	1.6	60.0%	31.0%	7.5%	49.1%
Dassault Systemes S.A.	$546.0	57.4%	14.3%	91.00	0	1.2	85.7%	28.2%	16.5%	33.0%
The Titan Corporation	$1,033.0	25.2%	73.3%	104.9	12.2	2.2	26.7%	1.5%	-1.8%	3.3%
RadiSys Corporation	$340.7	24.3%	65.7%	129.8	86.8	1.3	34.3%	10.0%	9.6%	12.9%
Convergys Corporation	$2,320.6	29.5%	54.7%	34.96	0	6.0	45.3%	15.8%	9.3%	70.0%
3COM	$2,820.9	64.3%	81.1%	39.04	32	1.6	18.9%	-45.4%	-34.2%	-54.9%
Enterasys Networks, Inc	$1,071.5	66.4%	52.1%	106.0	64.2	1.1	47.9%	-18.5%	-56.6%	-15.0%
Jack Henry and Associates	$345.5	19.1%	56.1%	93.71	0	2.7	43.9%	24.8%	16.1%	49.8%
Novell, Inc.	$1,040.1	80.1%	31.5%	50.66	1.00	1.3	68.5%	-11.6%	-26.2%	-11.8%
Reynolds and Reynolds	$1,004.0	38.8%	44.1%	24.34	8.90	4.7	55.9%	17.1%	9.9%	60.0%
Cerner Corporation	$404.5	71.4%	22.3%	148.6	8.91	1.9	77.7%	6.3%	26.0%	8.9%
The Black Box Corporation	$827.0	26.1%	59.7%	78.78	37.8	4.1	40.3%	14.1%	7.8%	43.7%
Integraph Corporation	$690.5	40.0%	63.5%	85.64	21.1	2.4	36.5%	-3.4%	1.5%	-6.3%
Entrada Networks, Inc.	$25.7	66.1%	66.9%	130.1	97.6	1.6	33.1%	-33.1%	-82.5%	-38.6%
Inrange Technologies Corp	$233.6	34.9%	44.9%	196.9	102	1.0	55.1%	20.2%	6.1%	15.6%
Computer Networks Industry	$100.0	35%	52%	58.27	19.7	1.2	48.0%	13.0%	2.4%	12.0%
Networking Solutions Q3	$38.9	50.1%	47.0%	NA	NA	NA	53.0%	2.8%	NA	NA
Storage Solutions Q3	$16.5	17.0%	90.9%	NA	NA	NA	9.1%	-7.9%	NA	NA
50th Percentile	$758.8	39.4%	53.4%	92.35	20.8	1.6	46.6%	10.9%	7.1%	10.9%
70th Percentile	$1,164.9	32.1%	40.6%	64.88	10.4	3.0	59.4%	18.6%	11.7%	32.4%
90th Percentile	$1,571.1	24.9%	27.8%	37.41	0	4.3	72.2%	26.2%	16.2%	53.9%

CHAPTER 5

Phase 2: Data, Benchmarks, and Competitive Requirements

▶ **May 2 and 9: Putting Performance in Perspective**

The objectives for these sessions are to review the work in progress from the data collection for each metric, review the industry comparison, prepare the SCORmark submission, set competitive requirements, and begin to think about the defect analysis. In terms of file mechanics, the project leader organized a simple file-management plan. First, he set up a global storage folder named "SCEProject." Inside the folder were four subfolders: Presentations (from the coach), Templates (also from the coach), Deliverables, and Reference (SCOR 10.0 from the Supply Chain Council). Inside of the deliverables folder, the coach recommended the following file-naming convention: phase number.deliverable name.date. For example, the supply chain definition matrix was labeled *1.supplychaindefinitionmatrix.022411*. Each time a team member needed to revise the file, he or she would change the date. Inside the deliverables folder, the project leader had set up another called *archive* to store older versions.

For the web conference, each file owner downloaded a copy of the deliverable to his or her desktop. The meeting leader was then able to display each presenter's files at the click of a button.

Initial Data Review

The first file to review was the industry comparison. The second set of files to review were the spreadsheet results of the metric data collection efforts. The last thing to do was fill out the SCORmark survey.

David Able presented the industry comparison findings of the computer network industry (Table 5-1) and conglomerates (Table 5-2). Even on first examination of the data, several things jumped out.

First, the wide range of figures for cost of goods as well as selling, general & administrative (SG&A) costs made it clear that there is no standard for reporting these numbers from one company to another. Operating income seemed to be a good comparison point for expenses. "But there's still no way to compare supply chain costs using the data we have so far," the coach pointed out. "You can't add cost of goods and SG&A and supply chain costs to create a working scorecard metric. Total supply chain management costs are more activity based, and they can borrow from the other two categories, so you'd be double-counting certain costs if you just added them." The SCORmark survey would help with that comparison.

Second, the metrics on the conglomerates comparison for cash-to-cash cycle (197 days) and asset turns (1.5) for Fowlers confirmed what many in the finance community seemed to think about the company: It used physical assets well and cash assets poorly.

Third, as the team members looked at the "parity opportunity" portion of the table, their eyes got wide. As a conglomerate with $1 billion in revenue, Fowlers' 7 percent operating income ($70 million) was only half the level of the conglomerate industry benchmark. To achieve parity in operating income, the company would need to find another $70 million of benefit through supply chain performance.

Table 5-1. Fowlers' comparison data for computer network industry.

Industry Comparison—Computer Network Industry—Hoovers.com	Revenue MM	SG&A	Cost of Goods	Cash-to-Cash Cycle Time	Inventory Days of Supply	Asset Turns	Gross Margin	Operating Income	Net Operating Income	Return on Assets
Network Appliance, Inc.	$1,006.0	29.0%	40.0%	58.28	20.4	1.6	60.0%	31.0%	7.5%	49.1%
Dassault Systemes S.A.	$546.0	57.4%	14.3%	91.00	0	1.2	85.7%	28.2%	16.5%	33.0%
The Titan Corporation	$1,033.0	25.2%	73.3%	104.9	12.2	2.2	26.7%	1.5%	-1.8%	3.3%
RadiSys Corporation	$340.7	24.3%	65.7%	129.8	86.8	1.3	34.3%	10.0%	9.6%	12.9%
Convergys Corporation	$2,320.6	29.5%	54.7%	34.96	0	6	45.3%	15.8%	9.3%	70.0%
3COM	$2,820.9	64.3%	81.1%	39.04	32	1.6	18.9%	-45.4%	-34.2%	-54.9%
Enterasys Networks, Inc	$1,071.5	66.4%	52.1%	106.0	64.2	1.1	47.9%	-18.5%	-56.6%	-15.0%
Jack Henry and Associates	$345.5	19.1%	56.1%	93.71	0	2.7	43.9%	24.8%	16.1%	49.8%
Novell, Inc.	$1,040.1	80.1%	31.5%	50.66	1.00	1.3	68.5%	-11.6%	-26.2%	-11.8%
Reynolds and Reynolds	$1,004.0	38.8%	44.1%	24.34	8.90	4.7	55.9%	17.1%	9.9%	60.0%
Cerner Corporation	$404.5	71.4%	22.3%	148.6	8.91	1.9	77.7%	6.3%	26.0%	8.9%
The Black Box Corporation	$827.0	26.1%	59.7%	78.78	37.8	4.1	40.3%	14.1%	7.8%	43.7%
Integraph Corporation	$690.5	40.0%	63.5%	85.64	21.1	2.4	36.5%	-3.4%	1.5%	-6.3%
Entrada Networks, Inc.	$25.7	66.1%	66.9%	130.1	97.6	1.6	33.1%	-33.1%	-82.5%	-38.6%
Inrange Technologies Corp	$233.6	34.9%	44.9%	196.9	102	1.0	55.1%	20.2%	6.1%	15.6%
Computer Networks Industry	$100.0	35.0%	52.0%	58.27	19.7	1.2	48.0%	13.0%	2.4%	12.0%
Networking Solutions Q3	$38.9	50.1%	47.0%	NA	NA	NA	53.0%	2.8%	NA	NA
Storage Solutions Q3	$16.5	17.0%	90.9%	NA	NA	NA	9.1%	-7.9%	NA	NA
50th Percentile	$827.0	38.8%	54.7%	91.0	20.4	1.6	45.3%	10.0%	7.5%	12.9%
70th Percentile	$1,027.6	29.1%	44.3%	62.4	8.9	2.4	55.7%	16.8%	9.5%	41.6%
90th Percentile	$1,821.0	24.7%	26.0%	36.6	0.0	4.5	74.0%	26.9%	16.3%	55.9%

Table 5-2. Fowlers' comparison data for conglomerates.

Industry Comparison—Conglomerate Industry—Hoovers.com	Revenue	SG&A	Cost of Goods	Cash-to-Cash Cycle Time	Inventory Days of Supply	Asset Turns	Gross Margin	Operating Income	Net Operating Income	Return on Assets
Fowlers	$1,000	7.0%	86.0%	196.7	91.3	1.5	14.0%	7.0%	3.5%	10.7%
National Service Industries	$563	32.3%	62.3%	47.6	20.0	0.6	37.7%	5.3%	4.8%	3.4%
Maxxam Inc	$2,448	6.9%	81.7%	120.1	82.4	0.5	18.3%	11.4%	1.4%	6.2%
US Industries	$3,088	23.3%	66.1%	119.5	88.4	1.2	33.9%	10.6%	1.2%	13.1%
Pacific Dunlop Limited	$2,120	29.7%	66.3%	131.8	105.2	1.6	33.7%	4.0%	−3.4%	4.8%
Sequa Corporation	$1,773	13.9%	75.3%	127.1	102.2	1.4	24.7%	10.8%	1.4%	11.1%
GenCorp Inc	$1,047	3.8%	81.7%	94.8	77.7	1.1	18.3%	14.5%	12.3%	11.5%
Olin Corporation	$1,549	8.5%	77.2%	82.3	65.9	1.8	22.8%	14.3%	5.2%	19.7%
Federal Signal Corporation	$1,106	20.0%	66.9%	103.2	77.8	1.5	33.1%	13.2%	5.2%	14.7%
Kawasaki Heavy Industries Ltd	$8,395	12.4%	87.2%	253.4	136.8	1.1	12.8%	0.4%	−1.0%	0.4%
Valhi Inc	$1,192	16.9%	63.2%	144.1	117.7	0.7	36.8%	19.9%	6.4%	10.5%
Pentair Inc	$2,748	17.1%	71.1%	105.5	73.4	1.4	28.9%	11.9%	2.0%	12.3%
Tomkins PLC	$5,875	7.0%	81.4%	87.6	51.7	2.0	18.6%	11.6%	1.6%	17.5%
ITT Industries Inc	$4,829	23.6%	62.0%	96.4	64.8	1.4	38.0%	14.4%	5.5%	15.1%
Six Continents PLC	$5,939	27.2%	48.7%	39.0	16.8	0.6	51.3%	24.0%	11.4%	10.7%
TRW Inc	$17,231	9.0%	80.5%	42.4	22.9	1.4	19.5%	10.5%	2.5%	11.0%
Textron	$13,090	11.3%	72.8%	231.0	71.6	1.1	27.2%	15.8%	1.7%	12.7%
Johnson Controls Inc	$18,427	8.9%	83.1%	41.8	13.8	2.5	16.9%	8.0%	2.6%	14.9%
Dover Corporation	$5,401	20.8%	59.8%	119.5	88.5	1.5	40.2%	19.4%	9.6%	21.4%

Raytheon Company	$16,895	10.3%	76.0%	122.9	54.3	0.8	24.0%	13.7%	0.8%	8.7%
ABB Ltd	$22,967	19.0%	75.0%	170.0	67.7	1.0	25.0%	6.0%	6.3%	4.5%
RWE AG	$48,182	26.6%	67.8%	95.1	30.4	0.9	32.2%	5.6%	2.2%	3.6%
Emerson Electric	$15,480	19.9%	60.8%	103.7	73.6	1.4	39.2%	19.3%	6.7%	19.9%
Honeywell International	$25,652	12.2%	70.5%	111.1	75.3	1.4	29.5%	17.2%	6.5%	17.6%
United Technologies	$26,206	17.1%	69.1%	107.6	75.7	1.4	30.9%	13.8%	6.9%	14.3%
Koninklijke Philips Electronics	$35,658	15.5%	69.7%	105.7	73.1	1.3	30.3%	13.8%	25.4%	13.6%
3M	$16,724	30.3%	46.4%	141.8	108.7	1.5	53.6%	23.3%	10.7%	26.8%
Vivendi Universal SA	$40,138	22.3%	61.8%	212.9	44.6	0.4	38.2%	15.9%	5.4%	4.5%
Siemens AG	$86,208	26.9%	66.2%	134.3	84.9	1.3	33.8%	6.8%	2.4%	6.6%
Tyco International Ltd	$34,037	21.5%	53.4%	488.1	102.4	0.4	46.6%	25.1%	11.7%	7.7%
General Electric Company	$129,417	36.7%	34.1%	565.8	64.7	0.4	65.9%	29.3%	9.8%	8.7%
Conglomerate Industry	$100	30.0%	54.3%	291.0	77.7	0.7	45.7%	15.7%	11.2%	8.7%
Food—Meat Products Industry	$100	13.1%	82.7%	49.4	52.1	2.1	17.3%	4.2%	2.9%	6.7%
Media—Movie, Television, & Music Production Services and Products	$100	54.6%	45.6%	82.8	19.2	0.7	54.5%	-0.2%	-4.2%	-0.1%
Diversified Services—Miscellaneous Business Services	$100	35.1%	61.0%	47.6	16.7	1.3	39.0%	3.8%	-0.4%	3.8%
50th Percentile	$10,742	18.0%	68.5%	115.3	73.5	1.3	31.5%	13.8%	5.2%	11.3%
70th Percentile	$19,789	12.3%	62.9%	101.2	64.8	1.4	37.1%	15.9%	6.5%	14.4%
90th Percentile	$40,943	8.4%	52.9%	47.1	22.6	1.6	47.1%	23.4%	11.4%	19.7%

David and the team were trying to figure out how much Technology Products would have to contribute toward the $70 million.

As the review turned to the scorecard, the corporate controller, director of logistics, and director of customer service shared their *data collection experience*. First, they said they had been able to segment the Perfect Order Fulfillment and Order Fulfillment Cycle Time by SKU make-to-stock (MTS) or make-to-order (MTO), by customer, by plant, by customer order and line number, and by sales hierarchy.

The toughest part, as anticipated, was assembling the *Perfect Order Fulfillment*. For each line they were able to identify the expected quantity, requested and committed date, actual ship date, customer receipt date, and orders that were paid on time. While this is not exactly like the SCOR metric definition, it was close enough to understand overall customer reliability. They used both the template noted in Chapter 4 as well as the SCORmark questionnaire. *Order Fulfillment Cycle Time* was a blended number between MTS and MTO items; for this metric they also used the combination of the Chapter 4 template and SCORmark. *Supply Chain Management Cost* used the calculations as defined in the SCORmark survey. Figure 5-1 illustrates the enterprise scorecard performance for each of their targeted metrics.

There was a collective gasp in the room as the scorecard made its way to the screen. Each measure in the customer-facing section was new to Fowlers; as bad as it looked, it was the first time the team had really considered overall delivery reliability through customers' eyes.

The ensuing discussion sounded a bit like a session with a grief counselor; there was denial, bargaining, anger, and eventually acceptance of the data. Every member of the team wanted to bolt from the room and jump right into firefighting the problem—as they had all done so many times before. Fortunately, it was the end of the day. Tomorrow's agenda would focus the team on something else, and a good night's sleep would put this information in perspective:

Figure 5-1. Fowlers' enterprise scorecard.

Fowlers Inc. —Enterprise Scorecard				Benchmark Data				
25-Apr-11	Performance Attribute or Category	Level 1 Performance Metrics	2010 Act	Parity 50th Percentile	Advantage 70th Percentile	Superior 90th Percentile	Gap	Source
External	Supply Chain Delivery Reliability	Perfect Order Fulfillment	50.5%					SCORmark
	Supply Chain Responsiveness	Order Fulfillment Cycle Time (Days)	15.0					SCORmark
	Supply Chain Flexibility	Upside Supply Chain Flexibility (Days)	91.5					SCORmark
	Supply Chain Cost	Cost of Goods	86.0%	68.5%	62.9%	52.9%		Hoovers
		Supply Chain Management Cost	15.5%					SCORmark
Internal	Supply Chain Asset Management Efficiency	Inventory Days of Supply	91.3	73.5	64.8	22.6		Hoovers

The team had found an opportunity for the kind of improvement it needed to make. The team agreed to submit the SCORmark "as is" rather than waste any more time justifying something the customers had been saying for years.

The SCORmark Survey

The SCORmark™ survey is a service provided to Supply Chain Council members that utilizes a subset of the APQC database to create a scorecard using SCOR metric definitions. The last time I used the survey, it was 57 questions covering 157 Excel rows. Figure 5-2 illustrates a sample output for supply chain management cost.

Competitive Requirements Analysis

The next step is composed of three tasks: conducting competitive requirements (prioritizing performance targets relative to competitors), assembling a plan to complete a defect analysis for each metric, and preparing for steering team review number one.

Rules for Prioritization

As illustrated in Figure 4-1, there are five attributes of supply chain performance:

1. Delivery reliability
2. Responsiveness
3. Flexibility
4. Supply chain cost
5. Asset management efficiency

The objective of the *competitive requirements exercise* is to prioritize your company against competitors with respect to the five attributes for each customer or market channel—determining whether you

Figure 5-2. Sample output of SCORmark supply chain management cost.

Supply Chain Management Cost	Your Score
	$7.18
Description of supply chain management costs (5.023) with references to the question number in the survey (5.027)	

You chose the advantage target for this metric. While you have scored above parity by –$1.72, your target gap is $2.08.

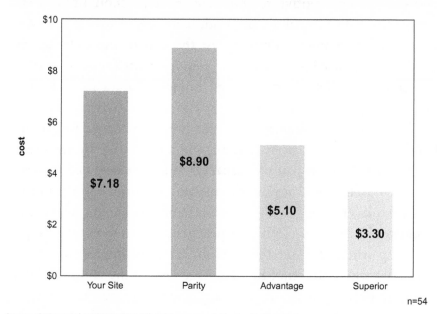

Source © Copyright APQC 2007. All rights reserved. Used with Permission.

need to perform at a superior level (90th percentile), at a level of advantage (70th percentile), or at parity (50th percentile).

There is a catch: For each customer or market channel, the team is allowed to set only one performance attribute at the superior level and two at the level of advantage. The other two attributes must be set at parity.

One last note: the requirements are established from the company's point of view as they relate to the competitive landscape of the future. This is not a firefighting exercise aimed at trying to identify where to improve the most; it's a strategic exercise, focused on how to differentiate against stiff competition in the future.

Many companies are using the strategic categories discussed in *The Discipline of Market Leaders* (written by Michael Treacy and Fred Wiersema, Basic Books, 1997), which define operational excellence, customer intimacy, or product innovation as the strategy driver. The results of the competitive requirements exercise should reflect and support the SWOT analysis and critical success factors as reviewed in the business context summary. At the end of the exercise, the team must reach consensus on the requirements for each market. Empirically, it might help to assign numeric values to each chip: three for superior, two for advantage, and one for parity.

The competitive requirements exercise is performed first by the design team, then the steering team, and a third time by each relevant business team as part of a separate data-gathering task. In each case, the coach should review the metric categories and definitions with the players along with available benchmarks, but actual data should not be revealed. That's because people tend to put the "superior" chip where they see the need for the most improvement, not necessarily where the strategic advantage lies. At the end of the day, leadership needs to make the decision based on its business strategy.

During the Fowlers web conference, the coach facilitated the design team through the exercise, the results of which are seen in Figure 5-3.

The team scored five channels and learned that there were two basic supply chain design configurations, plus one with a twist. The U.S. *retail markets* was typical for the store- and consumer-oriented retail sector: superior service (meaning perfect order fulfillment), better-than-average order cycle times, and better-than-average flexibility to respond to demand fluctuation within the quarter. Promotions, short product life cycles, and order policy are examples affecting demand variability.

Figure 5-3. Fowlers Technology Products Group competitive requirements summary.

SCOR 10.0 Strategic Metric Performance Attribute	Technology Products Group Competitive Requirements					
	U.S. Retail Markets	U.S. Distributor Markets	U.S. Direct-to-Consumer Markets	U.S. OEM and Key Accounts	U.S. Government	
Supply Chain Delivery Reliability	Superior	Parity	Superior	Superior	Superior	
Supply Chain Responsiveness	Advantage	Parity	Advantage	Advantage	Advantage	
Supply Chain Flexibility	Advantage	Parity	Parity	Advantage	Advantage	
Supply Chain Cost	Parity	Advantage	Parity	Parity	Parity	
Supply Chain Asset Management Efficiency	Parity	Superior	Advantage	Parity	Parity	

The U.S. *OEM and key accounts*, as well as the U.S. *government market,* shared similar requirements.

The U.S. *distributor market* is characterized by regular weekly shipments of goods in truckload quantity; effective inventory management practices would both support high turns for Fowlers and increase the gross margin return-on-investment for the distributor.

Last, the U.S. *direct-to-consumer markets*—though similar to retail—needed to give Fowlers the opportunity to shape demand patterns in order to mitigate inventory risk.

The team made plans to validate these preliminary results with the durables, food, and technology business teams and refine the input prior to the next weekly session.

Metric Defect Analysis

Metric defect analysis is borrowed from the Six Sigma and Total Quality Management disciplines. The basic idea is that for each metric identified in the scorecard, the data teams define and analyze the failures or defects.

This is not root-cause analysis. Many experienced master black belts would suggest that root cause is approached after the fifth or sixth "why" question. The objective here is to use the system (in this case SAP software) and simple analytical tools such as Pareto charts, run charts, histograms, control charts, and so forth, to help answer the first and second "why did this fail" question, as well as the "which question" relating to SKU, customer, location, etc.

Why use the system? Many companies resort to manual research right away. Although it is sometimes unavoidable, starting with manual research generally reduces the frequency of analysis, further reinforces "not using the system," and limits the sample size for analysis. Most important, the objective is to refresh the defect analysis each time the metric is refreshed—be it daily, weekly, monthly, quarterly, or semiannually.

The Fowlers data teams caught on quickly and started to think about what they would call a defect for each metric, and to brainstorm the data that would be required to get to the desired conclusion. The expectation would be to present the actual metric performance, the definition of what was deemed a failure or "defective" for the metric, the various ways the data could be segmented, the first sort (sortation) of failures (largest to smallest), a second sort of failures at the next level (largest to smallest), and an estimate of the level of effort required to get to the final root cause (often considered the fifth sort of failures).

Sponsor Update Considerations

In advance of the review of content with the sponsors and steering team members, the Fowlers design team considered the following points:

- The project manager, David, should be the principal person consolidating and preparing the presentation.

- Prior to the review, the team would conduct informal one-on-one discussions with sponsors and steering team members who may be surprised by the content.

- Any rumors, objections, and other cultural issues that arise during the one-on-one meetings would be addressed in a design team meeting and should be discussed candidly.

- Speaking roles for design team members would be determined for the steering team review. In addition to David, design team members who did a lot of homework would be given a chance for exposure.

Overall, the objectives of this update are to review supply chain metric definitions and preliminary query data, conduct the competi-

tive requirements exercise with the entire steering team, review preliminary industry comparison sample and benchmark data, and
establish expectations for the steering team review on May 16.

The corporate controller, the vice president of sales and marketing of the food products group, the director of logistics, and the
director of customer service worked with David to prepare the first
update. The topics included:

- Conduct competitive priority exercise with the steering
  team—review design team results.
- Review preliminary supply chain metric data.
- Review preliminary benchmark data.
- Set expectations for the steering team review.

Phase 2: Scorecards and Gap Analysis

▶ **May 16 and 23: Estimating the Size of the Opportunity**

After a proper debrief of highlights from the sponsor and steering team updates, the design team starts to work on the objectives for the next set of deliverables: review data on the scorecard and begin the process of calculating and assigning financial value to gaps.

The Scorecard Review

For a scorecard to be complete, it must include actual data for each metric, appropriate industry benchmarks, competitive requirements, and gap calculations. In a perfect world, scorecards would cascade neatly from the enterprise level to each business or from the enterprise level to each market segment. But that rarely happens, as the Fowlers design team learned.

As the review process took shape, the team discovered that courageous conversations were necessary to make sense of the data and focus the design effort. The first part of the meeting centered on the actual and benchmark columns.

Discussion of the enterprise scorecard (Table 6-1), led by

Table 6-1. Fowlers' enterprise scorecard.

Fowlers Inc.

2-May-11	Performance Attribute or Category	Level 1 Performance Metrics	2010 Act	Benchmark Data			Parity Gap	Source
				Parity 50th Percentile	Advantage 70th Percentile	Superior 90th Percentile		
External	Supply Chain Delivery Reliability	Perfect Order Fulfillment	50.5%	74.0%	81.0%	88.0%	−23.5%	SCORmark
	Supply Chain Responsiveness	Order Fulfillment Cycle Time	15.0	10.0	6.50	3.0	−5.0	SCORmark
	Supply Chain Flexibility	Upside Supply Chain Flexibility	91.5	60	45.0	29	−31.5	SCORmark
Internal	Supply Chain Cost	Cost of Goods	86.0%	68.5%	62.9%	52.9%	−17.5%	Hoovers
		Supply Chain Management Cost	15.5%	9.5%	6.8%	3.9%	−6.0%	SCORmark
	Supply Chain Asset Management Efficiency	Inventory Days of Supply	91.3	73.5	64.8	22.6	−17.8	Hoovers

the corporate controller and director of logistics, considered three issues. First, although enterprise-wide customer-facing data indicated "below parity" performance, the aggregate data were not helpful in pinpointing the severity of some of the issues. The team agreed that, in order to understand the issues and the potential opportunity, it was necessary to *segment the reliability, responsiveness, and flexibility metrics* by (1) business group, (2) stock-keeping unit (SKU), and (3) customer.

A second issue had to do with the fact that balance-sheet data were available only at the corporate level; trying to precisely allocate that information back to the supply chains (as defined by the definition matrix) would have taken a major balance-sheet restructuring and countless hours of allocating. As a result, the team simply used *percent of sales to total* as a means to allocate inventory on the product group scorecards.

Third, and most important, the scorecard wasn't organized in the same way as were the supply chain competitive performance requirements. The scorecard was organized by business—because that's how the data existed. The supply chain requirements were determined by market/customer channel—because that represented the ideal situation the team wanted to create. Translating from the competitive requirements to the scorecard would be a challenge.

"You'll come up against more than one roadblock like this," the SCOR coach said. "We're not always going to have complete data or perfect alignment. What is your preference? Go back and do some more homework, or pick a direction to go forward?" The team was impatient, and a few minutes of conversation made it clear that there probably was no perfect solution. In the interest of moving forward, the team agreed to apply the priorities of the retail channel because it represented the operating unit's largest share of revenue.

Discussion led by David Able about the technology products group (Table 6-2), summarized three unique learning points and considered two compromises.

Table 6-2. Fowlers' technology products scorecard with competitive requirements.

Technology Products Group				Benchmark Data						
2-May-11	Performance Attribute or Category	Level 1 Performance Metrics	2010 Act	Parity 50th Percentile	Advantage 70th Percentile	Superior 90th Percentile	Parity Gap	Competitive Gap	Competitive Gap Analysis	Source
External	Supply Chain Delivery Reliability	Perfect Order Fulfillment	30.2%	74.0%	81.0%	88.0%	–43.8%	–57.8%		SCORmark
	Supply Chain Responsiveness	Order Fulfillment Cycle Time	11.0	10.0	6.50	3.0	–1.0	–4.5	$6,750,000	SCORmark
	Supply Chain Flexibility	Upside Supply Chain Flexibility	91.5	60	45.0	29	–31.5	–46.5		SCORmark
		Cost of Goods	63.6%	54.7%	44.3%	26.0%	–8.9%	NA	$40,050,000	Hoovers
Internal	Supply Chain Cost	Supply Chain Management Cost	12.8%	9.5%	6.8%	3.9%	–3.3%	–3.3%	$14,850,000	SCORmark
	Supply Chain Asset Management Efficiency	Inventory Days of Supply	60.5	20.4	8.9	0.0	–40.1	–40.1	$31,442,000	Hoovers

The first learning point was this: Although the decision to out-source manufacture of several products succeeded at achieving low-est unit cost, it drastically reduced the flexibility metric, which in turn affected inventory levels. The second learning point was that the new metrics on service reliability provided empirical evidence in support of complaints by customers that the company was "hard to do business with." The third learning point was that by assem-bling supply chain costs through the SCORmark, it became clear that material acquisition expenses outpaced all other cost increases. Inbound transportation, normally calculated as a cost of material, was isolated for all to see. The last learning point was similar in all busi-ness units: There was considerable opportunity to improve operating income by attacking supply chain costs, improving use of working capital, and better leveraging SAP functionality.

The technology products group's first necessary compromise fo-cused on how to distribute the market/customer channel perfor-mance requirements onto the technology products scorecard. Like corporate, the technology products business team agreed to adopt the retail superior/advantage/advantage/parity/parity (SAAPP) pri-orities for its scorecard gap baseline.

The Scorecard Gap Analysis

The next item on the agenda is focused on completing the competi-tive gap analysis. The gap analysis occurs from both top down (this section) and bottom up, using our defect analysis (Chapter 7). The first step in the *top-down process* is to calculate the mathematical op-portunity for each metric. This is done by calculating the parity gap and/or the competitive gap, and then subtracting actual performance for each metric from the benchmark number determined by the competitive requirement for the category.

If the gap analysis results in a negative number (bad), it means actual performance is less than the benchmark (e.g., the gap between an actual delivery performance of 78 percent and competitive requirements of 92 percent is -14). The next step is to translate each gap number into a profit potential; the most frequently used measure is operating income.

The calculations are straightforward for the internal metrics but can be subjective for customer-facing metrics. The basic calculation that the design team, and ultimately the business team, must agree on is the anticipated effect on revenue through improvements to delivery reliability, responsiveness, and flexibility. This is often more art than science, but there are some accepted approaches:

- *The Lost Opportunity Measure.* This calculates the revenue lost before order entry because of lack of availability of a product.

- *The Canceled Order Measure.* This measure calculates revenue lost after order entry because of canceled orders that result from poor delivery performance.

- *The Market Share Measure.* This measure attempts to project a revenue increase based on achieving competitive advantage in the customer-facing metric categories.

Because any approach will have its tradeoffs, just make sure to document the assumptions and details for the financial analysis and identify some of the steering team or business team members to help validate preliminary numbers.

In Fowlers' case, the design team agreed on the organization of the gap analysis itself, agreeing with the norm that all the opportunity dollars should be calculated using an operating income; this would allow the team to add up the numbers for the "opportunity" of the scorecard. Here are some other conclusions reached by the team based on the information in Table 6-2:

- All customer-facing metrics must be grouped, and "lost opportunity" and "canceled order" calculation methods must be used. The technology products group's 2010 revenue was $450,000,000; the design team's analysis showed that 1.5 percent of the group's sales were either not entered, cut from the order due to availability, or canceled due to poor response to unanticipated demand. The $6,750,000 was calculated by multiplying revenue times 1.5 percent.

- Cost of goods for 2010 was $286,200,000. An 8.9 percent gain was valued at $40,050,000.

- Ending inventory for 2010 was $47,437,000, representing about $784,100 per day. A 40.1–day improvement is equivalent to a $31,442,000 inventory reduction.

- Supply chain management cost for 2010 was $57,601,000. A reduction of 3.3 points is the equivalent of a $14,850,000 reduction in expenses.

Phase 2: Defect Analysis

➤ **May 30 and June 6: Answering the Questions of Who, What, Where, When, and How Much and Then Telling the Steering Team**

The concept of defect analysis now becomes the central focus for the design team, along with preparing the first performance review of the supply chain for the steering team. Specifically, the team will define data points for each metric considered to be a failure; segment the data by product, location, customer, supplier, etc.; and then answer with system-generated data at as many levels of "why" questions as possible.

Defect Analysis

Initiated on April 25, the preliminary results of the defect analysis for each metric are now ready for review. As noted in the web-based meeting agenda, the stated expectation was for each team to present the actual metric performance; review the definition of what was deemed a failure or "defective," the various ways the data could be segmented, the first sort of failures (largest to smallest), and a second sort of failures at the next level (largest to smallest); and build an estimate of the level of effort to get to the final root cause—(often considered the fifth sort of failures).

Whereas the benchmark and competitive requirements (Chapter 6) provide a top-down means of estimating the performance improvement opportunity, the defect analysis is a more precise bottom-up method. In fact, if a decision needed to be made as to how much time is allocated to benchmarking versus thorough defect analysis, I would allocate one hour to benchmarking for every ten hours of defect analysis. It is the ultimate source for prioritizing projects and estimating benefits, as illustrated in the next phase.

The entire design team agreed that the hardest task was to use the system alone to generate the first- and second-level sorts. Most of the team was accustomed to using the manual research method on the most recent issue of the day. They all agreed that while the system's sorts may not be perfect, they were repeatable each time the metric performance was reported. The following were their findings.

Perfect Order Fulfillment

As documented on the technology products group scorecard (Table 6-2), the actual perfect order fulfillment is 30.2 percent, which means that 69.8 percent of Fowlers' orders failed to be perfect for some reason. The customer-facing metric team defined failures for perfect order fulfillment as sales orders not meeting the quantity, commit date, delivery quality, pricing, and documentation expectations of the customer, as documented in Fowlers' sales order, invoice, and shipment documents. The team was able to segment sales orders by customer number, ship-to location, Fowlers shipping location, manufacturing plant, supplier ship-from location, SKU line number, shipping lane, and freight provider.

The first and second sorts (Figure 7-1) of the failures included three primary categories and twelve subcategories:

1. Sales Order Shipped Not Complete

♦ Product Not Available at Initial Available-to-Promise Check

♦ Manufacturing Late

Figure 7-1. Perfect order fulfillment defect analysis, first and second sorts.

Perfect Order Fulfillment Defect Analysis	41.0%	15.0%	13.8%
First Sort Categories (Columns)	**Sales Order Shipped Not Complete**	**Sales Order Delivered Late**	**Sales Order in Late-Pay Status**
Second Sort Categories (Rows)			
Product Not Available at Initial Available-to-Promise Check	11.0%		
Manufacturing Late	5.0%		
Inventory Reallocated to Another Customer	5.0%		
Actual Demand Exceeded Forecast	20.0%		
Warehouse Shipped Late		2.5%	
Credit Hold		5.0%	
Order Released to Warehouse Too Late		2.0%	
Freight Provider Delivered Late		0.5%	
Customer Picked Up Late			4.0%
Price Discrepancy		5.0%	5.0%
Delivery Issue Including Quality			4.8%

- ◆ Inventory Reallocated to Another Customer
- ◆ Actual Demand Exceeded Forecast

2. Sales Order Delivered Late

- ◆ Warehouse Shipped Late
- ◆ Credit Hold
- ◆ Order Released to Warehouse Too Late
- ◆ Freight Provider Delivered Late
- ◆ Customer Picked Up Late

3. Sales Order in Late-Pay Status

- ◆ Customer Picked Up Late
- ◆ Price Discrepancy
- ◆ Delivery Issue Including Quality

Order Fulfillment Cycle Time

As documented in the technology products group scorecard, the actual order fulfillment cycle time (blended MTO and MTS) is 11. Failure definition for this metric was tricky. First, the team assembled a histogram of a sample of 224 orders (Figure 7-2). Second, the team needed to *define a failure*. Their competitive target was 6.5 days; if they chose that number, all but 48 orders failed. The team settled on nine days, better than parity and on the way to their competitive target. So, if the actual days were greater than nine, the sales order was deemed a failure. There were 97 failed orders in the sample. For each failed sales order, the team also looked at time subsegments as defined in the SCOR metric definition and compared the actual subsegment time to what was defined in the master data for expected lead time. They used this data as the second sort of failures (Figure 7-3). The team was able to use the same segmentation strategies as defined in perfect order fulfillment.

Upside Supply Chain Flexibility

As documented in the scorecard, the actual upside supply chain flexibility (averaged across all SKUs in the project scope) is 91.5

Figure 7-2. Order fulfillment cycle time histogram.

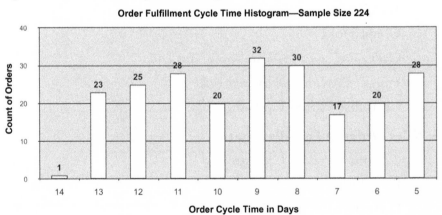

Figure 7-3. Order fulfillment cycle time defect analysis.

Order Fulfillment Cycle Time Defect Analysis	Defect Rate	Failed Orders	Target Days
Order Receipt to Order Confirmed	18.3%	41	1
Order Confirmed to Shipment Created	12.1%	27	2
Shipment Created to Order Picked	4.9%	11	1
Order Picked to Order Shipped	3.6%	8	1
Order Shipped to Order Delivered	4.5%	10	4

days. Failure definition for this metric included two parts: comparing actual to master data, and comparing master data to strategic requirement. First the team compared the overall actual stacked lead times of each SKU to the expected lead time as noted in the SKU master data. If the total actual days were greater than expected, the SKU was deemed a failure.

A second sort of this data took the analysis one step further. For each failed SKU, the team looked at time subsegments as defined in SCOR (including PLAN, SOURCE, and MAKE lead times) and compared the actual subsegment time to what was defined in the master data for expected lead time.

To compare the strategic requirement, the team used the histogram (Figure 7-4) of SKU total lead times; defined a targeted lead time–based competitive requirement; and defined as failures all SKUs above the target. They sorted the failures from highest to lowest in annual volume; this view of failures initiated a number of questions as to how to develop supply chain strategies that would make the macro supply chain more flexible to marketplace demand fluctuations. The team was able to segment upside supply chain flexibility data using the product hierarchy, bill of material, plant, DC location, volume, and sales and operations planning (S&OP) family groupings.

Figure 7-5 illustrates four part numbers that were strategic-

Figure 7-4. Upside supply chain flexibility histogram.

Figure 7-5. Strategic requirement failures by part number.

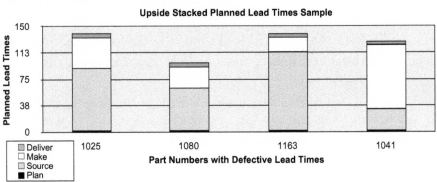

requirement failures. They were high-volume SKUs with lead times greater than 60 days (the parity requirement for U.S. Distributor Markets and U.S. Direct-to-Consumer Markets determined in the competitive requirements exercise).

Supply Chain Management Cost

As documented in the technology products group scorecard, the actual supply chain management cost is 12.8 percent cost-to-sales.

The defect analysis for this metric was a little more arbitrary than the previous three. The team members first developed a Pareto chart of supply chain costs (Table 7-1). They then defined failure modes for each category. As an example, failure modes for outbound transportation cost were defined as expedited freight, cost centers over budget, and routes that exceeded the expected cost per pound. The results gave the team a good indication of which process areas most affected cost-to-serve, and helped it visualize which failure modes

Table 7-1. Pareto chart of supply chain costs.

2010 Supply Chain Management Cost			
Cum		57,601	
34.8%	34.8%	$20,033	Outbound Transportation Cost
57.2%	22.4%	$12,929	Finished Goods Warehouse Cost
70.9%	13.7%	$7,896	Inbound Transportation Cost
77.3%	6.4%	$3,694	Opportunity Cost
81.5%	4.2%	$2,401	Obsolescence Cost
84.6%	3.1%	$1,781	Supply Chain Finance Control Cost
87.5%	2.9%	$1,672	Purchasing Cost
89.8%	2.3%	$1,345	Customer Service Cost
91.5%	1.7%	$981	Supply Chain Application Cost
93.1%	1.6%	$946	Supply Planning Cost
94.6%	1.5%	$850	Supplier Quality Cost
95.7%	1.1%	$646	Shrinkage Cost
96.7%	1.0%	$562	Component Engineering and Tooling Cost
97.6%	0.9%	$504	Demand Planning Cost
98.4%	0.7%	$432	Raw Material Warehouse Cost
99.1%	0.7%	$403	IT Operational Cost for Supply Chain
99.6%	0.5%	$284	Accounts Receivable Cost
100.0%	0.4%	$242	Accounts Payable Cost

were making the biggest dent in gross profit. The team was able to segment metric data using the cost center hierarchy and S&OP defined business unit.

Inventory Days of Supply

As documented in the scorecard, the actual inventory days of supply (DOS) is 60.5 days. The defect analysis for this metric utilized both the classification (i.e., finished goods, work in progress, purchased finished goods, raw materials, packaging, etc.) and activity level as defined by customer, finance, and annual volume (i.e., A, B, C, D, Customer Liable, Excess, Shrink, and Obsolete). The team also determined that it needed to illustrate the defects using both inventory dollars ($) and days of supply. Defects were defined as:

   All: Excess, Shrink, and Obsolete

   A: High-volume SKUs with DOS greater than 15

   B: Mid-volume SKUs with DOS greater than 30

   C: Lower-volume SKUs with DOS greater than 60

   D: Lowest-volume SKUs with DOS greater than 90

The results summarized where the most inventory dollars were invested and which SKUs were the poorest performing. The team was able to segment metric data using the product hierarchy, inventory classification, and S&OP defined business unit.

Planning for the First Team On-Site

The metric defect analysis sets the stage for the first on-site visit. As discussed in the project scheduling options, the first on-site with the team can focus on assembling the AS IS SCOR Level 3 processes diagram using the "staple yourself to an order" interview process. Alternatively, the first on-site may be the process diagram and brainstorm event initiating the next phase of the project: project portfolio development. Chapter 14 illustrates the techniques, instructions, and examples of the process analyses for either case.

The Steering Team Review

The initial focus on the agenda is for each assigned subteam to review its scorecard gap analysis, including revised assumptions, calculations, and feedback from validation resources. The goal is for the entire design team to achieve consensus for each metric on the total opportunity calculated on the scorecard. This review doubles as a dry run for a portion of the steering team review. As part of this review, each metric team must identify the design team member who will make the presentation. Do not underestimate the impact of a crisp, clear, and concise presentation delivered by the people who did the work. This review will be the first in which data that are presented may be contentious.

The agenda for this steering team *review* includes the following:

- Competitive requirements
- Scorecards
- Gap analysis
- Defect analysis
- On-site plans for process analyses and brainstorm event

For Fowlers, the validation effort ultimately did not change the numbers or assumptions, but the process did reveal some change-management stages that would have to occur. The careful organization of the subteams for each metric and the choice of influential validation resources helped to manage the length of these stages as the wider Fowlers audience was introduced to "the numbers."

Change Management: Dealing with Denial

In the first stage, reactions are predictable as the design team's work spreads through the organization: The numbers are wrong; we aren't that bad.

The technology products business team members, when presented with the scorecard gap analysis, reacted predictably: They challenged the numbers. This happens in almost all projects. That's why it's important to have the right design team members from each of the product groups present to explain the data and have their validation resources sitting right next to them (as opposed to having a consultant). For people seeing the data for the first time, this builds confidence that the numbers are, in fact, reliable and quickly puts the focus on the issues.

Change Management: Placing Blame

The second reaction is to allocate blame, which is easier than taking responsibility for the results. Positioning design team members to share their personal perspectives on the gap analysis, and to review competitive performance facts, helps accelerate business unit leaders through this stage and moves them beyond the convenient catchall phrase: "But we're unique."

Change Management: Book the Numbers

The third reaction is to confuse acceptance of the analysis with actually having solved the problem. Agreeing on the opportunity does not improve anything. At this point, the business team is excited at the value of improving supply chain performance; based on benchmarks and competitive requirements, the numbers can add up fast. But it's too soon to start booking the savings in corporate forecasts and memos to the board. The real value of change will show up as part of the next phase.

In closing out the scorecard deliverable, the Fowlers project team members learned an important lesson—one that would be repeated again and again. They learned that the main goal of the analysis and validation effort is to manage change, not just to complete a deliverable. Their ability to quickly learn the *Supply Chain Excellence* process, understand the main idea of the deliverables, and then carefully transfer that knowledge to the wider Fowlers audience was critical. With advanced apologies to *Dilbert*, they realized the essential change management value of "greasing the skids," "getting others up to speed," and "touching base."

Phase 3: Develop the Project Portfolio

▶ **June 16 and July 11–15: Building Shared Vision and the Project List**

What do the numbers 50, 20, 1,000, 15, and 3 have in common? They're the typical results of a successful project portfolio phase that is founded in data (defect analysis), experience (through the brainstorm event), and process (using SCOR).

Fifty can be the number of people who participate in a daylong brainstorm event. Twenty is how many disconnects or issues a typical person can come up with in an hour. A thousand is the number of disconnects or issues the whole team can generate in the same amount of time. Fifteen is a common number of projects that will be identified to eliminate the issues. Three is the percent of savings (relative to sales) that an average performing company will achieve by implementing these projects. In other words, a supply chain supporting $100 million in revenue can yield $3 million in gross opportunity savings split between revenue growth, productivity improvement, cost reduction, and asset turnover.

The objectives for the June 16 session are to plan and set the date for the brainstorm event (the week of July 11–15), conduct and document the on-site event, assemble the preliminary project portfolio, and begin to validate the metric impact.

Planning the Brainstorm Event

A well-planned brainstorm event takes the information collected and analyzed through the metric defect analysis and integrates it with employee experience and SCOR processes. The combination creates a positive feeling of teamwork, shared vision of the real issues, and confidence in the size of potential benefit. It also provides for greater stakeholder involvement in the project, giving extended team members and other invited participants a feeling of contribution, common understanding, and, ultimately, ownership of the changes.

There are six ingredients to a good brainstorming event:

1. An appropriate invitee list
2. Effective communication, including advance invitation, project overview, and instructions for event preparation
3. Organized brainstorm categories using the metric defect analysis and scorecard data
4. An appropriate venue
5. Predefined leadership roles for the design team that carry through from defect analysis to opportunity analysis
6. Documentation that captures the individual disconnects, problem groups, preliminary projects, and benefits estimate

Invitees

Select participants from among those people who are close to the day-to-day and week-to-week details of all facets of the movement of materials. Attempt to represent expertise from planning, sourcing, manufacturing, marketing and sales, warehouse, transportation, finance, and customer service. For the brainstorm event, the quantity of issues, with examples, is a critical factor. Don't reach too high in the organization; participants at higher levels of management have more trouble generating a detailed list and often cannot point to specific examples. The examples help drive the root cause analysis. Invitees can be considered part of the extended team listed in the project charter or invited guests. In either case, proper communication makes a big difference in the quality of the output.

Effective Communication

The invitation letter needs to clearly convey the purpose of the event, preparation instructions, and the basics of where, when, and so on. The invitation needs to be in participants' hands one to two weeks in advance; anything less gives the impression that the project is poorly planned and limits the quality of individual preparation. A project overview session conducted before the event provides participants with a wide-angle view of the project, including a status report on the key deliverables of the scorecard gap analysis and metric defect analysis. Further, it gives them a short tutorial on their homework assignment: understanding the defect analysis for their metric and coming up with 20 or so potential causes of the second sort of defects.

Many companies have automated collection of the disconnects using an Excel spreadsheet. The entire workbook might be labeled as *Disconnect Detail*. Each subsequent worksheet can be labeled with the participant's name. Filling out the worksheet (Figure 8-1) can be accomplished by using one file, with each person taking a turn, or by sending a copy of the file to each participant, with the files to be returned and consolidated prior to the event. The benefits of an electronic template are threefold. First, the disconnect IDs are easily referenced for future use using the "find" function in Excel. Second,

Figure 8-1. Sample disconnect detail worksheet.

Description for Disconnect or Issue—Example	Initials	ID	SCOR Process
Item master data-setup errors cause poor planning data to pass to plants and suppliers, resulting in poorer forecasts—item 093232	PB	1	EP.3
No visibility to customer demand—consumption rate leads to unpredicted spikes in demand, resulting in customer shortages—order 0930211	PB	2	P1.1
		3	
		4	
		5	
		6	
		7	
		8	
		9	
		10	
		11	
		12	
		13	
		14	
		15	
		16	
		17	
		18	
		19	
		20	

and more important, labels can be generated and applied to electronic sticky notes prior to the session, speeding up the process and making the output more legible. Third, the Excel worksheets are easy to share and review using a web-based meeting platform that allows you to share a desktop and provides file-sharing commands.

Organized Brainstorm Categories

Setting up brainstorm categories and teams in advance helps the participants stay focused, leverages their knowledge and experience, and ultimately provides better ideas about the causes of defects. Using the SCOR metrics from the scorecard as the brainstorm categories has proven to be the most effective way of organizing the teams and relating projects to benefit estimates.

The Appropriate Venue

The ideal venue is a large rectangular room with enough seating for all attendees. Tape the category titles (typed in large print on 8.5″ × 11″ paper), defect analysis (also in handout form), and scorecard data on the walls, spacing them evenly around the room. Many teams have used sticky notes, flip-chart paper, or butcher-block paper to capture the participants' ideas on causes for defects. Most of the time will be spent in small groups, frequently standing next to the collected items in a brainstorm category; therefore the activity does not work as well in a small conference room.

Predefined Leadership Roles

For the brainstorm event, design team members formalize their role in the knowledge-transfer process, transitioning from student to teacher. The project manager (or coach) serves as the master of ceremonies, reviewing the agenda and instructions for each step. He or she also serves as pace keeper, moderator of conflict, and general role model for everyone. Each design team member is assigned to lead (co-lead) a brainstorm category and facilitate the brainstorm steps. As will be discussed, this includes grouping similar issues by SCOR process, defining problem statements, estimating the weight of each problem, and assembling the preliminary project portfolio benefits. Be sure to keep those involved in each metric defect analysis together on the same team.

Documentation Approach

The project portfolio worksheet is the primary documentation tool for the next few chapters. It is prepared in advance with some of the fields being filled out in real time during the brainstorm event. Figure 8-2 illustrates the template and offers instructions defining the type of data required for each problem identified.

Based on our experience of facilitating more than 90 of these events, two lessons stand out. The first is that *preparation pays*. The more the participants understand about the metric and the first and second sorts of the defect analysis, the more effective they will be in identifying potential causes (answers to third-, fourth-, and fifth-level "why" questions).

The second lesson has to do with the process of *identifying the issues*; it can either be individual or group. The method that has been discussed so far has each participant identifying issues from his or her point of view, based on knowledge of the defect analysis and direct experience with issues. During the event, the team then groups individual ideas into a problem. The group method focuses on generating the problems through discussion and consensus, rather than generating individual issues.

Both methods have pluses and minuses. The first method has detail, and builds shared understanding and vision; the second builds consensus quickly. The risk with the first method is that it can take longer to eliminate redundancies. The risk with the second method is that it aggregates too quickly and misses some things. In addition, outspoken individuals can influence the output.

Conducting the Brainstorm Session

The day of the event, July 13, had finally arrived. The Fowlers brainstorm team included the entire design team; Chief Operating Officer Brian Dowell; product development managers; buyer/planners; customer service representatives; cost accountants; marketing

Figure 8-2. Sample project portfolio worksheet data definitions.

Metric	Level 1 Defect	Problem Statement Number	Problem Statement Phrase	Problem Statement Description	Individual Disconnect IDs	Level 2 Defect	Defect Rate	Problem Weight	Problem Impact	SCOR Process
Title of the brainstorm category is listed here; e.g., Perfect Order Fulfillment.	Label of the first sort of the Defect Analysis.	After the disconnects have been aggregated to problems, a number is assigned; e.g., 1.01, 1.02, etc.	Brief description of the problem using a noun, adjective, and verb.	A sentence or two that describes the problem. It must be relevant to all of the individual disconnects and include an example; e.g., part number, supplier, or customer.	The individual disconnect IDs are recorded here.	The label of the second sort of the Defect Analysis.	This is the overall defect rate for the Level 2 defect and is taken directly off the Defect Analysis Pareto chart.	This is the weight the team assigns to the problem. The sum of the problem weights within a Level 2 defect category can be no more than 100% and oftentimes less if not all the problems are known.	This is a calculated field multiplying the defect rate times the problem weight. This is the estimated impact to the SCOR Level 1 metric. For sure, this is the most difficult number to estimate.	Ideally, the team would have already attended a SCOR Framework class. Two or three team members will identify the SCOR element(s) where the problem occurs. SCOR Level 1, 2, or 3 can apply here.

analysts; material planners; focus factory managers; sales managers; product line managers from both the technology and food products groups (the latter was the next SCOR project candidate); functional experts for purchasing, order management, planning, distribution, and manufacturing from the corporate applications group; a transportation manager; an import/export manager; a warehouse manager from corporate logistics; a market research analyst; forecast analysts for each of the product families; and a business development manager from the corporate marketing group. In all, there were forty people on the list. As mentioned earlier, the design team agreed to use its six SCOR Level 1 metrics as the brainstorm categories. The rationale was to get the extended team thinking about the relationship of each issue to the defect data and why things failed.

The team took the coach's advice and stayed with the metric and defect analysis teams. Design team leaders were assigned. The planning director was assigned to be team leader for the perfect order fulfillment category. Order fulfillment cycle time was led by the purchasing director; the director of manufacturing oversaw discussion of upside supply chain flexibility; supply chain management cost was handled by the director of logistics/customer service; the corporate controller led the cost of goods discussion; and the vice president of sales and marketing for the food products group led inventory days of supply with help from the director of applications. David Able served as the master of ceremonies, and the coach was used as a floater among teams, helping them as needed.

The Fowlers Brainstorm Event

The agenda for the brainstorm event at Fowlers had five line items and looked like this:

1. *Introduction*. David reviewed the agenda, room layout, brainstorm categories (perfect order fulfillment, order fulfillment cycle time, upside supply chain flexibility, supply

chain management cost, cost of goods, and inventory days of supply), and associated defect analysis, and introduced the category leaders.

2. *Initial Brainstorm: 60 Minutes.* David facilitated the brainstorming activity, getting all those involved to place their 20 individual causes of Level 2 defects onto the appropriate metric charts. Brian insisted on the electronic method, through which participants had entered their data the previous week and labels were put on sticky notes prior to the session.

3. *Affinity Diagrams: 120 Minutes.* By using the predetermined team lists, David moved people to their appropriate metrics with their team leaders. They spent two hours reading through the ideas, grouping them into similar problems within each Level 2 defect category.

4. *Documentation: 120 Minutes.* The team was tasked with completing the project portfolio worksheet. The team leader had assigned a documentation role and had prepared the worksheet template ahead of time. This was the most difficult part of the day; gaining agreement on the problem definition and the metric impact of eliminating the issue spawned many passionate discussions.

5. *Question-and-Answer Review: 60 Minutes.* Fowlers' disconnect analysis session yielded 838 individual disconnects in six brainstorm categories, and an initial 62 problem groups with their own statements. David then facilitated a public question-and-answer review of each team's problem statements to conclude the event.

Figures 8-3A and 8-3B illustrate a portion of the perfect order fulfillment team's project portfolio worksheet. In Figure 8-3A, the planning director had already filtered the defect Level 1 column to isolate "sales order shipped not complete" and the Level 2 column to isolate "actual demand exceeded forecast." Twenty-seven individual disconnects for the defect were grouped into three problems: "Poor Visibility to External Customer Sales Plan," "Poor Forecast Management," and "New Product-Manufacturing Lead Time & Planning Not Aligned."

Figure 8-3B illustrates that if all three of these problems were eliminated, the *impact* to perfect order fulfillment would be 20 percent (7.4 plus 7.4 plus 5.2). The formula takes the defect rate times the problem weight for each problem. Problem weights are the most difficult part of the exercise. Everyone is uncomfortable. This is the moment of truth at which experience has to help the data arrive at

Figure 8-3A. Fowlers' perfect order fulfillment team project portfolio worksheet, filtered.

Metric	Level 1 Defect	Problem Statement Number	Problem Statement Phrase	Problem Statement Description	Disconnect IDs	Level 2 Defect	Defect Rate
Perfect Order Fulfillment	Sales Order Shipped Not Complete	7.01	Poor Visibility to External Customer Sales Plan	For 70% of our planning, we have a lack of visibility to the customer's demand or promotions resulting in no forecast and a 36% sales plan error.	321, 255, 193, 157, 142, 689, 703, 567, 234, 6, 59, 43	Actual Demand Exceeded Forecast	20.0%
Perfect Order Fulfillment	Sales Order Shipped Not Complete	7.02	Poor Forecast Management	SKU level forecasts are inaccurate due to minimal analysis, poor input from known sales and marketing input, and a lack of corporate discipline to support one forecast.	217, 26, 267, 469, 551, 242, 431, 181, 236, 308	Actual Demand Exceeded Forecast	20.0%
Perfect Order Fulfillment	Sales Order Shipped Not Complete	7.03	New Product- Manufacturing Lead Time & Planning Not Aligned	New Product Development items are not planned and released to production with enough lead time for production to meet customer orders/demand in units and timetable.	385, 142, 203, 257, 418	Actual Demand Exceeded Forecast	20.0%

Figure 8-3B. Fowlers' perfect order fulfillment team project portfolio worksheet, with demonstration of impact.

Problem Statement Phrase	Problem Statement Description	Level 2 Defect	Defect Rate	Problem Weight	Impact
Poor Visibility to External Customer Sales Plan	For 70% of our planning, we have a lack of visibility to the customer's demand or promotions resulting in no forecast and a 36% sales plan error.	Actual Demand Exceeded Forecast	20.0%	37.0%	7.4%
Poor Forecast Management	SKU level forecasts are inaccurate due to minimal analysis, poor input from known sales and marketing input, and a lack of corporate discipline to support one forecast.	Actual Demand Exceeded Forecast	20.0%	37.0%	7.4%
New Product-Manufacturing Lead Time & Planning Not Aligned	New Product Development items are not planned and released to production with enough lead time for production to meet customer orders/demand in units and timetable.	Actual Demand Exceeded Forecast	20.0%	26.0%	5.2%

a realistic number. Conservative realism is ideal; gross sandbagging is not helpful. As the weight is assigned, participants are usually already thinking about how to validate the numbers and document their assumptions. An important note: The sum of the problem weights within a Level 2 defect category can never be more than 100 percent. Less than 100 percent means that not all of the problems have been identified; more than 100 percent means the team is being overly optimistic.

CHAPTER 9

Phase 3: Refine the Project Portfolio

▶ **July 11–15: Validating the Project Benefits and SCOR Processes**

There is no easy way to take the impacts and process areas documented in the brainstorm session and validate them at the level of confidence "to simply book the numbers" with leadership. But that's the challenge for this session: consolidating the 62 problems across six metrics into a concise set of SCOR process–based projects and finalizing impacts for each of them.

Consolidating Problems to Projects Using SCOR

Consolidating problems into projects is an easier task when someone is experienced with the filter and sort functions of Excel spreadsheets. The ability to organize a pivot table is even more useful.

In preparation for the first day's meeting, the project manager consolidates the problems from all of the metric worksheets by copying and pasting them onto a single worksheet called *Project Portfolio*. With the Auto Filter on, the consolidation process begins.

The first step in the process is to filter the heading "SCOR Process" by SCOR Level 3 process ID. At this point, some problems may have more than one SCOR Level 3 ID, such as P1.1, D1.3, and P1.3; and some may have Level 2 IDs, such as P1. In the case of multiple Level 3 IDs, gain consensus on which process area is the most influential relating to the problem. In the case of Level 2 IDs, try to pick the most influential Level 3 process relating to the problem.

The second step in the process is to assign an arbitrary project number to all the problems resulting from the SCOR Level 3 filter; for example, all problems containing the SCOR Level 3 ID D1.3 get assigned the same project number. This routine is repeated for each SCOR Level 3 ID until all problems have a project number assigned.

To be clear, after the filtering, all problem statements should have a project number. It is conceivable (though not probable) that there could be 184 projects—one for each SCOR Level 3 element: 20 for PLAN, 17 for SOURCE, 22 for MAKE, 52 for DELIVER, 26 for RETURN, and 47 for ENABLE.

The focus for the next level of filtering, called *Process Similarity*, again uses the field called SCOR Process. This time the team uses a custom filter containing a SCOR Level 2 ID (i.e., S1, M2, P1, or D3). For this filter, the team attempts to consolidate projects based on process scope. For example, a filter using S1 may yield five projects—one each for S1.1, S1.2, S1.3, S1.4, and S1.5. There are at least *four factors* that influence project consolidation within a SCOR Level 2 process. The *first* is the physical location of where the process occurs. For example, S1.2, S1.3, and S1.4 (receiving, quality assurance, and "put-away") are typically carried out in the raw material warehouse and therefore are candidates for consolidation.

The *second* factor is the function or functions performing the process. For example, if your suppliers drop-ship their products to your customer's warehouse, purchasing may not only have to schedule the product but also enter the receipt transaction in the system when the shipment is physically received by the customer warehouse. In that case, S1.1 and S1.2 would be candidates for consolidation. The *third* factor is the degree of impact. If improving the scheduling process with suppliers accounts for 50 percent of the inventory benefit in the portfolio, the degree of effort and focus may warrant isolating the process with only one project. Likewise, consolidation is good if the benefit for each process is small but when added together they create a significant impact.

A *fourth* factor, consolidating plan projects, requires one more decision: horizontal vs. vertical grouping. For example, a frequent horizontal consolidation involves grouping P4.1, P4.2, P4.3, and P4.4 into a project called *distribution requirements planning*; or grouping P3.1, P3.2, P3.3, and P3.4 into a project called *master production scheduling*. Another horizontal grouping could involve grouping all P4, P3, and P2 processes into a project called *tactical planning*.

A common vertical grouping that focuses on improving capacity planning (both long term and near term) and scheduling and might include P1.2, all P3 processes, and M1.1. The decision for vertical vs. horizontal grouping sometimes can be as much art as science. Factors that influence a vertical grouping include linking rough-cut planning to scheduling, forecasts to available inventory at distribution centers, and annual volume commitments of suppliers to near-term purchase order releases. The main factors that influence a horizontal grouping are synchronizing customer orders, manufacturing schedules, and planned supplier receipts.

The focus of the next filtering step is called *strategic similarity*, which attempts to consolidate projects across the strategies of *make-to-stock, make-to-order, and engineer-to-order*. This custom filter uses an "or" statement in an effort to identify projects within the same process but in another strategy. For example, using the custom filter "contains P2, S1 or S2 or S3" will yield projects containing any of the SOURCE-related projects. The team would use the same four grouping strategies discussed in the preceding paragraphs.

The last filtering step, called *ENABLE*, again uses the SCOR Process field. This time the team uses the custom auto filter containing "E." This leaves all problem statements that are connected to some form of enabling process.

ENABLE filters can go three directions. First, often they are *grouped across the Enable process categories* EP.3, ES.3, EM.3, and ED.3 and may be consolidated into a project focused only on master data accuracy—including planning item data, source list, routings and recipes, and customer list. Second, they are often *grouped vertically with their associated planning and execution processes*. For example, a project focused on P1 (sales and operations planning) may also include EP.1, EP.3, EP.4, and EP.10. Third, if the scope is big enough, ENABLE elements *can be left as individual projects*. For example, EP.7 may be the process that includes an overall physical network evaluation using a sophisticated logistics engineering tool.

Figure 9-1 is the result of the Fowlers P1.1 filter. The team discussed each of the three problems and agreed to consolidate 7.01 and 7.02 into Project 1, and put 7.03 into another—Project 6—already identified and associated with ED.7, manage product life cycle.

Validating the Problem Weight

As already stated at least once, the hardest task to date is validating the problem weights, which were estimates based on team experience during the brainstorm event. These problem weights have the largest influence on the projected size of the benefit pool—and therefore are of the highest interest to the steering team.

Validating the problem weight follows a four-step process:

1. Collect a small random sample of data focusing on instances of the Level 2 Defect;

Figure 9-1. Fowlers' problem validation P1.1 filter.

Metric	Level 1 Defect	Problem Statement Number	Problem Statement Phrase	Problem Statement Description	Level 2 Defect	Impact	SCOR Process	Project Number
Perfect Order Fulfillment	Sales Order Shipped Not Complete	7.01	Poor Visibility to External Customer Sales Plan	For 70% of our planning, we have a lack of visibility to the customer's demand or promotions resulting in no forecast and a 36% sales plan error.	Actual Demand Exceeded Forecast	7.4%	P1.1 EP.3	1
Perfect Order Fulfillment	Sales Order Shipped Not Complete	7.02	Poor Forecast Management	SKU level forecasts are inaccurate due to minimal analysis, poor input from known sales and marketing input, and a lack of corporate discipline to support one forecast.	Actual Demand Exceeded Forecast	7.4%	P1.1	1
Perfect Order Fulfillment	Sales Order Shipped Not Complete	7.03	New Product-Manufacturing Lead Time & Planning Not Aligned	New Product Development items are not planned and released to production with enough lead time for production to meet customer orders/demand in units and timetable.	Actual Demand Exceeded Forecast	5.2%	P1.1 ED.7	6

2. Conduct root cause analysis for each instance;

3. Compare results to initial problem weight estimates;

4. Adjust accordingly.

The Fowlers perfect order fulfillment team started its validation effort by defining a query to extract sales-order data for the last forecasted month. For each item on these sales orders, members compared the forecast to the actual order volume and filtered for those items that were a part of Level 2 Defect, *actual demand exceeded forecast*. The good news is that the 20 percent overall rate used for the brainstorm event was validated.

To validate the 37 percent estimate surrounding *Poor Visibility to External Customer Sales Plan*, the team sorted the items by customer where order volume exceeded forecast. They found that 32 customers were involved. Of those, only five were providing some kind of forecast, planogram, sales plan, and/or point-of-sale data. For an additional seven customers, there had been a desire to gather demand data but none was being provided. This group of 12 customers represented 25 percent of the sample size. The team recommended changing the problem weight from 37 percent to 25 percent, changing the overall impact from 7.4 percent to 5 percent.

To validate the 26 percent estimate surrounding *New Product-Manufacturing Lead Time & Planning Not Aligned*, the team focused on items for the twenty non-strategic customers. New products were defined as any part number introduced in the previous six months. This filter isolated 20 percent of all orders in which demand for new items exceeded forecast. The team recommended changing the problem weight from 26 percent to 20 percent, changing the overall impact from 5.2 percent to 4 percent.

To validate the 37 percent estimate surrounding *Poor Forecast Management*, the team analyzed the remaining items (55 percent of the total) that were not new and were not part of the strategic customers' order count. The team refined the criteria to identify items where the best statistical model, for some reason, had not been used. This filter isolated 15 percent of the orders that were characterized by low-volume items. The team recommended changing the problem weight from 37 percent to 15 percent, changing the overall impact from 7.4 percent to 3 percent. Figure 9-2 illustrates the results of the validation for this single Level 2 Defect category.

As illustrated, the team changed the problem statement for Poor Forecast Management to *Poor Forecast Model*. It also changed the weights as specified in this section. The overall impact now totaled 12 percent. The team also acknowledged that the remaining 40 percent of the instances in which an item's order volume exceeded forecast was in a category of "other"—which it did not have time to analyze. The team proceeded in the next week with this validation method for every Level 2 Defect for each of the six metrics considered in the brainstorm. The result of the effort was a first view of the technology products group project portfolio summary (Figure 9-3)—which would be the first subject on the agenda for the next session.

Figure 9-2. Fowlers' poor forecast management Level 2 validation.

Problem Statement Phrase	Problem Statement Description	Level 2 Defect	Defect Rate	Problem Weight	Impact	SCOR Process	Project Number
Poor Visibility to External Customer Sales Plan	For 70% of our planning, we have a lack of visibility to the customer's demand or promotions resulting in no forecast and a 36% sales plan error.	Actual Demand Exceeded Forecast	20.0%	25.0%	5.0%	P1.1 EP.3	1
Poor Forecast Model	Poor SKU level statistical models were used to generate demand plans.	Actual Demand Exceeded Forecast	20.0%	15.0%	3.0%	P1.1	1
New Product-Manufacturing Lead Time & Planning Not Aligned	New Product Development items are not planned and released to production with enough lead time for production to meet customer orders/demand in units and timetable.	Actual Demand Exceeded Forecast	20.0%	20.0%	4.0%	P1.1 ED.7	6

Figure 9-3. Fowlers' technology products group project portfolio summary, first draft.

Project Number	Project Phrase	Project Description	Revenue ($)	Perfect Order Fulfillment (%)	Order Fulfillment Cycle Time (days)	Upside Supply Chain Flexibility (days)	Total Supply Chain Management Cost ($)	COGS ($)	Inventory ($)
	Baseline		$450,000,000	30.2%	11.0	91.5	$57,601,000	$286,200,000	$47,437,000
1	Improve Demand Management and Forecasting	This project will improve poorly defined practices, underutilized modeling techniques, and untrained personnel.		8.0%					$1,660,000
2	Optimize Supply Management Practices	This project will focus on enabling and execution of tactical processes with targeted suppliers.				5.0		$5,000,000	$1,550,000
3	Improve SAP Utilization	This project will focus on scaling up more effective and efficient data warehouse capability, and improve the business units' utilization of the PP and MM reporting.					$1,350,000		
4	Improve Data Integrity	This project will define a master data management process and correct errors in supplier, item, and customer master data.		5.0%	2.0	7.5			
5	Improve Supplier Flexibility	This project will focus on developing vendors' capability to respond to near-term demand fluctuations for source-to-stock and source-to-order items.				15.0	$1,350,000	$2,500,000	$1,320,000
6	Implement Formal Product Life Cycle Management Process	This project will design, develop, and implement an integrated management process for all phases of a product's life cycle, from introduction through commercialization to retirement.		4.0%		7.5		$5,000,000	$2,500,000

(continues)

Figure 9-3. (continued)

#	Project Name	Description	Benefit						
7	Engineer an Integrated Tactical Planning Process	This project will design, develop, and implement effective and efficient tactical planning processes to help manage the short-term horizon balancing customer orders, stocking levels, replenishment orders to factories, and purchase orders to suppliers.		5.0%	1.0		$1,350,000	$2,500,000	$1,000,000
8	Implement Sales and Operations Planning	This project will implement a Sales and Operations Planning process integrating demand and supply planning with business plans and reconciliation to financial objectives.		25.0%			$3,375,540	$1,182,000	$4,400,000
9	Improve the Efficiency and Effectiveness of the Physical Supply Chain Network	This project will focus on short- and long-term physical network strategy improving cycle time, transportation and warehouse spend, and align long-term capacity requirements.			-4.0		$5,400,000		$1,650,000
10	Tighten Up Order Management Discipline	This project will cover entry errors, EDI errors, and business rules from inquiry and quote through order entry and inventory allocation.		15.0%	2.0		$540,000		$500,000
11	Establish Formal Return Management	This project will define and implement a reverse logistics processes from goods movement to policy to the authorization process.					$1,350,000		$660,000
12	Eliminate Poor Inventory Control Practices	This project will focus on defects that relate to inventory record accuracy, shrinkage, and cycle counting.		2.5%					$1,660,000
	Benefit		$4,500,000	64.5%	1.0	35.0	$14,715,540	$16,182,000	$16,900,000
	Projected Performance Level		$454,500,000	94.7%	10.0	56.5	$42,885,460	$270,018,000	$30,537,000

CHAPTER 10

Phase 3: Opportunity Analysis

▶ **July 11–15: Due Diligence for the Project List**

Three percent profit improvement to the sales value of the supply chain: As described in Chapter 1, that's the rule-of-thumb opportunity before the data are prepared (read: sanitized) for presentation to executives and the board. For every $100 million in revenue, that means an opportunity for an extra $3 million in earnings. This gem is worth repeating.

Where any company comes in against this rule, however, depends on its distance from parity on six key metrics: revenue, perfect order fulfillment, order fulfillment cycle time, upside supply chain flexibility, cost of goods, and total supply chain management cost. The more of these metrics to which a company performs at or better than parity, the more likely it is that the discovery and analysis process will yield opportunity of approximately 1.5 percent. Companies that perform below parity with respect to these metrics typically will find opportunities in excess of that amount—up to 4.5 percent.

Depending on how experienced design team members are at the budgeting process, the opportunity assessment will range from simple to mind-bending. The objectives of this last session in the July 11 to 15 on-site are to create, refine, and prioritize the weights and impact analyses for each of the projects in the portfolio (Figure 9-3), and prepare for the third formal steering team review.

Summarizing the Opportunity

The objective for this portion of the session is to educate the team about the process of finalizing the project benefits through validating weights and impacts, documenting important assumptions, and beginning to think about implementation scope, sequence, and resources.

The final validation process follows six principles.

♦ *Principle One.* At a minimum, the subteams must, again, revisit the problem weights and the defect analysis with a critical view of the validation data, sample size, and relevancy.

♦ *Principle Two.* Factor out the effect of forecasted growth by assuming constant revenue for the financial period; usually savings are annualized. If the sponsor is willing, it's acceptable to include the profit improvement from revenue growth.

♦ *Principle Three.* Be realistic in the savings estimates; the steering team and ultimately the executive team should add the appropriate safety buffer to the numbers, observing the doctrine of "under-promise and over-deliver." As stated previously, conservative realism is normal; gross sandbagging is not helpful at this point.

♦ *Principle Four.* Document all assumptions behind the problem weight estimates and resulting impacts. This is the most important principle; any push-back by the steering team typically has more to do with the assumptions than the numbers.

♦ *Principle Five.* Identify finance and other resources that can objectively test or spar with the numbers and assumptions—before the estimates are shared with the steering team.

◆ *Principle Six.* Identify what type of savings this project will have: revenue growth, cost reduction, productivity improvement, or cost avoidance.

The Project Opportunity Worksheet

Each project requires some form of a spreadsheet (Table 10-1). The first section—*project phrase, project number, and project description*—is taken from the preliminary project portfolio. The first column is taken from the revenue, cost of goods sold, and supply chain management cost metrics. The columns under 2012, 2013, 2014, and 2015 are where the team needs to enter estimated savings recorded as a negative number for costs and a positive number for revenue. The bottom line—*operating income/economic value added impact*—simply adds the absolute value of *total cost of sales* benefits to *total supply chain management cost* benefits. The most frequent question from design teams at this point is how to portray project savings over multiple years. There is only one answer to this: It depends!

The finance and executive leadership teams will have the answer. The most common guideline is to count only new savings to be recorded in each year. To illustrate, let's use the inbound transportation example from Table 10-1 of cost savings over four years. Year one nets $110,100, or 10 percent of the total from savings in the western region; years two and three net another $275,300 or twenty-five percent each in savings in the central and eastern regions; and year four nets $440,400, or 40 percent in savings, by focusing on imports. By using the *new savings* guideline, the four-year total is $1,101,100.

The assumptions are the most important part of this exercise. There's no magic in assembling a good one. Each metric *category* (row) that shows benefit gets its own statement of assumption. It could include an item number or numbers by type (i.e., raw mate-

Table 10.1. Project Opportunity Analysis

	Project Phrase:	Implement Sales and Operations Planning				
	Project Number:	8				
	Project Description:	This project will implement a Sales and Operations Planning process integrating demand and supply planning with business plans and reconciliation to financial objectives.				
		YEAR OF IMPACT				
		2012	**2013**	**2014**	**2015**	
Revenue		$450.0	$1,125.0	$1,125.0	$1,800.0	**1**
Cost of Sales						
	Labor					
	Material	−$295.5	−$591.0	−$295.5	—	**2**
	Indirect					
Total Cost of Sales		−$295.5	−$591.0	−$295.5	$0.0	
Total Supply Chain Management Cost						
	Order Management Cost					
	Customer Service Cost					
	Finished Goods Warehouse Cost	−$79.0	−$79.0	−$79.0	−$79.0	**3**
	Outbound Transportation Cost					
	Material (Product) Acquisition Cost					
	Purchasing Cost					
	Raw Material Warehouse Cost					
	Supplier Quality Cost					
	Component Engineering and Tooling Cost					
	Inbound Transportation Cost	−$110.1	−$275.3	−$275.3	−$440.4	**4**
	Planning and Finance Cost					
	Demand Planning Cost					
	Supply Planning Cost					

	Supply Chain Finance Control Cost					
	Inventory Carrying Cost					
	Opportunity Cost	−$85.7	−$85.7	−$137.0	−$34.2	6
	Obsolescence Cost	−$240.0	−$240.0	−$240.0	−$240.0	5
	Shrinkage Cost					
	Taxes and Insurance Cost					
	IT Cost for Supply Chain					
	Supply Chain Application Cost					
	IT Operational Cost for Supply Chain					
Total Supply Chain Management Cost		−$514.8	−$680.0	−$731.3	−$793.6	
Operating Income/ EVA Impact		$1,260.3	$2,396.0	$2,151.8	$2,593.6	

rial, work in progress, finished goods, or returns); estimated volume, calculated using such data as market share, geographic segment, unit volume, or unit forecast; cost or revenue impact, calculated by cost per unit or margin per unit; and/or delivery reliability, lead time, and necessary business conditions.

There are different kinds of assumptions. One kind describes the impact of cost reduction or productivity improvement in direct or indirect categories. Another describes the revenue impact of delivery reliability through fewer lost opportunities or pure growth. Yet another type of assumption describes the working-capital impact of lead time and delivery performance, as measured in inventory, payables, and/or receivables.

As an example, in addition to the service and inventory improvements documented on the project portfolio, the Fowlers team validated assumptions for the major income statement opportunities that would result from Project 8 (Figure 9-3). The team aligned these opportunity assumptions with the numbers in the last column as summarized in the following:

1. By improving perfect order fulfillment by 25 percent, Fowlers would reduce lost opportunity orders, validated as 1.5 percent of total orders, or 18,000 orders missed on account of no immediate material availability or cancellations. At $250 average value per order, the four year revenue opportunity calculates to $4,500,000. *Metric: Revenue.*

2. Achieve a 1 percent decrease in price per part for the ability to provide accurate forecast data to all suppliers. At $1,182,000 material cost, that equates to a $1,182,000 cost decrease. *Metric: COGS.*

3. Have inventory immediately available. This will reduce 10 percent of the amount of time spent per order picking multiple times, expediting inventory transfer orders, and providing phone status to customer service representatives. At $4.40 warehouse cost per order with 71,818 orders per year, this equates to $316,000. *Metric: Total Supply Chain Management Cost.*

4. Reduce unplanned changes to purchase orders, decreasing the number of instances of expedited transportation within lead time. Sixty-five percent of purchase orders are currently expedited, incurring 35 percent higher inbound transportation costs than necessary. Inbound transportation totals $7,896,000; improvement would reduce cost by $1,101,100. *Metric: Total Supply Chain Management Cost.*

5. Reduce the annualized rate of accrual for obsolescence by $240,000. *Metric: Total Supply Chain Management Cost.*

6. Reduce working inventory for low-volume products equivalent to 9.2 percent decrease of overall inventory value. For the balance-sheet measure of inventory this is equivalent to $20,000,000; for the economic value add (EVA) measure of inventory this is equivalent to $2,000,000. *Metrics: Inventory, and Total Supply Chain Management Cost as illustrated in Table 10-1.*

Identify Further Validation Resources

As the team tweaks the assumptions, it also reviews the list of names of people involved in building them and considers additional validation resources.

There are two reasons to add more names. First, it may be necessary to add more content expertise about details to further refine assumptions. For example, one might include a marketing research analyst to help refine market share and volume numbers or a cost accountant to calculate the impact of accruals or balance sheet changes. Second, adding these subject matter experts gives them extra time to digest the information before deciding to stand behind the numbers and therefore widen support for the project. It is normal for the numbers from the preliminary project portfolio to change; as the team digs deeper into the numbers and assumptions behind them, confidence will grow. Now is the time when documentation discipline will start to pay off. The opportunity spreadsheets and the project metric summary are two of the most important items to keep accurate. For example, teams often need to add *Revenue Impact* to the project metric summary and adjust the benefit dollars as they are refined. The next session initiates implementation with time spent assembling implementation charters for each of the projects and putting them in an implementation plan. With the path to the next week clear, the team turns toward preparing for steering team review two.

Conducting Steering Team Review Number Three

Prepare and conduct steering team review number three with the following agenda items:

- Review project portfolio
- Review project benefits, assumptions, and validation logic
- Review brainstorm event highlights

Phase 4: Lay Groundwork to Implement Projects

➤ **Mapping Out the Details and Portfolio Implementation Plans**

Who, what, when, where, and how are the questions the team faces now that the "how much" question has been answered. The challenge in preparing to initiate this next phase is to complete implementation project charters and prioritize launch dates based on effort, impact, and dependencies, and then implement the projects. On the Fowlers technology products group schedule, the implementation timeframe officially starts August 1, 2011. The meeting format would be project dependent but includes periodic face-to-face meetings, remote web-based conferences, and site visits where necessary.

Implementation Project Charters

An implementation project charter is intended to be the one document that has all the answers. It begins with the project title and description. The *project title* is a short phrase describing the action and process targeted for change.

The *project description* attempts to identify known changes and best practices that will guide the project.

The *problem statement* summarizes the phrase from the brainstorm event and other relevant individual disconnects that accurately describe the issues at hand.

Project objectives include known outcomes that need to occur for the project to be considered successful and for benefits to be realized. These will include impact or changes regarding trading partners, the organization, processes, people, technology, goals, and metrics.

Scope potentially specifies the product, customer, supplier, process, metric, system (data), and organizational functions that will be used to identify the future solution. Scope may be equal to the one defined in Phase 1; it also is common to refine the scope yet again knowing that the implementation will scale as needed.

Potential issues and other assorted *barriers* are presented in a bulleted list in the implementation project charter that attempts to highlight known "show stoppers"—things that will prevent the project from successful implementation. For example, a project aimed at implementing a good forecasting process requires focus from a person who can manage the assembly of a forecast, and it requires a good tool that can provide a statistical model. Potential issues and barriers to this project could be the organization's unwillingness to assign or hire a forecaster and/or the investment probability of buying an adequate statistical forecasting tool. The concept is to list only the big issues rather than provide an exhaustive narrative of every potential barrier.

The benefit section simply copies and pastes, from the project portfolio, the summary of the project's impact from each metric. The detailed opportunity analysis, with assumptions, is attached as an appendix to the implementation project charter.

The action plan steps offer project milestones. There are 13 of these:

1. Identify and approve project resource plan

2. Establish project schedule, including informal kickoff date

3. Review project charter, background, and expectations with project team

4. Develop baseline for metrics selected as in-scope

5. Conduct AS IS Level 3 and Level 4 process gap analysis (synchronizing with any previous analysis)

6. Develop action plans to close "quick hit" gaps

7. Assemble TO BE Level 3 and Level 4 process based on leading practice

8. Develop and approve solution design storyboard

9. Build and test solution

10. Pilot and verify solution

11. Roll out solution to project scope and evaluate metric impact

12. Define process control measures

13. Scale implementation to targeted supply chains in the definition matrix

Implementation resources specify by name the project champion or sponsor from the steering team; the project leader, which is generally a priority time role; subject matter expert; and team members. The subject matter expert role can vary depending on the scope of the project. The role could be a software expert if the primary idea is to roll out system functionality. It could be a best-practice expert if process is the primary idea. It could be two roles if process and tools need to work together. The team-member role can be somewhat complicated. The analytical role may be straightforward, but the implementation may change the nature of the team members' jobs. For example, implementing sales and operations planning in an organization that doesn't yet have such a process will include the new roles of demand and supply planners on the project team—which will also define how these individuals do a significant part of their jobs in the pilot and beyond.

Schedule essentially puts dates against the milestones in the preceding list, and can be represented in a list form or a Gantt chart managed by the leader. The typical rhythm of an implementation project is six months, with the team meeting each week—even if the meeting's duration is short. The first month addresses milestones 1 through 4, and the second month completes milestones 5 through 7. The third month has two parallel activities, closing the actions in milestone 6 and completing milestones 8 through 10. The fourth, fifth, and sixth months focus on milestones 11 and 12 in a continuous improvement loop, and the sixth month completes milestone 13. Rollout speed is dependent on the complexity of the solution, but can range from one month to six months. In most cases, a well-run project takes no longer than twelve months to move through all thirteen milestones. The portfolio itself typically covers three to four waves over a three-year span (Figure 11-1).

Figure 11-1. Fowlers' high-level implementation time line.

Wave	2011			2012				2013				2014			
	Q2	Q3	Q4	Q1	Q2	Q3	Q4	Q1	Q2	Q3	Q4	Q1	Q2	Q3	Q4
1															
2															
3															
4															

Develop
Pilot
Roll Out

Excerpts from the Fowlers Project 7 Implementation Charter—Engineer an Integrated Tactical Planning Process

Project Description

This project will design, develop, and implement effective and efficient tactical planning processes to help manage overall capacity, customer orders, stocking levels, replenishment orders to factories, and purchase orders to suppliers. Best-practice models suggest three tiers of planning including long-term capacity and inventory planning (4–18 months), master scheduling (3–13 weeks), and plant scheduling (1–14 days). The project would also develop master data maintenance policies and programs, and assess and recommend changes to the supply chain organization.

Problem Statement

The planning and scheduling processes are not integrated between the PLAN and MAKE and DELIVER processes, nor with SAP utilization of functionality, which creates a void between the sales forecast, inventory replenishment, sales order commitments to customers, and the plant scheduling processes. In addition, capacity management cannot be performed in the system due to inaccurate master data fields (i.e. routes, run rates, and yield). Last, the organizational structure does not facilitate productive analysis and response to issues and, more important, also does not facilitate effort and attention to proactive supply planning.

Project Objectives

1. Produce an achievable production schedule (M1.1)
2. Develop effective rough-cut capacity plans (P1.2 and P1.3)
3. Comprehend inventory and customer demand in the master schedule (P3)
4. Align the production schedule to the master production plan (M1.1)
5. Update and maintain production master data (EM3)
6. Develop policies to support an effective production plan (EM1)
7. Develop process measures to drive accountability (EP2 and EM2)
8. Measure and analyze production schedule adherence (M1.3)
9. Recommend organizational changes to support future-state process

Scope of the Project

◆ Product and Channel: Top SKUs that contribute 50% of sales in retail channel
◆ Process: P1.2, M1.1, P3
◆ System: PP, MM, and SD

◆   Metrics
  ◆ Manufacturing schedule adherence: weekly
  ◆ Master plan adherence: monthly
  ◆ Rough-cut capacity: monthly
  ◆ Master data accuracy: weekly (rotating)
  ◆ Percent of target stock: weekly

Potential Issues & Barriers

1. Approval to hire additional resources into the supply chain organization.
2. Resistance from business to change the supply chain organizational structure.

Benefits Summary

◆   The project benefits are summarized in Figure 11-2.

Action Plan (Milestones)

1. Identify and approve project resource plan
2. Establish project schedule, including informal kickoff date
3. Review project charter, background, and expectations with project team
4. Develop baseline for metrics selected as in-scope
5. Conduct AS IS Level 4 process gap analysis
6. Develop action to close "quick hit" gaps
7. Assemble TO BE Level 3 and Level 4 process based on leading practice
8. Develop and approve solution design storyboard
9. Build and test solution
10. Pilot and verify solution
11. Roll out solution to project scope and evaluate metric effect
12. Define process control measures
13. Scale implementation to targeted supply chains in the definition matrix

Implementation Resources

Champion
Leader
Subject matter expert
Team members

Figure 11-2. Project 7 benefits.

Project #	Project Phrase	Project Description	Perfect Order Fulfillment (%)	Order Fulfillment Cycle Time (days)	Total Supply Chain Management Cost ($)	COGS ($)	Inventory ($)
		Baseline	30.2%	11.0	$57,600,000	$286,200,000	$47,437,000
7	Engineer an Integrated Tactical Planning Process	This project will design, develop, and implement effective and efficient tactical planning processes to help manage the short-term horizon, balancing customer orders, stocking levels, replenishment orders to factories, and purchase orders to suppliers.	5.0%	1.0	$1,350,000	$2,500,000	$1,000,000

CHAPTER 12

Phase 4: From Portfolio Development to Implementation

> ➤ **Organizing Supply Chain Improvement as Part of Daily Life: Faster, Better, and Cheaper**

The finish line! Or is it? After one of the toughest graduate classes at the University of Minnesota, Prof. Richard Swanson said, as he handed out the final exam, "True learning is a painful experience . . . I can see that all of you have learned a great deal in this course."

As the last of the students left the room at the end of the hour, he offered one more piece of advice: "Remember," he said, "the road never ends. It's the journey that must be your home."

In the first and second editions, this chapter was at the end of the book. In the third edition it finds its way to the middle. For the benefit of those who have followed the *Supply Chain Excellence* method since it was introduced publicly in 2003, we offer the following five reasons for this significant change. *First,* as with all operational improvement initiatives, *faster, better, cheaper is a driver of change.* To compete in a worldwide marketplace, the rate of supply chain performance improvement needed to increase; 17 weeks is too

145

much time just to arrive at a list. The "new and improved" timeline of *Supply Chain Excellence* gets the project team to a validated project portfolio 25 percent faster, and to initiating the first project 50 percent faster. *Second*, increasingly *global projects* necessitated a change in the schedule. It is hard to meet every week in a face-to-face environment when the team needs to travel from several locations around the world. There certainly are milestones at which team members need to look each other in the eye, but for many other meetings, using teleconferencing technology is appropriate. *Third*, companies that had used the method more than five times were desiring to make *Supply Chain Excellence* an *implementation method*, not simply portfolio identification. This is because they were trying to eliminate loss of momentum between final approval of the portfolio and the approval to begin the first project; in cases requiring system investments, this could be six months or more. They also sought to minimize knowledge loss between the design team and the implementation teams—which also cost time.

The *fourth* reason the timeline has changed is to enable centralized supply chain leaders to *send a stronger message* to the business units (their customers) that the job wouldn't be finished until the needle was moved on key supply chain metrics. In earlier efforts, *Supply Chain Excellence* was "sold" in two parts: identify the project list and then implement it. While portfolio development was effective, attention waned at times during the implementation. The nuance is that the "new and improved" *Supply Chain Excellence* is "sold" on moving the needle in one effort—and therefore the timeline needed to include both pieces: project identification and implementation. *Fifth*, the relationship between continuous improvement resources, infrastructure, and already-invested Lean and Six Sigma training needed to be *integrated throughout* the *Supply Chain Excellence* timeline—not simply taking a hand-off at the end or providing data analysis in the beginning.

Design teams end the portfolio-development phase weary, but

also transformed, enlightened, broadened, deepened . . . changed. In many respects, individuals knew the answers to the problems the first day. When asked why they still needed this much time, most would summarize it something like this: "Each of us had our own biases, ideas, and agendas. The analysis and reflection time helped us put data behind the ideas, replace individual agendas with a shared vision, document every assumption, educate our leaders on the real issues, and gain support for some tough changes. Our company is about to undergo massive transformation; the time was necessary to change us, the foundation, first."

Initiating Implementation

Chapter 11 listed 13 milestone steps that define "implementation" of a single project from the portfolio. The remaining sections of *Supply Chain Excellence* will discuss key concepts and Fowlers' progress through to step 13—scale of implementation. The Fowlers technology products team picked Project 7, Engineer an Integrated Tactical Planning Process, as the one to initiate first.

Chapter 13

- Identify and approve project resource plan
- Establish project schedule, including informal kickoff date
- Review project charter, background, and expectations with project team
- Develop baseline for metrics selected as in-scope

Chapter 14

- Conduct AS IS Level 3 and 4 process gap analysis
- Develop action to close "quick hit" gaps

Chapter 15

- Assemble TO BE Level 3 process based on leading practice

Chapter 16

- ◆ Assemble TO BE Level 4 process based on leading practice
- ◆ Develop and approve solution design storyboard
- ◆ Define process control measures

Chapter 17

- ◆ Build and test solution
- ◆ Pilot and verify solution
- ◆ Roll out solution to project scope and evaluate metric impact

Phase 4: Initiate Implementation

> **Getting Organized, Getting People, Getting Data**

There are several points during a Supply Chain Operations Reference (SCOR) project that seem to draw people into reflecting on the significance of their work. The scorecard gap analysis is often such an occasion. Initiating the first implementation project is another.

At this point, members of the design team have reason to feel that they've produced something of great value to their company—measured in millions of dollars and improved customer satisfaction. Better still is the feeling of confidence instilled by a detailed understanding of the improvements—knowing that the selected projects will deliver results.

The momentum has reached something close to full speed, and other people throughout the organization are looking for ways to participate, knowing that this work is in the executive team's center of attention. The organization stands poised for a transition to something big and new. After twelve weeks of analysis on metrics and portfolio development, everyone is eager to get started with implementing something.

With these thoughts as background, the objectives for initiating an implementation project are to identify and approve the project resource plan; establish the project schedule, including an informal kickoff date; review the project charter, background, and expectations with the project team; and develop baseline for metrics selected as in-scope.

Identify and Approve Project Resource Plan

Picking the team for implementation of change is critical to the sustained improvement. There are four considerations:

1. RACI (Responsible, Accountable, Consulted, and Informed) analysis is the first guide: determining who is responsible for doing the work, identifying the one accountable owner for the process, and figuring out who needs to be consulted prior to taking action as well as who needs to be informed afterward. Ideally the project leader is the person primarily responsible for doing the work or guiding the process and the project champion (sponsor) is the one person accountable for the process.

2. Each team needs appropriate subject matter experts. Expertise could relate to a certain best practice, such as vendor managed inventory; collaborative planning, forecasting, and replenishment; or an analytical continuous-improvement practice like Lean or Six Sigma. On large-scale, complex projects it is not uncommon for there to be multiple subject matter experts.

3. On projects for which there will be new system requirements, it is ideal for systems functionality experts to be on the team to translate business needs into software requirements and teach the team members how the software is supposed to work. This accelerates the *detail design, configure, and test phases* in the software development part of the project.

4. The project team should also have at least one former design team member either on the team or assigned to it as a mentor to help avoid re-analyzing past work and to provide access and perspective on the defect analysis, benefit projections, and assumptions.

With the Project Seven kickoff date set for the Thursday of the following week, the team roster started clearing its calendars. The team members included:

- Champion (sponsor): VP operations in the technology products group (David Able)
- Leader: director of planning and production control
- Subject matter experts: SAP expert for materials management and production planning; leading practice expert in rough-cut capacity planning (RCCP) and master scheduling
- Team members: forecast analyst, plant scheduler, distribution requirements planner, supply planner, and order fulfillment supervisor

Establish the Project Schedule and Kickoff Date

Implementation project schedules follow a discipline similar to that of the *Supply Chain Excellence* roadmap: regular, weekly, and focused on deliverables. Though the nomenclature is a bit different, the schedule also follows a path similar to AcceleratedSAP implementation methodology, from project preparation through to business blueprint, realization, final preparation, go-live, and support.

The project schedule essentially puts dates around each of the 13 action steps highlighted in the implementation project charter. A regular team meeting was set for Thursday mornings from 9 a.m.

to noon, and it became the focal point for review and approval of deliverables. The project task summary and schedule is as follows:

1. Identify and approve project resource plan: week of August 1

2. Establish project schedule, including informal kickoff date: week of August 8, kickoff August 11

3. Review project charter, background, and expectations with project team: kickoff August 11

4. Develop baseline for metrics selected as in-scope: week of August 15

5. Conduct AS IS Level 3 and 4 process gap analysis: week of August 22

6. Develop action plans to close "quick hit" gaps: week of August 22

7. Assemble TO BE Level 3 and 4 process based on leading practice: weeks of August 29 and September 5

8. Develop and approve solution-design storyboard: weeks of September 12 and 19

9. Build and test solution: weeks of September 26 and October 3

10. Pilot and verify solution: weeks of October 10, 17, 24, and 31

11. Roll out solution to project scope and evaluate metric impact: month of November

12. Define process control measures: month of November

13. Scale implementation to targeted supply chains in the definition matrix: initiate in December

Steps 8, 9, and 12 are the most variable, driven mostly by the complexity of necessary system solutions. In Fowlers' case, SAP functionality for Materials Management and Production Planning was already installed but was not working at its fullest potential. In fact, people at the plant level were so frustrated that they stopped using some of the functionality. The team members did admit that they were not strict with setting up the resources in their plant. They also alluded to the fact that leading-practice master-scheduling concepts were secondary to correctly setting SAP master data elements to automate existing processes. Step 10 focuses on piloting the solution on a subset of the project scope. In Fowlers' case, the pilot focused on an important set of resources (production lines) in one plant. Step 11 would roll out the solution to the rest of the plant. Step 13 would roll out the solution to the rest of the division plants.

Review Project Background and Develop the Performance Baseline

The kickoff meeting included a candid discussion presented by David Able, the project sponsor. He set the strategic challenge as to why this project was critically important and why it was selected. He put the problem statement, project description, and project objectives into his own words and emphasized both the timing and the size of expected benefits (see Figure 11-1 and the sidebar that follows it).

The project leader then reviewed the scope, including the product and channels, process, SAP modules (PP and MM), plants (North America manufacturing and distribution centers), and the metrics. The product and channel scope includes the SKUs contributing 50 percent of sales in the retail channel. The process scope includes P1.2 Identify, Prioritize and Aggregate Supply-Chain Resources (RCCP), all the P3 PLAN MAKE elements (master scheduling), and M1.1 Schedule Manufacturing Activities (factory floor or finite scheduling).

The team suggested that the processes that touch these should also be added for contextual (not analytical) purposes. The rest of the P1.1 Identify, Prioritize and Aggregate Supply Chain Requirements (demand plan or forecast), P1.3 Balance Supply Chain Resources with SC Requirements (demand-supply imbalance), P2 Plan Source (resulting MRP by component), and P4 Plan Deliver (distribution requirements plan) were added. The metric scope included manufacturing schedule adherence on a weekly basis, master plan adherence each month, rough-cut capacity plan each month, master data accuracy on a weekly rotating basis, and in-stock percentage each week.

The next task was to assemble the data collection plan to establish the project's performance baseline. The data collection, like building the scorecard, required a consensus around the definition of each metric, a reasonable sample size, and the identification of the source for the data. The Fowlers leadership team members admitted that in their haste to "get the SAP system in," they grossly underestimated the requirements for data warehousing and extracting information out of system using the standard reports. This implementation project, then, would be considered an opportunity to learn relevant SAP standard reports, develop a more robust data warehouse strategy (see Data Warehouse Strategy sidebar), and figure out how to better utilize the ways in which SAP data can be exported to both Microsoft Excel and Access. The following is a summary of the Fowlers Project 7 data collection plan.

Manufacturing schedule adherence is defined using the principles of perfect order fulfillment. The three critical pieces are quantity, ship date, and product quality. A schedule is defined as a collection of process orders. If each process order meets the quantity, date, and quality requirement, it is considered good. If a process order misses one of the three criteria, it is considered bad. The method for defining schedule adherence is to divide good process orders by total process orders for the week. The team established a 26-week baseline using a run-chart format. At the moment, the team was sorting through the list of standard SAP reports, looking for the one that could help satisfy the data requirements to calculate the baseline. CO46, Order Progress Report, seemed to contain all the data necessary to judge schedule adherence.

Master schedule adherence looks at the plant's ability to achieve the overall volume and mix requirements, and the ability of the planner to resolve capacity constraints in the future. A master plan is a collection of resource (production lines) plans one week in the past and 13 weeks in the future. If a resource's volume commitment was met for the previous week within a tolerance of ± 5 percent and there are no over-capacity circumstances in the next 13 weeks, it is considered good. The definition of master schedule adherence is the number of resources achieving "good" volume and capacity commitments divided by the total number of resources. The team chose the same 26-week baseline and likewise needed to develop a report similar to that of the schedule attainment. CM01, capacity planning, would be the SAP data source for this metric; though not a report, it relates requirements to planned capacity in hours or units and highlights capacity concerns when requirements are greater than capacity. It can be viewed in weeks or months.

Rough-cut capacity planning is similar to master schedule adherence but looks at monthly volume commitments over 18 months as part of the sales and operations planning process. The definition of rough-cut capacity plan is the number of resources achieving "good" volume and capacity commitments divided by the total number of resources. In this case, the team selected the next month's rough-cut capacity performance as the baseline. CM01 would also be the data source for this measure.

Master data accuracy, while conceptually understood, lacked the systematic analytic discipline to make it a real performance metric. To make it more realistic, the team agreed the measure would be modeled after inventory record accuracy, which relied on cycle counting to publish its performance. Thus, the team identified four categories of SKUs: large volume, medium volume, low volume, and no usage. Each category was assigned a different frequency of review. The team then identified the SAP item master data transactions and settings that were the most critical to daily operation, and verified the accuracy of the data. Master data accuracy then was the aggregate accuracy of the SKUs reviewed for the week. For a SKU to be considered good, all fields needed to be valid. Since the team did not measure this, the baseline would be established by the initial week of data collection.

In-stock percentage was a measure for SKUs defined as make-to-stock. It simply measured whether or not a SKU had available stock in a given week. This measure was similar to a historical measure called *fill rate*. The team suggested using the fill rate by week for the previous 52 weeks as the baseline. This would help illustrate seasonality and manufacturing performance. There are a number of inventory reports in the standard SAP report list. The team was considering the following as options: MB52, Plant Stock Availability; MB5B, Stock On Posting Date; and MC44, Inventory Turnover.

With the metric data collection plans in place, the team members challenged themselves to have some data samples by the following Thursday. On your mark, get set, measure!

Data Warehouse Strategy

With the help of the business intelligence expert, the Fowlers project team reviewed two options, a vision, and more than a dozen goals in creating the data warehouse strategy.

Data warehouses (DW) are distinct from transactional systems. Transactional systems are designed to move information efficiently, and they generally have low data retention. DW are built for reporting and analysis and are good at retaining data. DW are also designed to integrate data from multiple sources.

There are *two* approaches to data warehousing that the Fowlers team discussed: conventional and holistic. The *conventional* approach, used since the 1990s, essentially utilizes *multiple single-purpose* data warehouse models (tables), each addressing a specific area of the business (purchasing fact table, production fact table, sales fact table, etc.) Each table has its own dimensions. For example, dimensions of the purchasing table include buyer, materials, and supplier (Figure 13-1).

Systems experts design ways to pull data from tables and associated dimensions and create reports for people to use. Anyone who has asked for a new report to be created within a conventional data warehouse model knows that this seemingly simple request can take a lot of time and money.

An alternative model, a *holistic* DW, is *one multi-purpose* data warehouse for all business intelligence needs (Figure 13-2). It can be implemented as a template, and is designed to adapt on the fly to additional requirements without modification (Figure 13-3).

The project team's *vision* was "one simple and easy system with minimal limitations, providing the one view over the whole business and its supply chain in which the user can use filtering techniques to select data that will appear on a report."

Data Warehouse Goals

- Minimize inconsistent reports and reconcile different views of the same data
- Improve quality of data
- Consolidate enterprise data from multiple sources and time periods
- Make the data easily accessible and provide transparency
- Enable common and flexible calendars
- Save time on report preparation and construction
- Address the weaknesses of current reporting systems
- Empower people with information
- Enable pre-emptive reporting of events that are expected to happen
- Develop and enable single cross-functional business reports (Figure 13-4)
- Offer all supply chain–related information (Figure 13-5)
- Effortlessly replace all "standard" reporting needs
- Address deficiencies in the operational systems
- Be capable of reporting "unlimited" measures
- Allow "unlimited" product hierarchies
- Utilize holistic data warehouse dedicated supply chain reporting capability (Figure 13-5).

Figure 13-1. Conventional data warehouse table dimensions for purchasing.

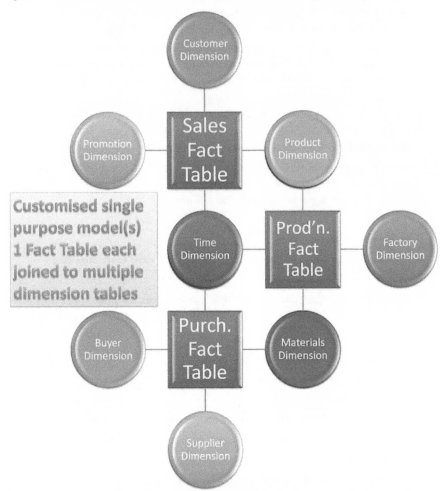

Figure 13-2. Structure of a holistic data warehouse.

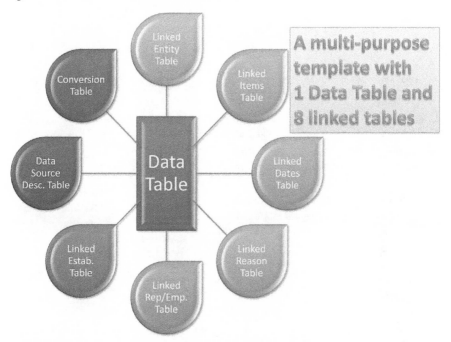

Copyright 2011. Reprinted from *Holistic Data Warehousing on Microsoft SQL Server 2008*, Gerry Phillips and Jane McCarthy; For-tee Too Sight Publishing, 2010. Used with permission.

Figure 13-3. Holistic data warehouse implemented as a template.

Customer Scan Data	Competitor Scan Data	Full Cost Breakdown History	Full Cost Breakdown Budgets	Full Cost Breakdown Latest
Customer Trading Terms Budget	Customer Marketing Co-op Actuals	Customer Marketing Co-op Estimate	Customer Marketing Co-op Budget	Consumer Complaints
Customer Special Deals Actuals	Customer Special Deals Estimates	Customer Special Deals Budgets	Customer Trading Terms Actuals	Customer Trading Terms Forecast
Purchases Actuals	Purchases on Order and Planned	Inventory Actuals	Inventory Projected	Sales Credit & Debit Notes
Labour Spend Actuals	Labour Recoveries Actuals & Planned	Overhead Recoveries Actuals & Planned	Production Out & In Actuals	Production Out & In Planned
Sales Actual/ Forecast	Customer Orders	Customer Shortages Actuals	Customer Shortages Projected	Today's Sales ½ hourly update
Sales Actuals	Sales Working Forecasts	Sales Live Forecast	Sales Budget	Sales & Operations Planning Forecast

Figure 13-4. Single cross-functional business report.

Frequency	Monthly						
ItemCategory	(All)		Sales and Operations Report				
ItemSubcategory	(All)						
Amt $'000			CMonth				
DataType	Cal Year	Version	Jan	Feb	Mar	Apr	May
Sales	2009	Actuals	$ 463,608	$ 848,663	$ 554,222	$ 570,051	$ 934,389
	2010	Act/Forecast	$ 490,342	$ 899,246	$ 521,655	$ 622,325	$ 905,926
	2010	Budget	$ 421,000	$ 936,000	$ 558,000	$ 566,000	$ 943,000
Cost of Sales	2009	Actuals	$ 214,860	$ 339,687	$ 225,302	$ 307,374	$ 386,347
	2010	Act/Forecast	$ 209,443	$ 363,285	$ 274,233	$ 251,283	$ 427,758
	2010	Budget	$ 209,831	$ 485,294	$ 262,074	$ 270,536	$ 442,397
Margin	2009	Actuals	$ 248,748	$ 508,976	$ 328,920	$ 262,677	$ 548,042
	2010	Act/Forecast	$ 280,899	$ 535,961	$ 247,422	$ 371,042	$ 478,168
	2010	Budget	$ 211,169	$ 450,706	$ 295,926	$ 295,464	$ 500,603
Margin%	2009	Actuals	53.7%	60.0%	59.3%	46.1%	58.7%
	2010	Act/Forecast	57.3%	59.6%	47.4%	59.6%	52.8%
	2010	Budget	50.2%	48.2%	53.0%	52.2%	53.1%
Purchases	2009	Actuals	$ 158,876	$ 242,787	$ 218,365	$ 203,310	$ 287,902
	2010	Act/Plan	$ 134,261	$ 232,693	$ 142,640	$ 137,367	$ 251,589
Prodn Out	2009	Actuals	$ 219,219	$ 341,146	$ 245,502	$ 299,191	$ 371,857
	2010	Act/Plan	$ 201,617	$ 344,089	$ 253,605	$ 242,706	$ 414,771
Prodn Scrap	2009	Actuals	$ 771	$ 2,733	$ 4,997	$ 8,945	$ 7,121
	2010	Act/Plan	$ 7,645	$ 10,703	$ 2,568	$ 2,500	$ 2,500
Prodn In	2009	Actuals	$ 146,817	$ 226,958	$ 205,909	$ 189,533	$ 277,862
	2010	Act/Plan	$ 134,194	$ 221,429	$ 138,425	$ 124,593	$ 230,544
Labour	2009	Actuals	$ 33,852	$ 53,728	$ 35,642	$ 46,160	$ 66,737
	2010	Act/Forecast	$ 33,569	$ 55,914	$ 44,903	$ 44,000	$ 72,000
	2010	Budget	$ 34,000	$ 79,000	$ 39,000	$ 42,000	$ 77,000
Inventory	2009	Actuals	$ 449,906	$ 467,195	$ 499,851	$ 505,445	$ 500,995
	2010	Act/Plan	$ 526,571	$ 518,638	$ 502,225	$ 506,421	$ 514,479
Inventory KPI	2009	Actuals	2.09	1.38	2.22	1.64	1.30
	2010	Act/Plan	2.51	1.43	1.83	2.02	1.20
Complaints	2009	Actuals	260	796	829	209	175
	2010	Actuals	133	558	336		

Figure 13-5. Holistic data warehouse dedicated supply chain reporting capability.

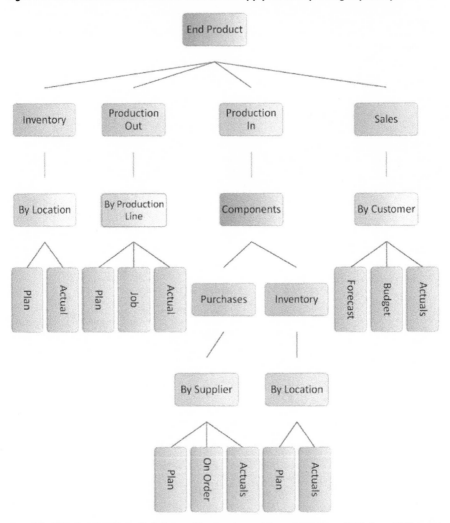

CHAPTER 14

Phases 2–4: The Staple Yourself Interview and SCOR Level 3 Process Diagram

> **June 13 to 17*: How the Work Really Gets Done; a Tool for All Phases**

The tasks for this set of deliverables can be applied during any one of three points during the project as part of the analysis, portfolio development, and/or project implementation. In fact, these tasks integrate very well with the AcceleratedSAP implementation methodology in the business blueprint phase. Girish Naagesh, Fowlers' CIO, commented in hindsight that if the team had completed this comprehensive SCOR Level 3 analysis either in advance or as part of the AcceleratedSAP deployment process, the details related to the Question and Answer Database (QAdb) and Customer Input Templates would have been easier to manage because the entire supply chain process would have been put in the proper context.

The first opportunity to use the interview and diagramming process is during Phase 2. In this case, the design team chose the recommended option of conducting an on-site process analysis in

*May also take place July 11 or the week of August 22, depending on organizational schedule (see the appendix).

preparation for the brainstorm event. The scope would include all relevant SCOR Level 3 process elements. More important, this option gives the team members an opportunity to meet and build relationships with members of the regional team with whom they are working, adding to the global perspective of the project. This option is represented in the schedule that is part of the Appendix.

The second option consolidates the activity into the first day of the brainstorm week. This scenario skips the face-to-face "staple yourself to an order" interviews and focuses the team on developing the process diagram in a conference room meeting format. Some project teams have introduced the staple yourself to an order worksheet the week before arrival using a web-based conference, with the expectation that the interviewees will do their best to complete it. The process scope, like the first option, includes all of the SCOR Level 3 elements.

The third option falls into the implementation phase of a project. This scenario uses the staple yourself to an order worksheets and assembles a process diagram—but only for those processes named in the scope for the project. On the project schedule, this deliverable can be noted as Staple Yourself to an Order Interviews and AS IS Process Diagram in Phase 2, or AS IS Process Diagram in Phase 3 and Conduct Level 3 and 4 Process Gap Analysis in Phase 4, as seen in the Appendix. In complex projects, teams have included both the first option and a refinement of the third.

The staple yourself interview is fieldwork that attempts to learn how things are done in the real world. The notion of a guided tour is discussed in the classic *Harvard Business Review* article "Staple Yourself to an Order" (July 1, 1992; Benson P. Shapiro, V. Kasteri Rangan, and John J. Sviokla). Guided by an interview plan, members of the project team travel to the site(s) where the processes scoped for the project begin and follow them to their closure—literally cradle to grave. For example, a sales-order field trip may start at a salesperson's home office, where the quote is generated; then move back to headquarters to see how the order is received, validated, and entered; then go to the warehouse to watch how the inventory is allocated to the order, so the customer service representative can communicate a delivery date to the customer; and ultimately end in accounts receivables, where reconciled invoices are archived.

Preparing for the Staple Yourself Interview

The preparation and interview process is composed of four basic steps. First, the project team thoroughly reviews the master data appropriate for the processes under review. This is a follow-up activity to data collection efforts of the past week (see "Master Data in SAP Capacity Planning Modules" sidebar). Second, also before the site visit, the team prepares the process analysis worksheets; this essentially means populating sections such as the name of the interviewee(s), accountable function, primary input(s), SCOR process element, and primary output(s). The inputs and outputs (stated in terms of the current state rather than SCOR) are especially important because they give the interviewees perspective on the beginning and end of the process.

Third, the project leader—on arriving at the site—provides a quick briefing to the interviewees about the SCOR Level 3 processes under investigation. This is normally done in a small conference room. After reviewing the inputs and outputs from the process analysis worksheets, the interviewees can help determine the best locations and strategies for conducting the interviews.

Fourth, the team and interviewees should proceed to the planned locations and complete the interviews. A location could be a desk, workstation, production line, warehouse, or any other place deemed appropriate. If the processes are completed primarily on the computer system, then physically the interview may be accomplished at the desk; the real tour will be through the computer system screens. In other cases, the design team may perform the main interview in a conference room with a live computer log-on, tour the system path, and then add the finishing details with a physical walk-through of the appropriate area.

Understanding the Staple Yourself Interview Worksheet

On the worksheet (Figure 14-1), interviewee and SCOR element sections are self-explanatory. Accountable Function and Responsible borrow the "R" and the "A" from the RACI (Responsible, Accountable, Consulted, Informed) analysis process. As noted previously, *responsible* refers to the roles that perform the work for a given process. *Accountable* is reserved for the one role that ultimately owns the process performance.

Primary Input(s) and Output(s) refer to the primary trigger(s) to start the process and the primary output(s) of the process. Level 4 Step and Description refers to a maximum of 10 tasks to complete the SCOR Level 3 process element. Why 10? Some teams need more processes to describe how they do their work; the important idea is to use the same maximum number of process steps for each SCOR element to help normalize the level of detail.

System Module refers to the information tools, screens, and/or transactions used to complete the tasks identified in each Level 4 step. The tools can range from a system functionality or module (SAP SD, MM, PP, FI, etc.) to SAP transaction codes, like CM01, VA01, CO09, MD04, etc.; Internet signal to a fax; EDI; Excel spreadsheet; phone call; or simple sticky note. Event Time is the time spent from start to finish on the Level 4 step, assuming no lag time; the team tries to normalize this to time per step.

Business Rules are policies and informal guidelines that govern decisions and behavior. Processing all orders by 3 p.m. may be a policy, but onsite supervisors might enforce an unwritten practice of accepting an order an hour later—with the same delivery expectations—as part of a customer-focused culture. Both are business rules.

Disconnects causing rework and/or extended wait time are issues

Figure 14-1. Staple yourself interview worksheet.

Interviewees	Enter the interviewees from the interview planning worksheet.				
Accountable Function	Enter the title of the ultimate role accountable to the performance of this SCOR Level 3 process.				

Primary Input(s)		SCOR Element		Primary Output(s)	
Enter the primary transactional input(s) to this process		Enter the SCOR Level 3 Process element ID and description, i.e., M1.1 Schedule Production Activities		Enter the primary transactional output(s) to this process	

	Level 4 Step	Description	System Module	Responsible	Event Time
Process Steps (>4 and <11)	1	Enter the description of each of the process steps; often referred to as Level 4 process steps	Enter the System Module and/or Transaction	Enter the title(s) of those doing the work	This is an effort of the amount of time (often calculated in minutes) and is normalized to one of five transactions, i.e., purchase order, work order, sales order, return authorization, or forecast
	2				
Total Event Time for Process Steps					0

Business Rules	Enter the business rules, both formal and informal, that directly or indirectly influence process performance		

	Disconnect Description	Initials	Relative Weight
Disconnects causing rework and/or extended wait time	Describe major disconnects that cause process steps to be reworked and/or add to process wait time (delay)	Interviewee's Initials	This compares the relative impact to the rest of the disconnects in the list

that result in gaps between elapsed time and event time—too much waiting—and/or cause unnecessary rework. Figure 14-2 illustrates a process analysis example for the SCOR element D1.2 Receive, Enter, and Validate Order.

Figure 14-2. Process analysis example: SCOR Element D1.2 Receive, Enter, and Validate Order.

Interviewees	Susan, Terri, Julie, Jane, Dan, and Mike				
Accountable Function	Customer Service Director				
Primary Input(s)		**SCOR Element**		**Primary Output(s)**	
Customer call, fax, or email Web order Field sales contact Customer profile		**D1.2** Receive, Enter, and Validate the Order		Entered sales order	
	Level Four Step	**Description**	**SAP Module--Transaction**	**Responsible**	**Event Time**
	1	Retrieve or enter new customer master record.	Sales & Distribution--VA01	Customer Service Representative	1
	2	Verify ship to/bill to addresses. Overview screen.	Sales & Distribution--VA01	Customer Service Representative	1
	3	Enter customer contact, payment terms, ship method and P.O. number. Overview screen.	Sales & Distribution--VA01	Customer Service Representative	1
	4	Enter requested ship date. Overview screen--sales tab.	Sales & Distribution--VA01	Customer Service Representative	1
Process Steps (>4 and <11)	5	Enter part number and quantity. Overview screen--sales tab.	Sales & Distribution--VA01	Customer Service Representative	1
	6	Review part description and modify as necessary. Overview screen--sales tab.	Sales & Distribution--VA01	Customer Service Representative	1
	7	Input default price and unit of measure. Overview screen--sales tab.	Sales & Distribution--VA01	Customer Service Representative	1
	8	Update or save order record. Overview screen--sales tab.	Sales & Distribution--VA01	Customer Service Representative	1
	9	Call back customer when inventory allocation fails and re-date the order. Allocation is checked when saving the order for each item line entered.	Sales & Distribution--VA01	Customer Service Representative	2
	Total Event Time for Process Steps				10
Business Rules	Formal--Orders can be held waiting for payment for a maximum of 30 days after stock is committed.				
	Formal--Credit reviews "holds" once daily.				
	Informal--Once an order is entered, each order line is manually reviewed for correct quantity, part number, and price.				
	Informal--If the ship-to address or bill-to address is modified or a new address is added, the order will go on a sales hold. Customer Service must review and approve the address change/addition before it becomes a permanent change/addition.				
	Disconnect Description			**Initials**	**Relative Weight**
	System pricing does not match spreadsheet version of the customer price.			JH	40
Disconnects causing rework and/or extended wait time	Manual entry to add new customer ship-to addresses for drop shipments from suppliers.			ST	20
	Customer requests different terms than contract.			MJ	20
	Customer order incorrect increments, i.e., unit of measure and order minimums.			DS	10
Copyright 2003 SCE Limited	Customer part number cross-reference is not correct.			JK	10

Fowlers Analysis of P3 Plan Make

The team members landed at the plant ready to go. They had followed all the rules. During the previous week, they and the plant manager had discussed the targeted interviewee list, which included the master scheduler, finite scheduler, and materials planner. They had memorized the SCOR element P3 Plan Make. Technically defined as "the development and establishment of courses of action over specified time periods that represent a projected appropriation of production resources to meet production requirements," it was synonymous with the leading practice of master scheduling. They entered the preliminary inputs and outputs and sorted out an interview approach to include all the Level 3 elements in one process analysis worksheet, thinking that the process would be smoother.

When they entered the conference room, there sat the plant manager and the scheduler, six months after their SAP go-live. The first lesson in these analyses is that the current state is not always as it seems. The second lesson is to not assume but simply observe; sometimes in supply chain your brain fills in the unknown with your conception of how you'd like it to work. The project leader introduced everyone and proceeded to review the process analysis worksheet. The first part of the discussion focused on the meaning of P3 Plan Make, which was a great learning opportunity that allowed all to get centered on the theory of master scheduling.

The next part of the interview attempted to dissect the inputs and outputs. After a rather animated philosophical discussion about master data, resource profiles, and smoothed eight-week schedules, the plant manager stated very plainly, "This is simple; I take the expected units for the month as committed to in the budget and divide by four. I then tell the scheduler what to run each week. There are three things that drive us crazy. The first is when we don't have parts to run something that is scheduled. The second is the customer orders that keep getting inserted in the schedule from corporate. Both cause more changeovers, unnecessary yield loss, and higher unit cost for me. The third is that the plan that spits out of the SAP scheduling module is not accurate; I can't trust it to hit my numbers."

When asked about his use of the SAP module, the scheduler said, "We tried it for a month but it didn't work. So we only use it to enter production orders, estimate material availability, report output and enter purchase orders for suppliers." Figure 14-3 summarizes the analysis.

Figure 14-3. Fowlers' P3 Plan Make staple yourself analysis.

Interviewee(s)	Barry and Jorge				
Accountable Function	Plant Manager				
Primary Input(s)		**SCOR Element**		**Primary Output(s)**	
Monthly Unit and Cost Objectives		P3 Plan Make		4 Week Schedule	
	Level 4 Step	**Description**	**SAP Module-- Transaction**	**Responsible**	**Event Time**
	1	Calculate the monthly plan by week.	Excel	Plant Manager	60
	2	Check work order status from last week.	Paperwork from Morning Scheduling Meeting	Scheduler	60
Process Steps (>4 and <11)	3	Re-sequence orders not completed from past week.	Paperwork from Morning Scheduling Meeting	Scheduler	15
	4	Work with supervisor to create this week's schedule using monthly plan.	Excel	Scheduler	15
	5	Calculate materials availability for the new schedule.	Materials Management--MD04	Scheduler	60
	6	Work with customer service to slot new orders in the near-term weeks.	Excel	Scheduler	60
		Total Event Time for Process Steps			270
Business Rules	Formal: Achieve plant unit cost objectives.				
	Informal: Exceeding the volume plan helps the plant overachieve performance expectations.				
	Disconnect Description			**Initials**	**Relative Weight**
Disconnects causing rework and/or extended wait time	Customer orders are inserted, causing unnecessary changeovers.			JP	30%
	The plant does not hit its commitments each week by SKU.			JP	30%
	Packaging and raw materials not available to run schedule.			BM	20%
	The system plan (resource load) is wrong.			BM	20%

Assembling the AS IS Process and RACI Diagrams

Coming off an intense on-site visit (assuming use of the recommended option one as described at the beginning of this chapter), the design team is armed with a packet of interview summaries covering more than 40 SCOR Level 3 process elements. Team members have discovered unwritten rules, policy shortcuts, work-arounds, and a real-time validation of how silo mentality is destroying productivity; they may have even learned a few words from the host country. Now they're ready to start assembling the picture of how their supply chain processes function (or not) in the current state. Process mapping is not a new technique for analyzing operational efficiency. Its effectiveness rests in the ability to pictorially portray how seemingly disparate processes are connected, to illustrate the essential information needed to drive the work, and ultimately to illustrate how process flow relates to organizational roles and responsibilities.

The SCOR approach to process mapping considers the Level 3 elements as the "work" in "work and information flow." The input–output is the "information" or transaction. The process mapper stands at the whiteboard, draws a box representing one SCOR element, adds the inputs and outputs from the interview worksheet, and then moves on to the next SCOR element in the list.

Figure 14-4 is a sample case involving multiple SCOR processes in PLAN, SOURCE, MAKE, and DELIVER. The system's material requirements planning (P2.1 and P2.2) generated planned requisitions for a planner to (1) balance, (2) convert (P2.3) to firm requisitions, and (3) release to the buyer (P2.4). The released requisitions are converted to purchase orders (S1.1) by a buyer; the purchase order record on the system and the physical delivery of the material and packing slip trigger receipt of the product (S1.2). The

172

Figure 14-4. Sample SCOR Level 3 process map illustrating PLAN, SOURCE, MAKE, and DELIVER.

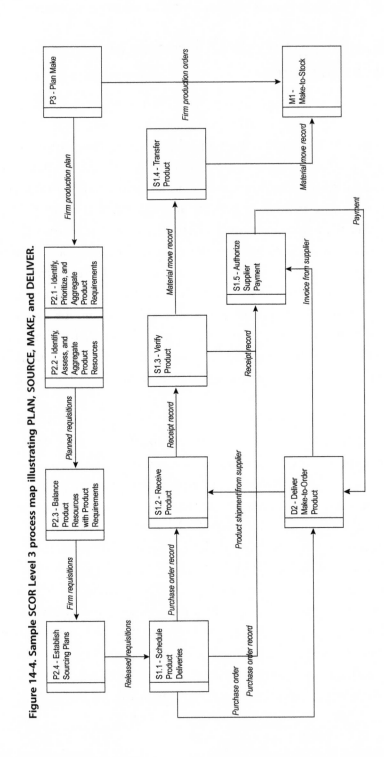

initial receipt record triggers appropriate quality checks (S1.3); then a material move record assigns the material to a warehouse location (S1.4). The purchase order record, receipt record, and invoice from the supplier (D2) trigger accounts payable to issue payment (S1.5). Meanwhile planning is transmitting the next firm production plan (P3), which triggers the manufacturing team to send a signal to issue stored raw material (M1) to a production line. The firm production plan also then begins the next cycle of material requirements planning (P3 to P2.1). Using an alternative mapping approach, the concept of a RACI diagram (Figure 14-5) can illustrate for each location the functions that participate in the performance of each SCOR process. Furthermore, it can also illustrate the role each function plays in each SCOR process (Figure 14-6).

The conclusion by the Fowlers team members around P3 Plan Make is that they really didn't have an AS IS Level 3 map; the processes discovered in the interviews were either scheduling or aligning to unit volume commitments.

Master Data in SAP Capacity Planning Modules

With the help of the SAP expert, the Fowlers project team reviewed five critical master data areas affecting the performance of the tactical planning process: plants, materials, work centers, bills of materials, and routings (or recipes). Following is a summary of the plant and materials discussion.

Plants within the SAP platform are used to define both factories and distribution centers, and are initially set up during the configuration part of *realization* (Figure 2-2). They typically are added only as a company grows and expands.

Materials in SAP are also commonly referred to as items, products, and SKUs; they are the hub of the information needed to run the supply chain. For Fowlers and other consumer products companies, this refers to materials that you SOURCE, MAKE, DELIVER, and RETURN. Basic material data include description, base unit of measure, weight, and size—all which are common to every plant in the Fowlers technology products group.

(*Text continues on page 176*)

174

Figure 14-5. Sample RACI diagram of functions by location in SCOR Level 3 processes.

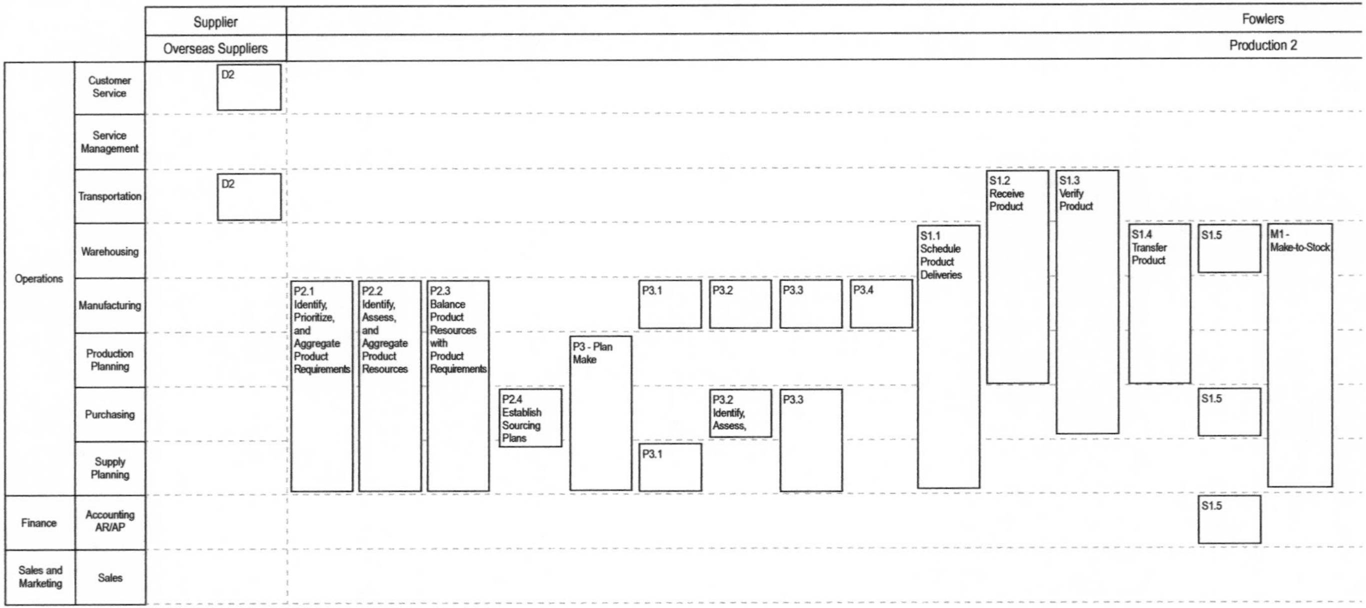

Figure 14-6. Sample RACI diagram of functions by SCOR Level 3 process.

	Customer Service	Transportation	Warehousing	Manufacturing	Production Planning	Purchasing	Supply Planning	Accounting AR/AP	Sales
P4 - Plan Deliver									
D2 - Deliver Make-to-Order Product									
P2.1									
P2.2				C	R		C		
P2.3						R, A			
P2.4 - Establish Sourcing Plans									
P3 - Plan Make					C	I	R, A		
S1.1 - Schedule Product Deliveries				C	R, A	C	I		
S1.2 - Receive Product		R	R, A	I					
S1.3 - Verify Product	C	R	R, A		I	I			
S1.4 - Transfer Product			R, A	C					
S1.5 - Authorize Supplier Payment			C			R, A		R	
M1 - Make-to-Stock				R, A	C				

Some material information is applicable to all plants and some can be different by plant. The SAP platform uses the term *transaction* to name a view of data within an SAP module of functionality. Using SAP transaction *MM03—Display Material*, the Fowlers team reviewed one of the materials in scope (Figure 14-7). Supply chain settings are found in the *MRP 1, MRP 2, MRP 3, and MRP 4* material master screens. The team reviewed critical parameters on the *MRP 1* tab including:

◆ *MRP type* influences the timing of receipts generated and firmed during a *Material Requirements Planning* (MRP) run.

◆ An *MRP controller* is the person or department that is typically the most familiar with the MRP data settings for the material, and also responsible for ensuring that sufficient stock of the material is available at the plant. For Fowlers, MRP controller "001" has been defined and assigned to the material reviewed. The MRP controller can be used to look at requirements exceptions for many materials at the same time, making the exception-management process more efficient.

◆ *Lot size* data governs the size of the receipts generated during the MRP planning run. At Fowlers, material F1000 has a lot size setting of WB, which causes all unfulfilled requirements within a week to be aggregated and served by one receipt.

◆ A *quantity rounding value* is used when generating new orders (receipts). For Fowlers, a value of 10 has been set. This adjusts the receipt quantity to a multiple that Fowlers believes is efficient when it is assembling the material.

On the *MRP 2* screen (Figure 14-8), Fowlers has maintained the following information:

◆ The *procurement type* "F" means that Fowlers will buy the material. This, combined with the *special procurement* setting of "40," which was defined when the system was configured, means that plant 2105 is "buying" the material from its sister plant 2106, where the product is assembled.

◆ The *scheduling* data, specifically the *planned deliv time* and the *GR processing time* (GR = goods receipt) controls the time the MRP planning run will use for determining when a product will become available to promise. For Fowlers, when running a standard availability check, any requirements outside of this lead time will be assumed to be fulfilled; the requirement will not be checked against actual stocks or future firmed receipts.

◆ The *scheduling margin key* is used to determine the types of order proposals—planned orders or purchase requisitions—that will be created. For Fowlers, a setting of "001" at plant 2105 generates purchase requisitions within the first 10 work days— the *opening period*—and planned orders further in the future. By using transactions ME55 or ME59N, this allows a buyer to collectively create purchase orders from purchase requisitions, while letting SAP MRP manage the generation or deletion of planned orders.

Figure 14-7. Fowlers' SAP display material MRP 1 tab.

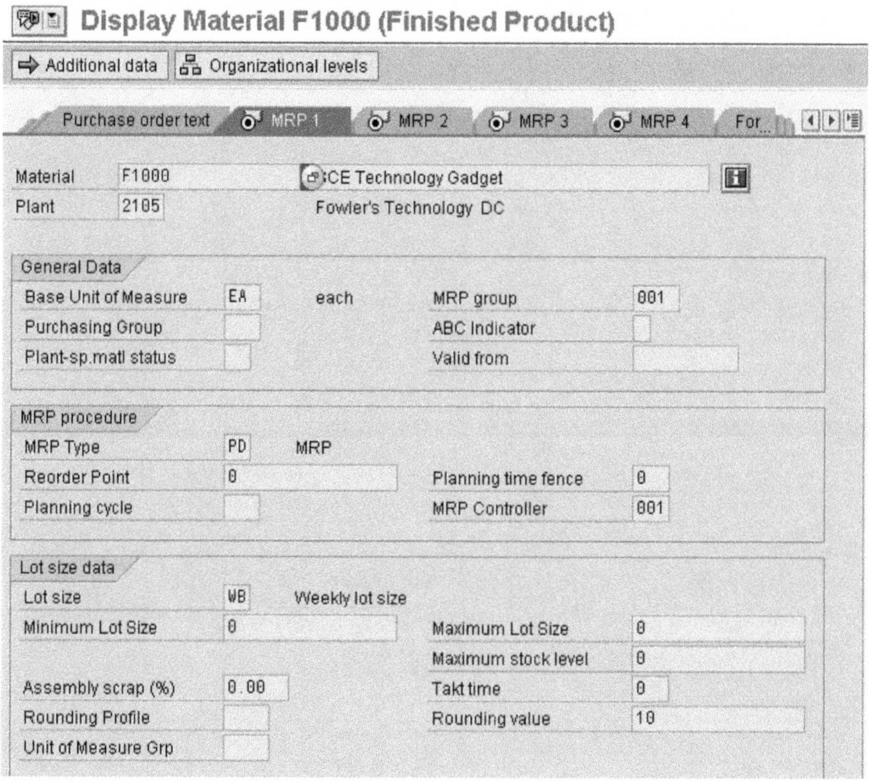

Display Material F1000 (Finished Product)

⇨ Additional data   🖧 Organizational levels

| Purchase order text | MRP 1 | MRP 2 | MRP 3 | MRP 4 | For... |

| Material | F1000 | CE Technology Gadget | |
| Plant | 2105 | Fowler's Technology DC | |

General Data

Base Unit of Measure	EA	each	MRP group	001
Purchasing Group			ABC Indicator	
Plant-sp.matl status			Valid from	

MRP procedure

MRP Type	PD	MRP	
Reorder Point	0	Planning time fence	0
Planning cycle		MRP Controller	001

Lot size data

Lot size	WB	Weekly lot size	
Minimum Lot Size	0	Maximum Lot Size	0
		Maximum stock level	0
Assembly scrap (%)	0.00	Takt time	0
Rounding Profile		Rounding value	10
Unit of Measure Grp			

Figure 14-8. Fowlers' SAP display material MRP 2 tab.

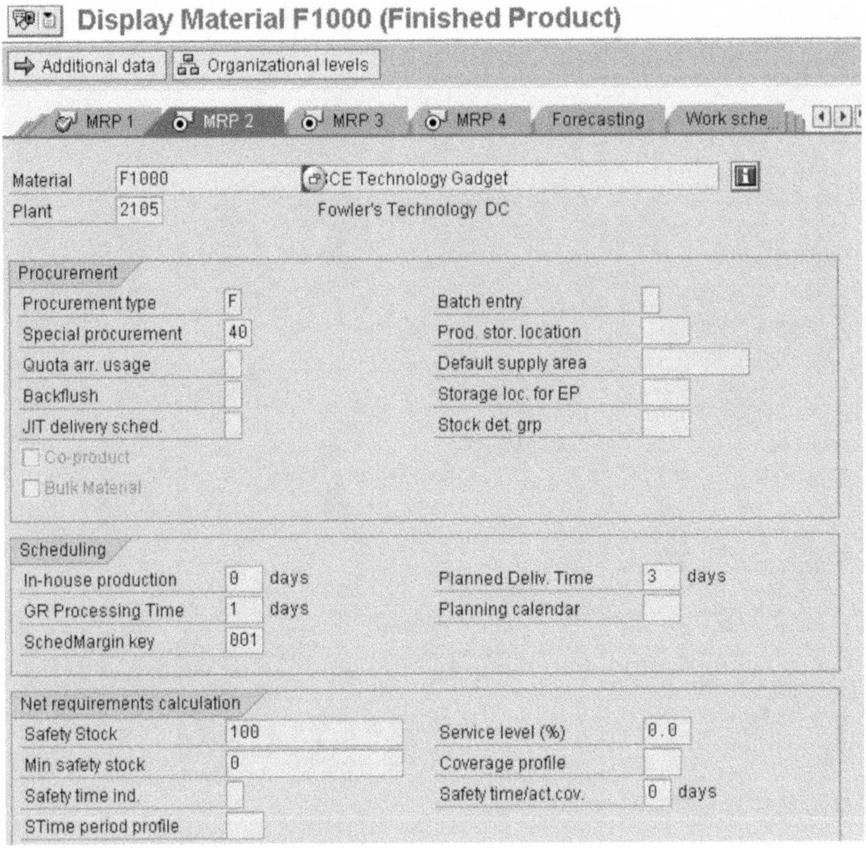

Display Material F1000 (Finished Product)

➡ Additional data | 🖳 Organizational levels

| 🔘 MRP 1 | 🔘 MRP 2 | 🔘 MRP 3 | 🔘 MRP 4 | Forecasting | Work sche |

| Material | F1000 | 🔘 CE Technology Gadget | ℹ |
| Plant | 2105 | Fowler's Technology DC |

Procurement

Procurement type	F		Batch entry	
Special procurement	40		Prod. stor. location	
Quota arr. usage			Default supply area	
Backflush			Storage loc. for EP	
JIT delivery sched.			Stock det. grp	
☐ Co-product				
☐ Bulk Material				

Scheduling

In-house production	0	days	Planned Deliv. Time	3	days
GR Processing Time	1	days	Planning calendar		
SchedMargin key	001				

Net requirements calculation

Safety Stock	100		Service level (%)	0.0	
Min safety stock	0		Coverage profile		
Safety time ind.			Safety time/act.cov.	0	days
STime period profile					

CHAPTER 15

Phase 4: Solution Design

► Defining How the Process Should Work at SCOR Level 3

The goal of many solution-development efforts is to "think outside the box." There was some kind of brain research from a college psychology class indicating that children who haven't yet started school will score an average of 95 percent on a creativity test, while third graders score 30 percent on the same test and adults in the workplace score 5 percent. So much for "outside the box."

Blend brain research with the fact that the relationships among supply chain processes are integrated and complex and you'll see that it's asking too much to expect a project team to start building TO BE processes from scratch. So the objectives for these steps of implementation are not fluid creativity; rather, they are to help define how the business should work using proven best practices, common sense, and native SAP functionality for organizations in that environment.

At Fowlers, as part of assembling the Project 7 solution design, the project team needed to understand the context of tactical planning within the rest of the SCOR Level 3 blueprint. The challenges were to understand how SAP capacity planning was supposed to work based on the original configuration, what other best practices would add to the process, and how to illustrate the TO BE blueprint with SCOR Level 3 elements (see the SAP Modules and Transactions sidebar).

The SCOR Level 3 Blueprint

The SCOR process blueprint (Figure 15-1) shows the integrated processes for five leading practices: sales and operations planning, distribution requirements planning, master production scheduling, material requirements planning, and available to promise. The blueprint also incorporates closed-loop execution processes for all SCOR Level 3 SOURCE, MAKE, DELIVER, and RETURN process elements.

The tour took the team sequentially from PLAN P1 to P4 to P3 to P2 to the SOURCE execution processes S1.1 through S1.5. Then it went on to the MAKE execution processes M1.1 to M1.7 and finally to DELIVER execution processes D1.1 to D1.14. Finally, the tour ended with the RETURN execution processes DR1.1 to DR1.4 and SR1.1 to SR1.5. The following section provides some of the words that go with the blueprint.

PLAN Supply Chain P1. This is the process of taking actual demand data and generating a supply plan for a given supply chain (defined in this case by customer, market channel, product, geography, or business entity). This process step is most closely associated with the discipline of sales and operations planning. The basic steps require a unit forecast that's adjusted for marketing and sales events; a supply plan that constrains the forecast based on resource availability (resources could be inventory, manufacturing capacity, or transportation); and a balance step in which demand/supply exceptions are resolved and updated in the system. The output between this process step and the next PLAN DELIVER (P4) is a constrained unit plan.

PLAN DELIVER P4. This is the process of comparing actual committed orders with the constrained forecast, and generating a

Figure 15-1. Typical SCOR Level 3 blueprint.

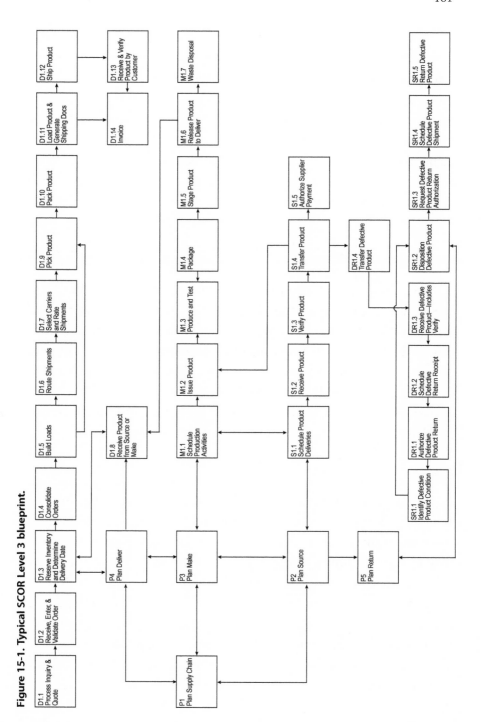

distribution resource plan to satisfy service, cost, and inventory goals. It is carried out for each warehouse stocking location and may be aggregated to region or another geography type. This process step is most closely associated with the discipline of distribution requirements planning. The relationship between this process step and PLAN MAKE P3 are replenishment requirements, which tell the plant manager how much product to plan for. Reserve inventory and promise date (D1.3) is a distribution requirements plan, which lets customer service know how much inventory will be available to promise.

PLAN MAKE P3. This is the process of comparing actual production orders plus replenishment orders with the constrained forecast, and then generating a master production schedule resource plan to satisfy service, cost, and inventory goals. It is carried out for each plant location and may be aggregated to region or another geography type. This process step is most closely associated with the discipline of master production scheduling. The relationship between this process step and PLAN SOURCE P2 are replenishment requirements, which tell the purchasing manager how much product to plan for. It's all passed down to schedule production activities (M1.1), which lets the plant scheduler know how much total product must be made by the ship date.

PLAN SOURCE P2. This is the process of comparing total material requirements with the constrained forecast, and generating a material requirements resource plan to satisfy landed cost and inventory goals by commodity type. It is carried out for items on the bill of materials and may be aggregated by supplier or commodity type. This process step is most closely associated with the discipline of material requirements planning. The relationship between this process step and schedule product deliveries is the material requirements plan, which lets the buyer know how much product must be purchased on the basis of current orders, inventory, and future requirements.

SOURCE Sx. The *x* in Sx is a wildcard-type indication that includes all of the SCOR Level 2 configurations. This set of execution processes involves the material acquisition process initiating and scheduling the purchase order, receiving and verifying product, transferring the product to available raw material, and authorizing supplier payment through. In the case of sourcing engineer-to-order products, there are accommodations to identify and select appropriate suppliers.

MAKE Mx. This set of execution processes encompasses the conversion process of raw materials to finished goods: scheduling production activities, issuing and staging the product, producing and testing, packaging, and releasing finished goods to customers or warehouses. In the case of making engineer-to-order products, there are accommodations to finalize engineering specifications before initiating a manufacturing work order.

DELIVER Dx. This set of execution processes involves the order fulfillment process: processing inquiries and quotes, entering orders, promising inventory, consolidating orders, planning and building loads, routing shipments, selecting carriers and rating shipments, receiving, picking, shipping, customer receipt, necessary installation, and final invoicing. In the case of delivering engineer-to-order products, there are accommodations to include the request for proposal or quote and negotiating contracts before order entry.

RETURN DRx and SR1x. This set of execution processes involves the return authorization process, return shipment and receipt, verification and disposition of product, and replacement or credit process for defective and excess inventory. In the third case of RETURN, more detailed scheduling, determination of product condition, and transfer of maintenance, repair, and overhaul items are modeled.

ENABLE Processes. Enable processes prepare, maintain, and manage information or relationships on which planning and execution processes rely. There is no decomposition of ENABLE elements. Think of them as necessary processes. There are eight management categories of ENABLE that are applied appropriately to PLAN, SOURCE, MAKE, DELIVER, and RETURN. They are business rules, performance improvement, data collection, inventory, capital assets, transportation, physical network configuration, and regulatory compliance. Another ENABLE process, unique to PLAN, manages alignment of the financial and unit plans; still another ENABLE process, unique to SOURCE, manages supplier agreements. Supply chains can have well-integrated planning and execution processes and still underperform if ENABLE processes are poorly managed. For example, a good sales and operations planning process cannot overcome a poor EP.9 align unit and financial plans.

Configuring the Level 3 Blueprint for Project 7

One of the first tasks in configuring the blueprint is to find a best-practices resource that can help define the proper ENABLE process elements. For Project 7, the project team picked the resource *Master Scheduling in the 21st Century: For Simplicity, Speed, and Success—Up and Down the Supply Chain* (by Thomas F. Wallace and Robert A. Stahl; T. F. Wallace & Co., 2003). Prior to configuring their blueprint the team members completed the master scheduling effectiveness checklist, assembled their first draft of a master scheduling policy, and outlined the basic responsibilities of a master scheduler, which the team considered part of the EP ENABLE PLAN processes.

The policy (EP.1) helped sort out some potentially contentious issues. First, the team defined the planning time zones: 0–14 days was considered fixed with no unauthorized changes; 3–8 weeks was considered firm with mix changes only by authorized roles; and 3–18 months was considered open, wherein volume decisions needed to reconcile with the rough-cut capacity plan as approved in the sales and operations planning process (P1).

Second, the decision-making authority for the fixed and firm zones were defined relative to the type of product, level of change, and date of impact. Third, the policy required use of the SAP order entry and available-to-promise (D1.2 and D1.3) in making customer commitments. Fourth, the forecasts (P1.1) were consumed properly using one of the SAP consumption algorithms.

Fifth, the master schedule could have no past-due production orders carried over into the new week. Sixth, production schedule attainment was defined and elevated to a critical metric with a target of 95 percent each week. Seventh, a weekly meeting with sales, marketing, and customer service would review the available capacity against customer orders to achieve consensus priority and resolution of issues.

Next, the team next constructed Level 3 process flow (Figure 15-2), adding appropriate SAP language as the inputs and outputs. The relationship between the supply planning step in sales and operations planning (P1.2) and the master scheduling process (P3) was labeled as rough-cut capacity plan. Essentially, it was a monthly view of the CM01 capacity from month 3 through month 12 that has netted the forecasted requirements (P1.1) against the resource capacities. The expectation, as part of the policy, is that there are no instances in which a resource (production line) is "red" (more requirements than capacity). The relationship between P4 and P3 is focused on the zero- to 8-week horizons, and is defined both by customer orders and replenishment orders called stock transport order (STO). An STO is a replenishment order that is generated when a product stock position in a warehouse has slipped below target, therefore putting product availability at risk. The relationship between D1.3 and P4 is where available-to-promise (ATP) functionality operates.

The point is that orders are now driving requirements in the master scheduling horizon. The other important factor in P4 is how the team has set forecast consumption logic in SAP master data settings. In the open-time horizon, forecasts define the requirements of capacity. As the time horizon approaches the current day, real orders

Figure 15-2. Fowlers' tactical planning SCOR process blueprint.

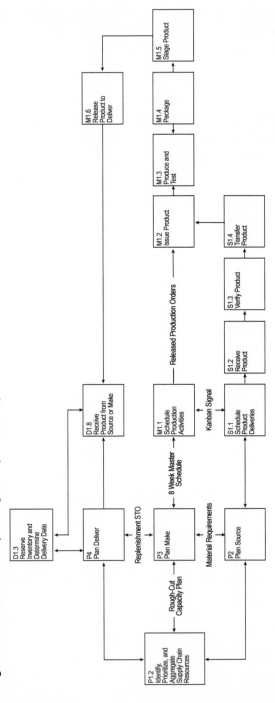

for needed stock replace (or consume) the forecasts. SAP functionality offers a number of ways that forecasts can be consumed.

The relationship of P3 to M1.1 is a two-week fixed plan that the scheduler can release for each product to each production line. If today is Thursday, then next week is considered fixed as Week 1 and the following week is considered fixed as Week 2. All materials should be available for Week 1, and the scheduler typically is working to confirm availability for Week 2. The relationship between P3 and P2 is called *material requirements*. It utilizes both the firm and the open capacity plans and converts them (using MRP) into material, packaging, and/or component requirements for suppliers. The important information includes date, quantity, and source. P2 then converts these requirements into requisitions that pass to S1.1, which then converts them to purchase orders.

Having finished the Level 3 process flow and the SAP module and transaction "should-be" education, the team is excited to dive into the detailed solution design, SCOR process Level 4 flows, and the SAP transaction storyboard.

SAP Modules and Transactions

Under the facilitative guidance of the SAP expert, the Fowlers project team reviewed all of the major *modules* that were part of the original configuration, along with their associated key *transaction codes*.

Modules for the SAP software are portions of functionality within an application *component* that are geared toward addressing specific business tasks. Figure 15-3 illustrates the modules that were a part of the original configuration using the SAP navigation screen for the Logistics component.

Transaction codes in the SAP software are alphanumeric codes (shortcuts) that are a subset of functionality (screens) under each module that help users complete necessary business tasks. For Fowlers, *CM01* capacity planning-work center load is a transaction that supports tasks to be completed in the SCOR processes of P3 PLAN MAKE. For most SAP transactions, the last number indicates the purpose of the transaction (1 to create, 2 to modify, 3 to display data). Figure 15-4 illustrates the SAP navigation screen the Fowlers team used to find the transaction CM01. Table 15-1 is a partial list of SCOR Level 3 elements, related SAP modules, common SAP transactions, and common SAP standard reports related to the Fowlers tactical planning solution.

Figure 15-3. SAP logistics modules.

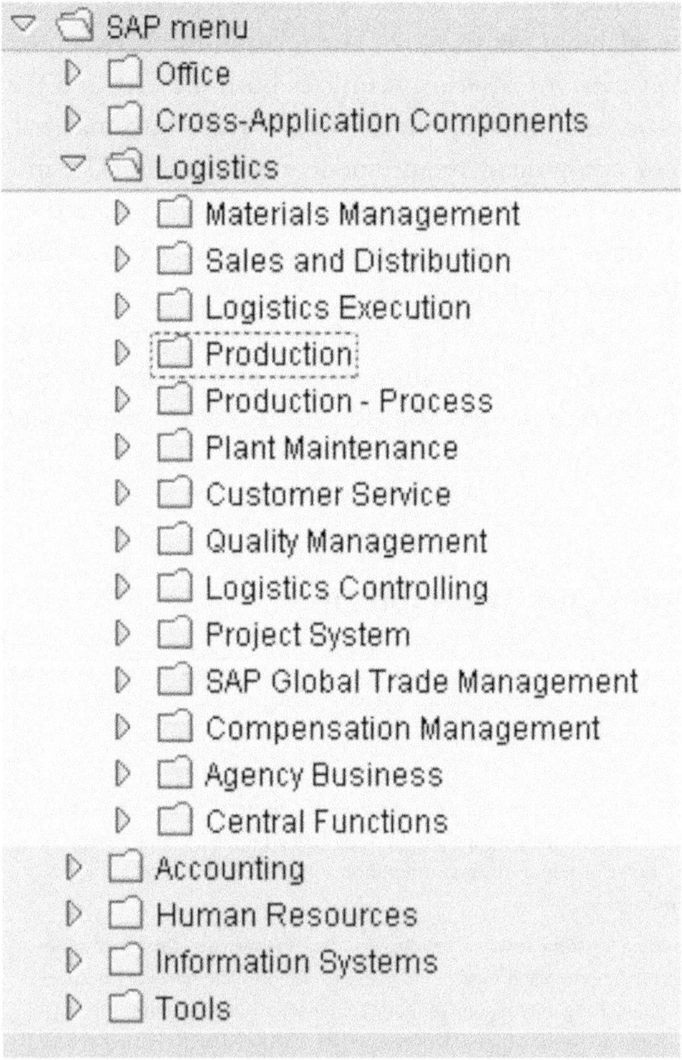

▽ 🗁 SAP menu
  ▷ 🗀 Office
  ▷ 🗀 Cross-Application Components
  ▽ 🗁 Logistics
    ▷ 🗀 Materials Management
    ▷ 🗀 Sales and Distribution
    ▷ 🗀 Logistics Execution
    ▷ 🗀 Production
    ▷ 🗀 Production - Process
    ▷ 🗀 Plant Maintenance
    ▷ 🗀 Customer Service
    ▷ 🗀 Quality Management
    ▷ 🗀 Logistics Controlling
    ▷ 🗀 Project System
    ▷ 🗀 SAP Global Trade Management
    ▷ 🗀 Compensation Management
    ▷ 🗀 Agency Business
    ▷ 🗀 Central Functions
  ▷ 🗀 Accounting
  ▷ 🗀 Human Resources
  ▷ 🗀 Information Systems
  ▷ 🗀 Tools

Figure 15-4. SAP menu drilldown to transaction CM01.

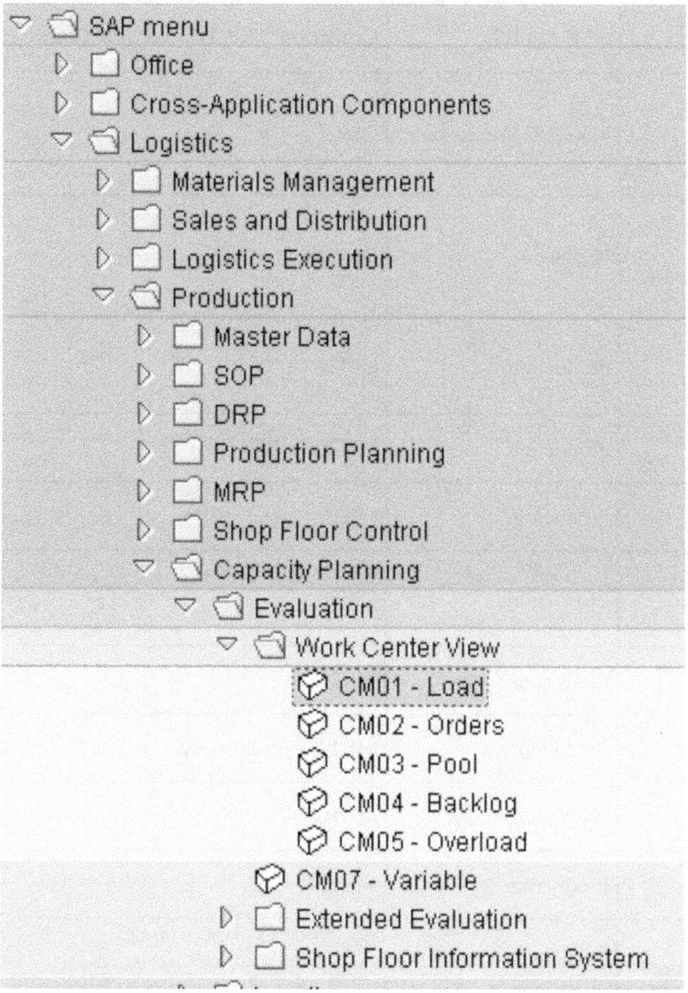

```
▽ ⬡ SAP menu
   ▷ ☐ Office
   ▷ ☐ Cross-Application Components
   ▽ ⬡ Logistics
      ▷ ☐ Materials Management
      ▷ ☐ Sales and Distribution
      ▷ ☐ Logistics Execution
      ▽ ⬡ Production
         ▷ ☐ Master Data
         ▷ ☐ SOP
         ▷ ☐ DRP
         ▷ ☐ Production Planning
         ▷ ☐ MRP
         ▷ ☐ Shop Floor Control
         ▽ ⬡ Capacity Planning
            ▽ ⬡ Evaluation
               ▽ ⬡ Work Center View
                     ⬠ CM01 - Load
                     ⬠ CM02 - Orders
                     ⬠ CM03 - Pool
                     ⬠ CM04 - Backlog
                     ⬠ CM05 - Overload
                  ⬠ CM07 - Variable
               ▷ ☐ Extended Evaluation
               ▷ ☐ Shop Floor Information System
```

Table 15-1. SCOR Level 3 elements related to SAP modules and common transactions.

SCOR 10.0 Level 3 Element	SAP Module	Common SAP Transaction Codes
P1.3 Balance Supply Chain Resources with Supply Chain Requirements	Materials Management	CM01
P2.3 Balance Product Resources with Product Requirements	Production	CM01
S1.1 Schedule Product Deliveries	Production	CM29
S1.2 Receive Product	Production	MIGO, MB31
S1.4 Transfer Product	Production	MB1B
M1.1 Schedule Production Activities	Production	CM29
M1.2 Issue Product	Production	MIGO
M1.3 Produce and Test	Production	MB1C—receipt only
M1.4 Package	Production	MB1C
M1.5 Stage Product	Production	MB1B
D1.1 Process Inquiry & Quote	Sales and Distribution	Inquiry: VA11, VA12, VA13 Quote: VA21, VA22, VA23
D1.2 Receive, Enter, & Validate Order	Sales and Distribution	VA01, VA02
D1.3 Reserve Inventory and Determine Delivery Date	Sales and Distribution	Within sales order processing VA01 or VA02 or via Backorder processing: C006 or via Rescheduling: V_V2
D1.8 Receive Product at Warehouse from Source or Make	Sales and Distribution	MIGO, MB31

CHAPTER 16

Phase 4: Level 4 Process Development and the Storyboard

▶ **How Business Process Improvement Is Like a Good Cartoon**

With the SCOR Level 3 blueprint and SAP transaction scope complete, the project team can begin to work on the SCOR Level 4 process details and the SAP transaction storyboard. Also on the docket is development of process control metrics. Recommendations for organizational changes and finalizing RACI analyses will be covered as part of supply chain strategy (Chapter 18).

In AcceleratedSAP terminology, the SCOR Level 3 blueprint (also referred to as high-level business requirements) is part of the business blueprint Phase 2; in the appendix we are on step eight. The blueprint should reflect how your company wants to do business and operate its supply chain and be consistent with the blueprint templates used as part of the QAdb input process. What many people refer to as SCOR Level 4 processes (or as detailed business requirements) are considered the transition blueprint from AcceleratedSAP business blueprint Phase 2 to realization Phase 3. SCOR Level 5 would be considered the baseline configuration for the system.

In fact, whether involving a system solution or not, SCOR Level 4 process details are necessary for any kind of SCOR process implementation activity to occur. While logical, this discussion is a bit of a misnomer because the SCOR model doesn't standardize definitions for Level 4 processes (Figure 16-1); although the model illustrates the relationship of Level 3 to Level 4, there are no Level 4 definitions to be found in the SCOR dictionary itself.

This chapter, then, is devoted to the concept of creating those definitions—blending system functionality, best practices, and data into a solution storyboard.

The concept of the storyboard is borrowed from the art of animation. At the start of a project, the animation director puts together milestone images on the storyboard. This is where the initial story line is developed, and it serves as a point of reference from which the details of the full-length film are later filled in. Similarly, the

Figure 16-1. SCOR Level 3 and Level 4 definitions.

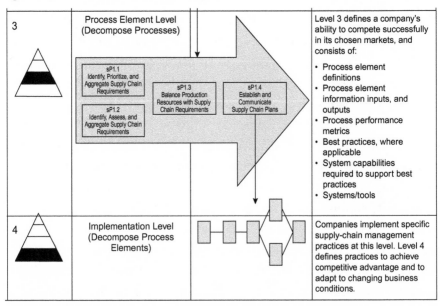

AcceleratedSAP Roadmap (Chapter 17) is the stage at which the solution goes through realization, final preparation, and go-live and support.

Constructing a SCOR Level 4 Process

There are eight steps to building a SCOR Level 4 process. The first four were completed in the last chapter; here is the full list:

1. Find an appropriate leading-practice book that can guide you through best-in-class characteristics.

2. Map your company's "best practice" processes to the SCOR Level 3 process blueprint. (Those who readily admit that they have no leading practices can skip this step).

3. Relate the processes as detailed in the book to appropriate SCOR Level 3 processes.

4. Identify the main system (SAP) transactions to be used, and cross-reference the transactions to the appropriate SCOR Level 3 process; this will help with the inputs and outputs and names for the transactions.

5. Use the transactions to help create a screen-shot storyboard that illustrates the different screens (features and functionality) from the beginning of the process blueprint to its end. The storyboard is relatively easy to produce; the "print screen" key on the computer keyboard allows for easy capture. The storyboard is not intended to replace technical documentation; the goal is to provide the design team and appropriate extended teams with a visual tour of the important functionality.

6. Use the storyboard and the leading-practice book to create the first draft of your Level 4 process.

7. Review the storyboard with appropriate design and extended team members, referencing the process map. The objective is to gain consensus on the features of the solution and understand the degree of change to either the process, the system, or both.

8. Use the feedback from step 7 to set up a system test environment, in which company data can be used to test the new processes and functionality without the risk of messing up the live system. In many cases, these "sandboxes" may have been set up as part of the original implementation effort.

Plan Supply Chain (P1) Level 4 Samples

This chapter includes a generic sample of the Level 4 processes that are commonly used for sales and operations planning. The best-practice resource is based in Thomas F. Wallace and Robert A. Stahl's *Sales & Operations Planning: The How-To Handbook*, 3rd Ed. (T. F. Wallace & Company, 2008). Figures 16-2 through 16-4 illustrate the level process flows for demand planning (P1.1), supply planning (P1.2), and reconciliation (P1.3), respectively.

As an added twist, the Level 4 processes are illustrated in time-phased groupings. In each figure the Level 4 processes are in one of four rows; each row relates to a week of a month (i.e., the first row contains all Week One activities for P1.1, P1.2, and P1.3). That way, a new demand planner can look at Figure 16-2 and understand what work needs to be completed during each week of the month.

Figure 16-5 is an SAP screen shot taken from a P1.1 storyboard that illustrates where the analytical effort from P1.1.4, P1.1.5, P1.1.7, and P1.1.8 (Figure 16-2) would be entered. The shot also illustrates the set of new names for minor transactions: that is, order forecast, marketing adjustment percentage, marketing/sales events, and so on.

(*Text continues on page 199*)

Figure 16-2. P1.1 Level 4 process blueprint for demand planning.

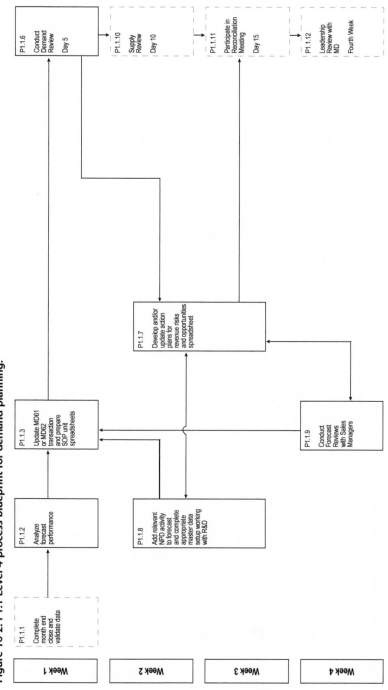

196

Figure 16-3. P1.2 Level 4 process blueprint for supply planning.

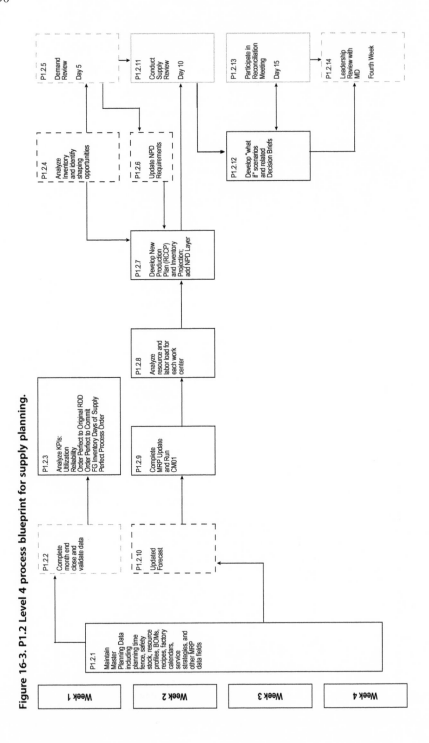

Figure 16-4. P1.3 Level 4 process blueprint for reconciliation.

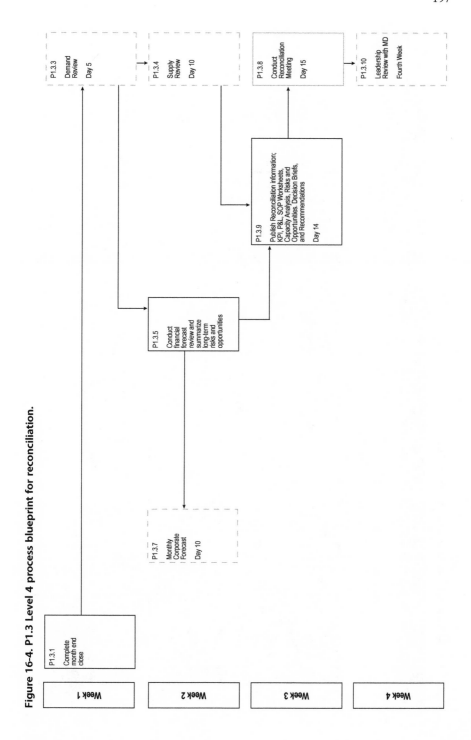

Figure 16-5. Sample storyboard screen shot from P1.1.

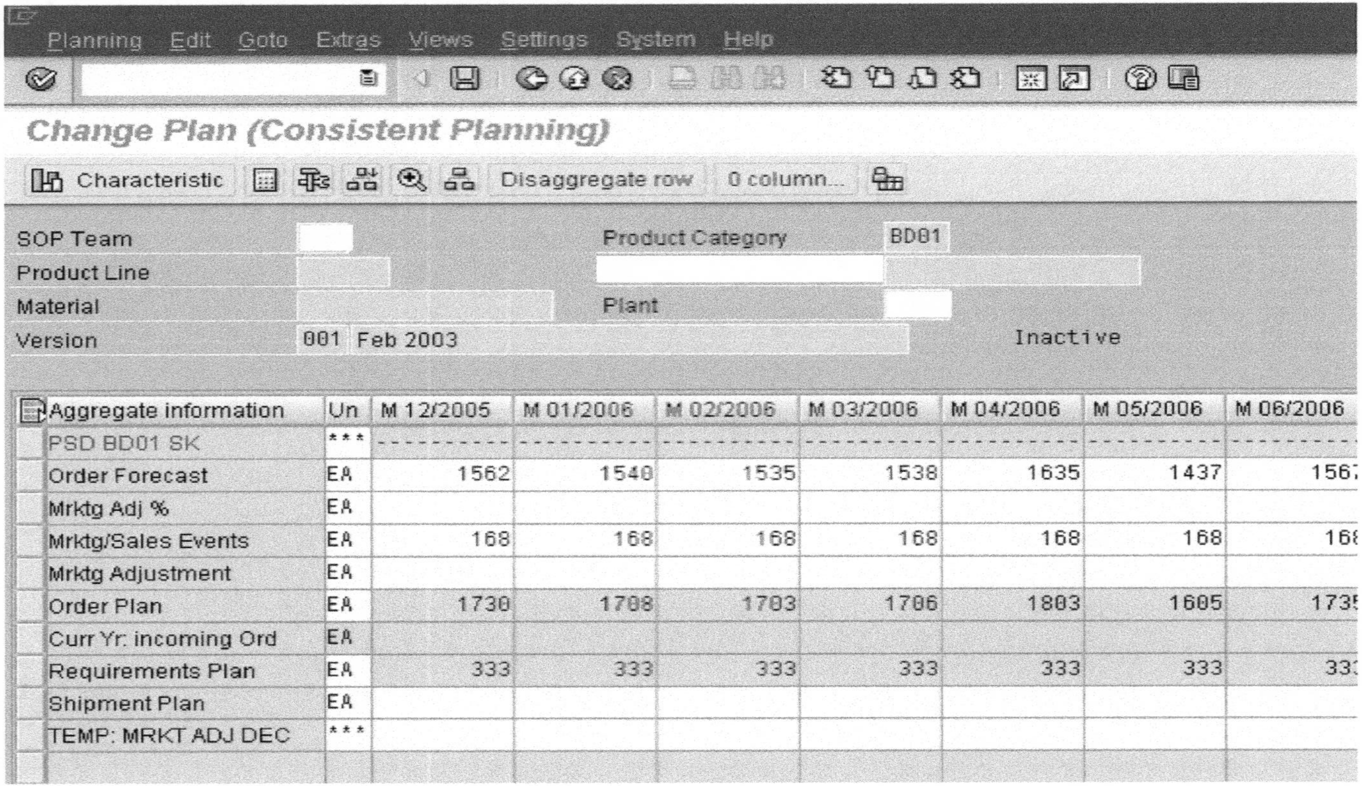

Fowlers P3 Level 4 Processes and Storyboard

Figure 16-6 is Fowlers' P3 PLAN MAKE Level 4 process flow for the Engineer a Tactical Planning Process project. As mentioned, the team members selected *Master Scheduling in the 21st Century* as their best practice resource. They found that it was difficult mapping each of the P3.1, P3.2, P3.3, and P3.4 processes independently, as SAP PP did not behave that way; the flow made more sense by blending the processes on the same page. The process references are consistent with SCOR Level 4.

Capacity Planning for the Storyboard

With the help of the SAP expert, the Fowlers project team started to assemble the resource capacity management storyboard. The first step was to affirm the overall goals—ensure that product will be made with enough lead time to be ready to ship on each sales order, and that adequate capacity, materials, and lead time are available to make this happen.

Second, the team needed to understand how the SAP system is supposed to work. It learned that SAP work centers—or resources—can be used to define the machines and people used to make or assemble materials. In this environment, capacity can be thought of both from a planning and a detailed scheduling point of view.

Capacity planning decisions are typically made for a future time period, commonly 2 to 13 weeks, when it's not yet critical to know exactly when a product will be produced—only that there is sufficient capacity to produce it. Capacity planning answers the question, "Do I have a reasonable chance to make enough product to fulfill a requirement placed on a specific work center within a specific timeframe such as a week or month?"

Detailed scheduling decisions, on the other hand, consider exactly when each product will be produced within the near term, commonly 0 to 2 weeks. The questions a scheduler has to answer are: When exactly (day and shift) do I need the product to be made to fill a specific requirement, such as a sales order or stock transport order? Will I have enough materials to make the product? Will my current production rate achieve the schedule?-And—a favorite of the plant manager and controller: How do I make all of these products and minimize all non-value-added work, such as setup time, changeover time, etc?

Third, the SAP expert worked with the Fowlers project team to piece together the *feature transactions* foundational to the storyboard. The storyboard focused on four areas:

200

Figure 16-6. Fowlers' P3 PLAN MAKE Level 4 process flow for the project: Engineer a Tactical Planning Process.

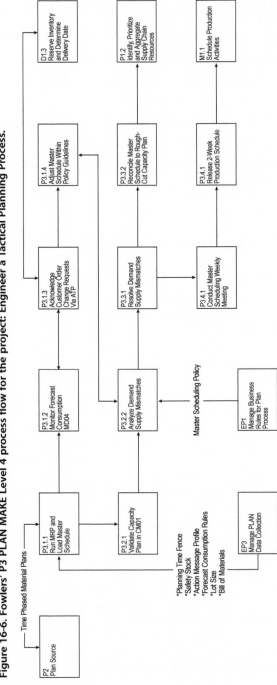

Resources (CRC2), recipes (C202), the capacity planning view (CM01), and the parameter settings for the MRP planning run (MD01). The team selected resource T100 and material F1000 to do a detailed review of the settings.

T100 CRC2 Resource Settings

The capacity formula "Z006" was correct. It calculated the amount of time it took to make one order as Setup Time (defined at Fowlers as the first standard value) plus Machine Time (defined as the second standard value) multiplied by the quantity of product produced (Figure 16-7). The team then checked the standard available capacity (Figure 16-8) and found something wasn't quite right. "We usually only get 85 percent resource capacity utilization but the capacity utilization was set to 100 percent," a team member observed. A note was made to change this field after the review was complete.

F1000 at Plant 2106 C202 Change Recipe

First the team members needed to look at the *Base Quantity* of the recipe to ensure they understood the *run rates* required for each step or operation to make the product. The Base Quantity was equal to 1 (Figure 16-9) The SAP expert explained that this meant the machine run rates would be equal to the amount of time required to make one each of material F1000. The First Standard Value—*setup time*—was equal to 1 hour. The second Standard Value—*machine time*—was equal to 0.1 hours (Figure 16-10).

The SAP expert also explained how capacity was calculated when making material F1000. Using the formula from the resource, he calculated the capacity required to produce one order of 200 Eaches (units) of F1000 as follows:

Setup time = 1.0 hour

Machine Time of 0.1 hour × 200 Eaches (or units) = 20.0 hours

Total time required = 21.0 hours

CM01 Capacity Planning

The first thing the team members noticed was that Week 11 was highlighted in red; capacity requirements exceeded available capacity (Figure 16-11). Clicking on the red line, they drilled down and found that there were two orders planned to be produced that week: orders 12022 and 12103. "Wait a second," one team member exclaimed, "Order 12022 is for a quantity of 1,090 EA of F1000, which would give us a total of 110 hours. But the capacity requirement is only equal to 80 hours. How can that be?" (Figure 16-12). Looking at the dates for order 12022, they were able to determine a start date of Friday, March 11, and completion on Monday, March 21. They went back to the main view of CM01, and by drilling into the prior and post weeks found the "missing" 30 hours. (Figure 16-13).

The capacity problem in Week 11 remained unresolved, but the team agreed it could be addressed when looking at the overall stock requirements for Material F1000, which prompted another team member to notice that there weren't any requirements in any of the future weeks. "We always load forecasts eight weeks into the future to ensure that when we run the MRP for planned orders we can estimate our future capacity requirements," he said. "I've seen planned orders in the future, but where are the requirements?"

MRP Planning Run MD01

To ensure accurate capacity requirements are generated, Scheduling Parameter 2 must be selected when running the MRP planning run (Figure 16-14). When using Scheduling Parameter 1, the system uses information contained within the material master—specifically the scheduling parameters *In-house Production Time, Goods Receipt Processing Time* and the *Scheduling Margin Key*—to calculate the basic start and finish dates for a planned order. Planned Orders created with basic dates do not appear on CM01. The team made a note to change the MD01 Scheduling parameter to "2" for future MRP planning runs.

Figure 16-7. T100 CRC2 resource settings in SAP capacities setup screen.

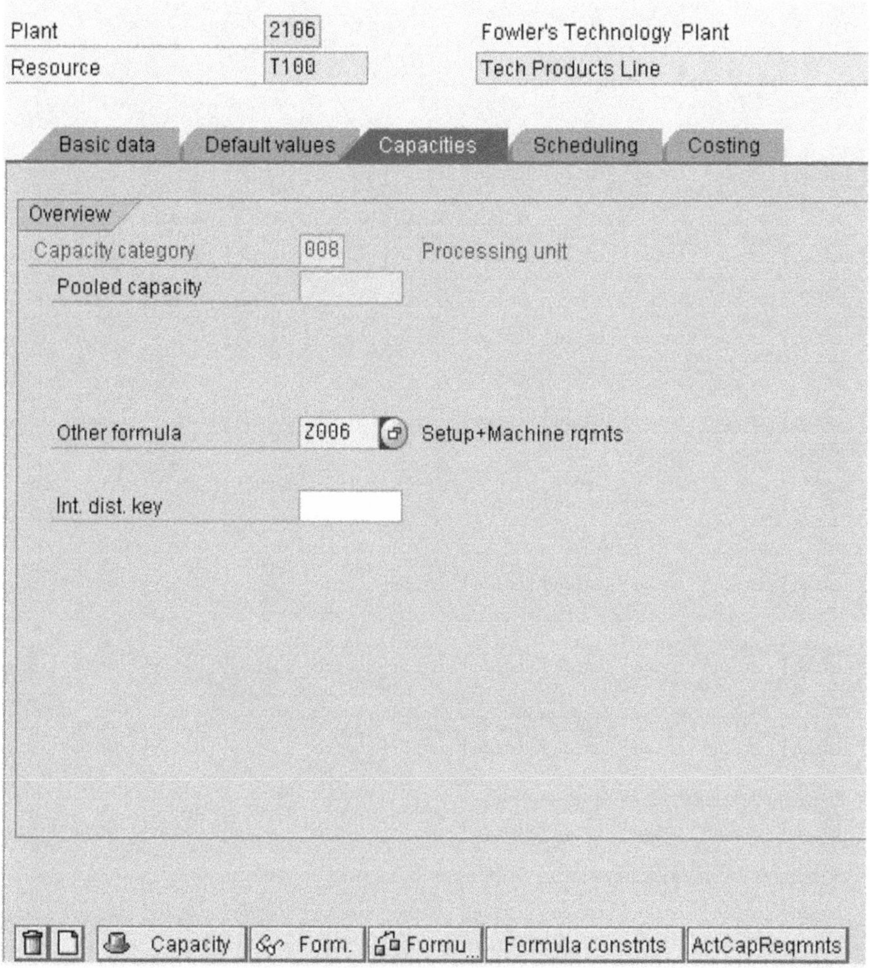

| Plant | 2106 | Fowler's Technology Plant |
| Resource | T100 | Tech Products Line |

| Basic data | Default values | Capacities | Scheduling | Costing |

Overview

Capacity category   008   Processing unit

Pooled capacity

Other formula   Z006 ⟳ Setup+Machine rqmts

Int. dist. key

| 🗑 🗋 | 🖴 Capacity | ⚙ Form. | 🔧 Formu.. | Formula constnts | ActCapReqmnts |

Figure 16-8. Standard available capacity in SAP capacity setup screen.

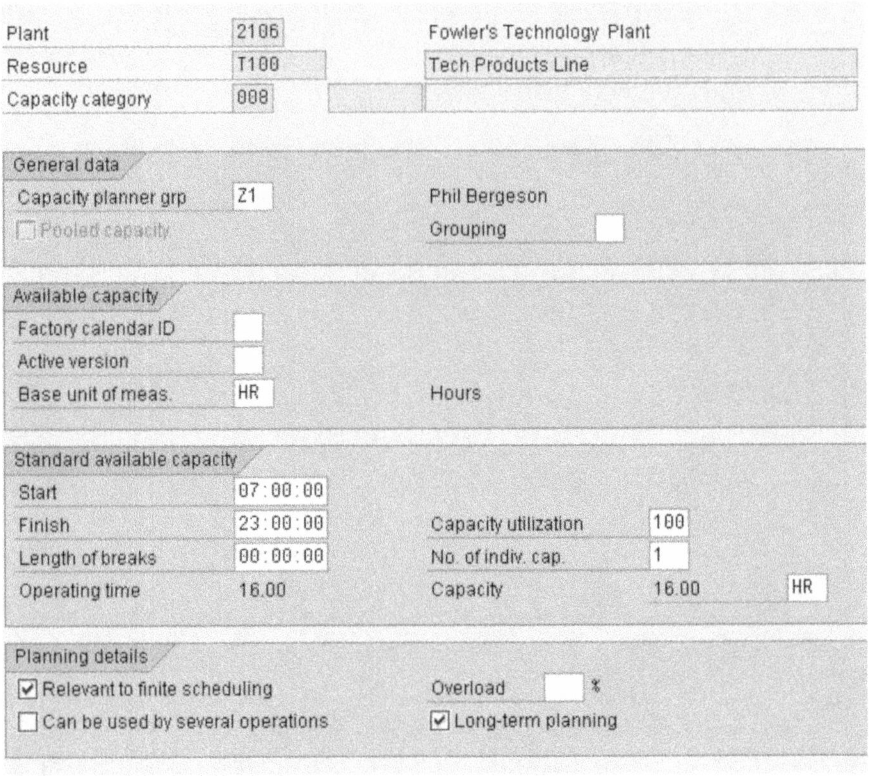

Plant	2106	Fowler's Technology Plant
Resource	T100	Tech Products Line
Capacity category	008	

General data

| Capacity planner grp | Z1 | Phil Bergeson |
| ☐ Pooled capacity | | Grouping |

Available capacity

Factory calendar ID	
Active version	
Base unit of meas.	HR	Hours

Standard available capacity

Start	07:00:00	
Finish	23:00:00	Capacity utilization	100
Length of breaks	00:00:00	No. of indiv. cap.	1
Operating time	16.00	Capacity	16.00	HR

Planning details

| ☑ Relevant to finite scheduling | Overload | ☐ % |
| ☐ Can be used by several operations | ☑ Long-term planning |

Figure 16-9. Setting of base quantity for required run rates.

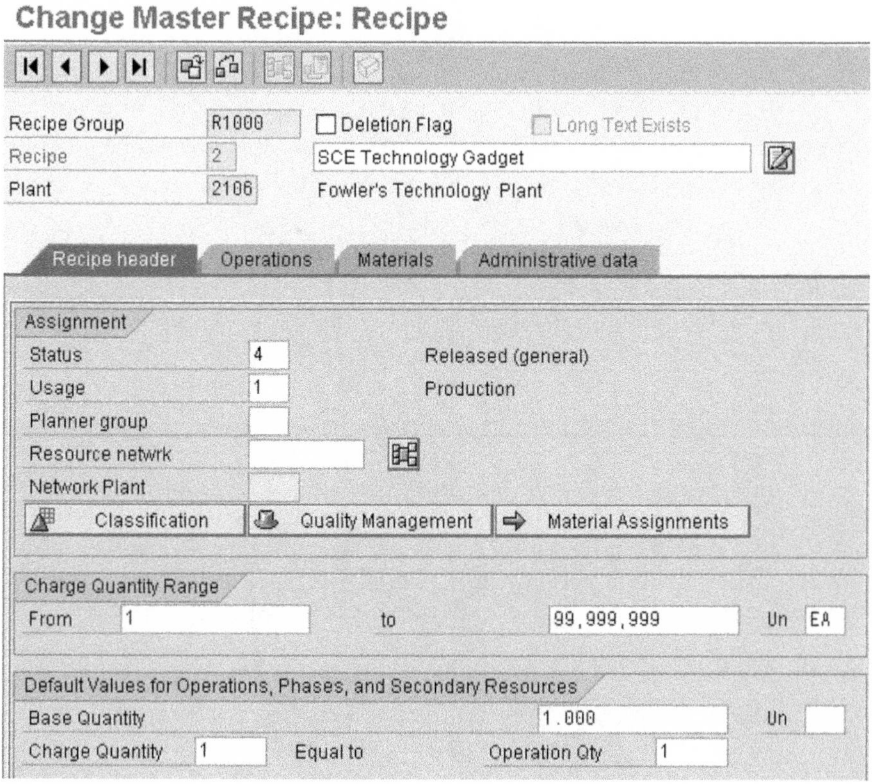

Change Master Recipe: Recipe

Recipe Group	R1000	☐ Deletion Flag	☐ Long Text Exists
Recipe	2	SCE Technology Gadget	
Plant	2106	Fowler's Technology Plant	

Recipe header | Operations | Materials | Administrative data

Assignment

Status	4	Released (general)
Usage	1	Production
Planner group		
Resource netwrk		
Network Plant		

⬛ Classification   🪣 Quality Management   ➡ Material Assignments

Charge Quantity Range

From	1	to	99,999,999	Un	EA

Default Values for Operations, Phases, and Secondary Resources

Base Quantity		1.000	Un	
Charge Quantity	1	Equal to	Operation Qty	1

206

Figure 16-10. Settings for set-up time and machine time.

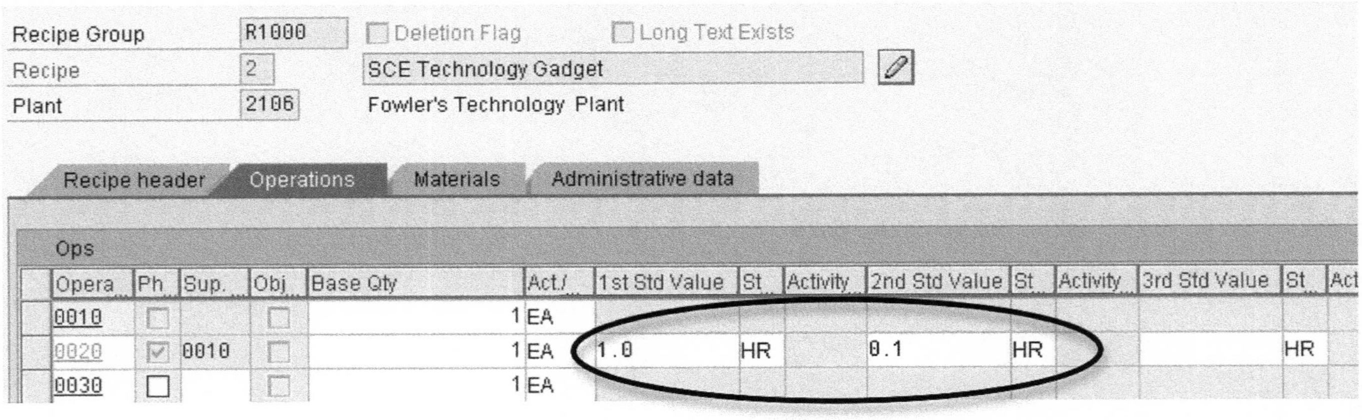

Recipe Group	R1000		Deletion Flag		Long Text Exists
Recipe	2		SCE Technology Gadget		
Plant	2106		Fowler's Technology Plant		

Recipe header | Operations | Materials | Administrative data

Ops

Opera.	Ph.	Sup.	Obj.	Base Qty	Act./	1st Std Value	St.	Activity	2nd Std Value	St.	Activity	3rd Std Value	St.	Act
0010					1 EA									
0020	▷	0010			1 EA	1.0	HR		0.1	HR			HR	
0030					1 EA									

Figure 16-11. SAP capacity planning screen showing requirements in excess of capacity.

Work center   T100   Tech Products Line   Plant   2106
Capacity cat.: 008   Processing unit

Week	Requirements	AvailCap.	CapLoad	RemAvailCap	Unit
10/2011	14.00	64.00	22 %	50.00	H
11/2011	121.00	80.00	151 %	41.00-	H
12/2011	16.00	80.00	20 %	64.00	H
13/2011	0.00	80.00	0 %	80.00	H
14/2011	0.00	80.00	0 %	80.00	H
15/2011	0.00	80.00	0 %	80.00	H
16/2011	0.00	80.00	0 %	80.00	H
17/2011	0.00	80.00	0 %	80.00	H
18/2011	0.00	80.00	0 %	80.00	H
Total >>>	151.00	704.00	21 %	553.00	H

Figure 16-12. SAP calendar week 11 capacity planning for Order 12022.

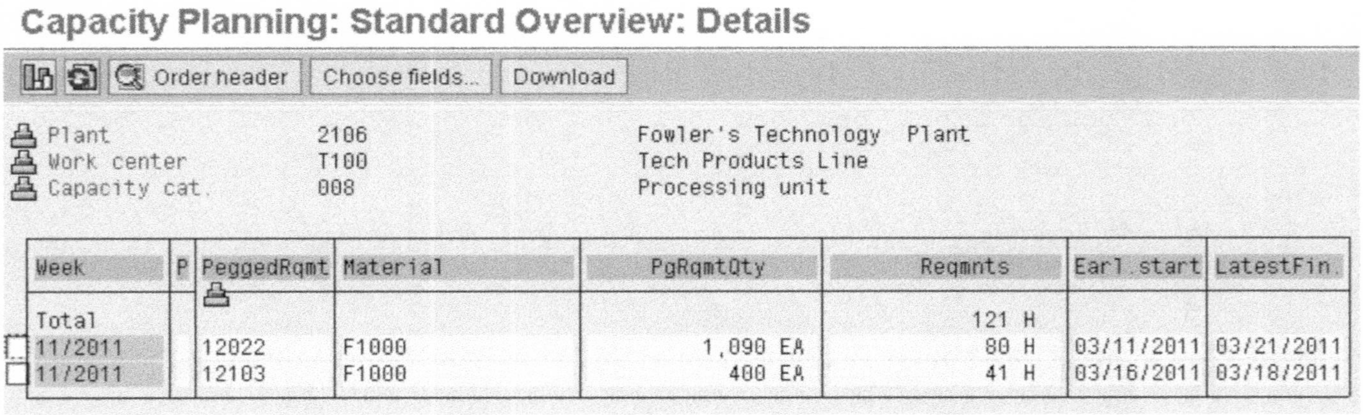

Capacity Planning: Standard Overview: Details

🔲 🔄 🔍	Order header	Choose fields...	Download

Plant   2106   Fowler's Technology Plant
Work center   T100   Tech Products Line
Capacity cat.   008   Processing unit

Week	P	PeggedRqmt	Material	PgRqmtQty	Reqmnts	Earl.start	LatestFin
Total					121 H		
11/2011		12022	F1000	1,090 EA	80 H	03/11/2011	03/21/2011
11/2011		12103	F1000	400 EA	41 H	03/16/2011	03/18/2011

Figure 16-13. Finding additional run time needed for Order 12022 in weeks 10 (top) and 12 (bottom).

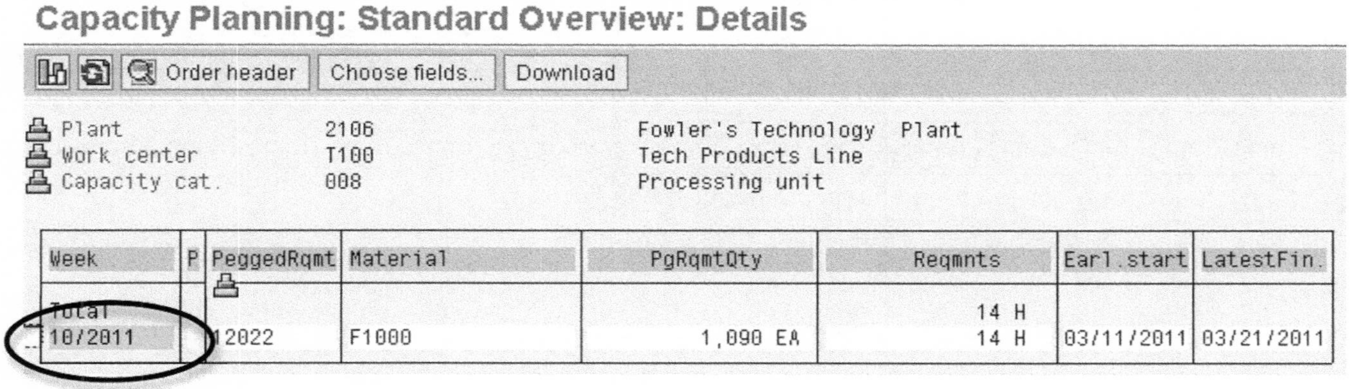

Capacity Planning: Standard Overview: Details

| 🔳 | 🔄 | Order header | Choose fields... | Download |

Plant   2106   Fowler's Technology Plant
Work center   T100   Tech Products Line
Capacity cat.   008   Processing unit

Week	P	PeggedRqmt	Material	PgRqmtQty	Reqmnts	Earl.start	LatestFin.
Total					14 H		
10/2011		12022	F1000	1,090 EA	14 H	03/11/2011	03/21/2011

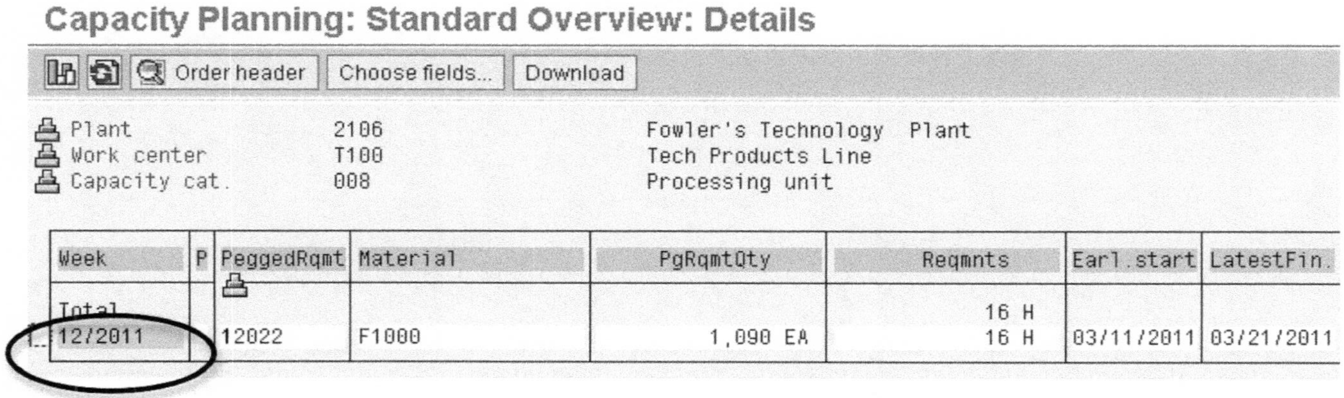

Capacity Planning: Standard Overview: Details

| 🔳 | 🔄 | Order header | Choose fields... | Download |

Plant   2106   Fowler's Technology Plant
Work center   T100   Tech Products Line
Capacity cat.   008   Processing unit

Week	P	PeggedRqmt	Material	PgRqmtQty	Reqmnts	Earl.start	LatestFin.
Total					16 H		
12/2011		12022	F1000	1,090 EA	16 H	03/11/2011	03/21/2011

210

Figure 16-14. Correcting SAP MRP scheduling parameters assures accurate capacity requirements.

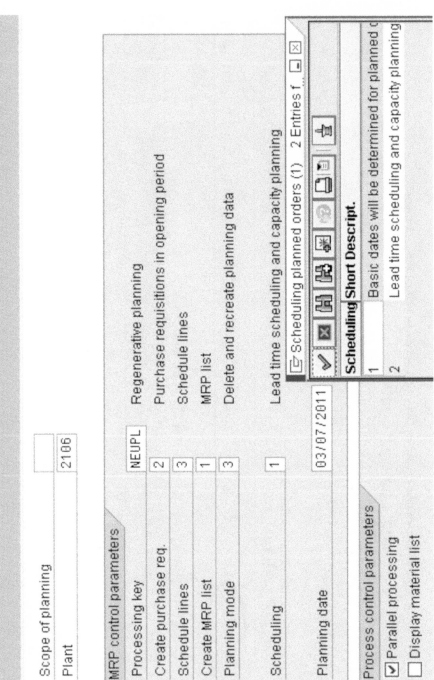

Stock Requirements for the Storyboard

Now that the team had the feature pieces of the capacity storyboard (sidebar: Capacity Planning for the Storyboard), the next step was to assemble the feature pieces of the planning process, including demand (requirements) and supply (receipts). The team picked product F1000, a make-to-stock item manufactured at a North American plant (SAP plant 2106) and typically shipped to a distribution center (SAP plant 2105) until required for a customer shipment.

As with all things in the SAP process, the team needed to understand some basic nomenclature. An SAP Material Requirements Planning (MRP) "run" uses *master and transactional data* to generate receipts to fulfill open requirements. Typical requirements are customer orders (*CusOrd*), planned independent requirements (*IndReq*), stock transfer requests to another plant, and safety stock (*SafeSt*). Receipts are represented by purchase requisitions (*PurRqs*) or planned orders (*PldOrd*). All of these MRP elements represent the current and future stock planning situation and can be seen using SAP transaction MD04—the Stock Requirements List (Figure 16-15).

The team first viewed MD04 for SAP plant 2105 and material F1000 and found the following receipt and requirement MRP elements:

Like a checkbook, each receipt (like a deposit) and requirement (like a debit) affects the available stock—SAP terminology is *available qty*. Note, the VSF requirements for 03/07/2011 and 03/14/2011 did not affect available stock; the SAP expert explained that configuration settings for some VSF forecasts, called *planned independent requirements* (PIRs), allow the requirements to be ignored within a specified short-term timeframe. This is helpful when it's desirable to respond only to customer orders in the short term, but do use the VSF forecast (PIRs) to help secure capacity and components.

Working over the same computer, the team members clicked on the summation sign at the left-hand side of the screen and were able to see *weekly aggregated receipts and requirements* (Figure 16-16). The team observed that there were no VSF forecast PIRs in week 12/2011. The SAP expert explained that they were "consumed" by customer orders to ensure that the requirements were not double-counted (900 in the requirements column). The details of this consumption could be found by navigating directly to the *total requirements display* (Figure 16-17) from transaction MD04. SAP Planning Strategy 40—*planning with final assembly*—designated F1000 as a make-to-stock item for which forecasts helped position available stock ahead of customer orders.

The last main feature in the storyboard was that of the planning time fence. On the MD04 screen for F1000 (Figure 16-18) the SAP expert pointed out that the purchase requisitions (additions to stock) would be fulfilled by plant 2106 as noted in the *Deliv/ Recv Plant* column, and that the customer ordering the product was "Super Tech" (subtractions from stock). On viewing the stock requirements list (Figure 16-19) for plant 2106, the SAP expert pointed out the *End of planning time fence* listed for date 03/22/

2011. The planning time fence for this material at this plant is set at 10 working days past the current date. Essentially, beyond the planning time fence, SAP MRP can recommend planned orders—*PldOrd*; within the planning time fence, only manual changes can be made by the scheduler. As demand increases within the time fence, planned orders are placed just outside the time fence, as in the case of *PldOrd 03/24/2011*.

Figure 16-15. SAP stock/requirements list for product F1000 at plant 2106.

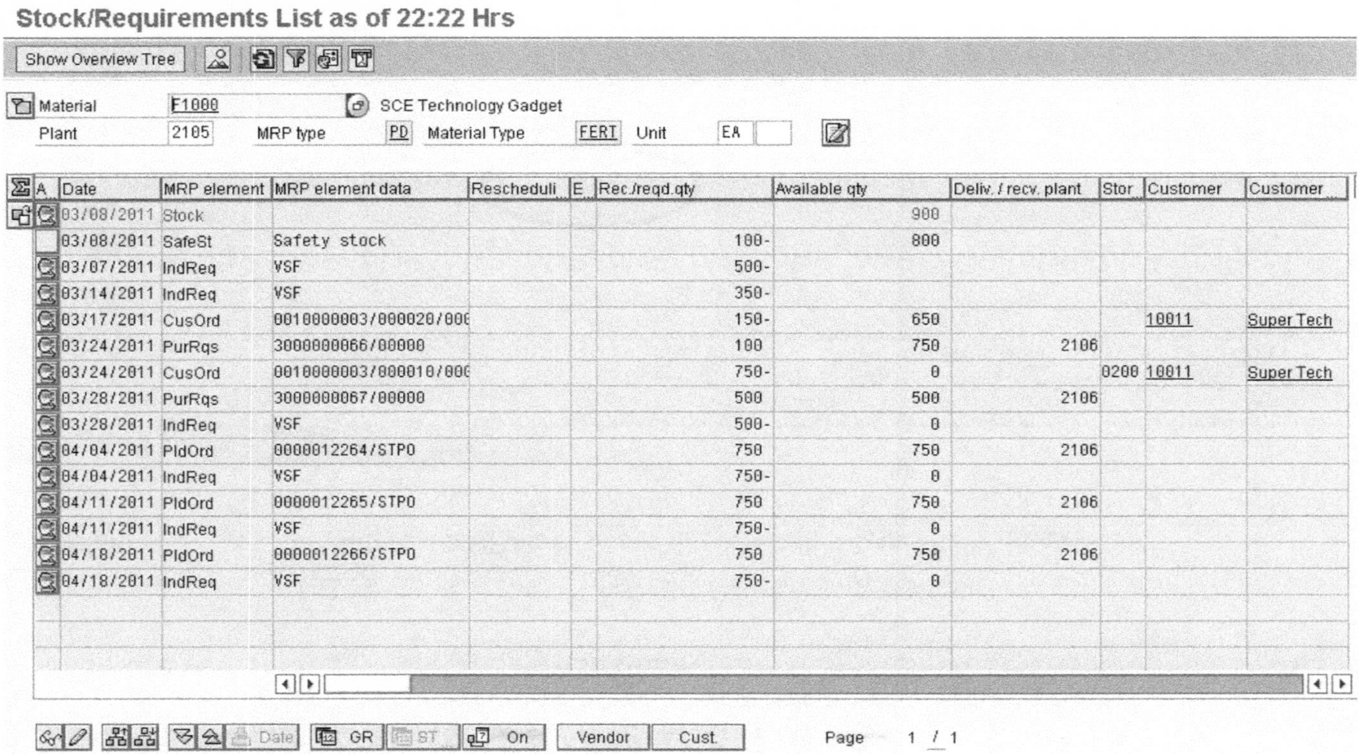

Stock/Requirements List as of 22:22 Hrs

Show Overview Tree

Material	F1000	SCE Technology Gadget
Plant	2105	MRP type PD Material Type FERT Unit EA

Date	MRP element	MRP element data	Rescheduli	E..	Rec./reqd.qty	Available qty	Deliv./recv. plant	Stor	Customer	Customer
03/08/2011	Stock					900				
03/08/2011	SafeSt	Safety stock			100-	800				
03/07/2011	IndReq	VSF			500-	500-				
03/14/2011	IndReq	VSF			350-	150-				
03/17/2011	CusOrd	0010000003/000020/000			150-	650			10011	Super Tech
03/24/2011	PurRqs	3000000066/00000			100	750	2106			
03/24/2011	CusOrd	0010000003/000010/000			750-	0		0200	10011	Super Tech
03/28/2011	PurRqs	3000000067/00000			500	500	2106			
03/28/2011	IndReq	VSF			500-	0				
04/04/2011	PldOrd	0000012264/STPO			750	750	2106			
04/04/2011	IndReq	VSF			750-	0				
04/11/2011	PldOrd	0000012265/STPO			750	750	2106			
04/11/2011	IndReq	VSF			750-	0				
04/18/2011	PldOrd	0000012266/STPO			750	750	2106			
04/18/2011	IndReq	VSF			750-	0				

Date GR ST On Vendor Cust

Page   1 / 1

Figure 16-16. Product F1000 Weekly Aggregated Receipts and Requirements, with "consumed" PIRs.

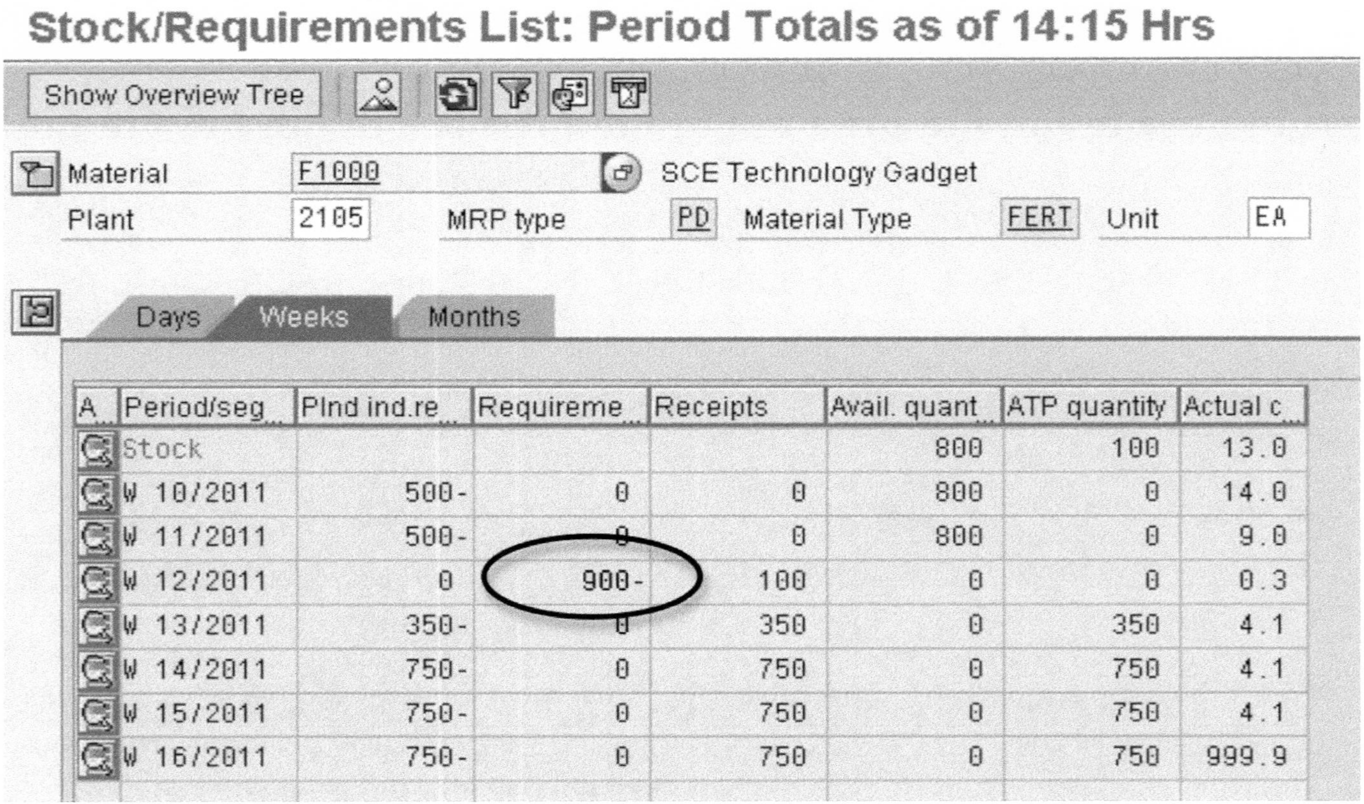

Stock/Requirements List: Period Totals as of 14:15 Hrs

Show Overview Tree

Material F1000 SCE Technology Gadget
Plant 2105 MRP type PD Material Type FERT Unit EA

Days | Weeks | Months

A.	Period/seg...	Plnd ind.re...	Requireme...	Receipts	Avail. quant...	ATP quantity	Actual c
	Stock				800	100	13.0
	W 10/2011	500-	0	0	800	0	14.0
	W 11/2011	500-	0	0	800	0	9.0
	W 12/2011	0	900-	100	0	0	0.3
	W 13/2011	350-	350	350	0	350	4.1
	W 14/2011	750-	0	750	0	750	4.1
	W 15/2011	750-	0	750	0	750	4.1
	W 16/2011	750-	0	750	0	750	999.9

Figure 16-17. Total requirements display detailing consumption of PIRs.

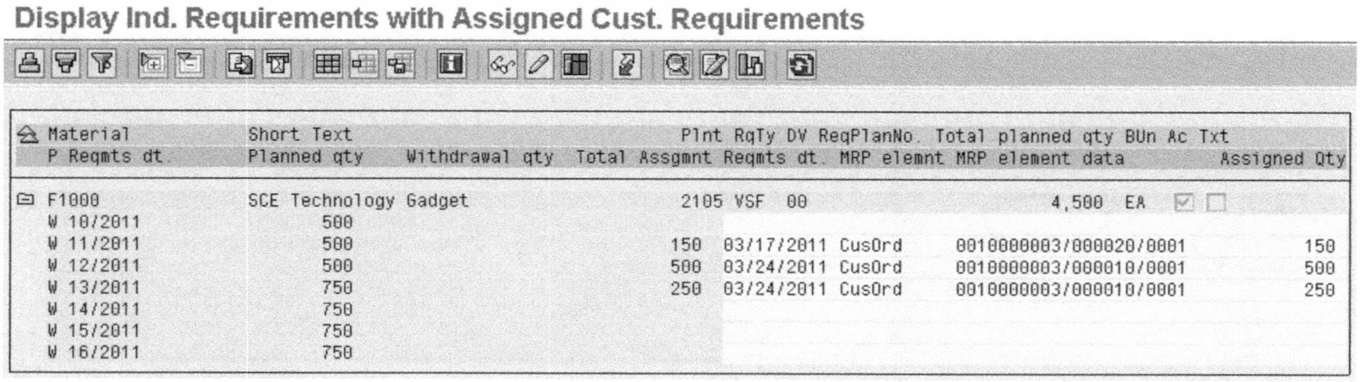

Display Ind. Requirements with Assigned Cust. Requirements

Material	Short Text				Plnt RqTy DV ReqPlanNo. Total planned qty BUn Ac Txt					
P Reqmts dt.	Planned qty	Withdrawal qty	Total Assgmnt Reqmts dt.	MRP element	MRP element data				Assigned Qty
F1000	SCE Technology Gadget				2105 VSF 00			4,500 EA ☑ ☐	
W 10/2011	500								
W 11/2011	500		150	03/17/2011	CusOrd	0010000003/000020/0001			150
W 12/2011	500		500	03/24/2011	CusOrd	0010000003/000010/0001			500
W 13/2011	750		250	03/24/2011	CusOrd	0010000003/000010/0001			250
W 14/2011	750								
W 15/2011	750								
W 16/2011	750								

Figure 16-18. Purchase requisitions are fulfilled by plant 2106; customer is "Super Tech."

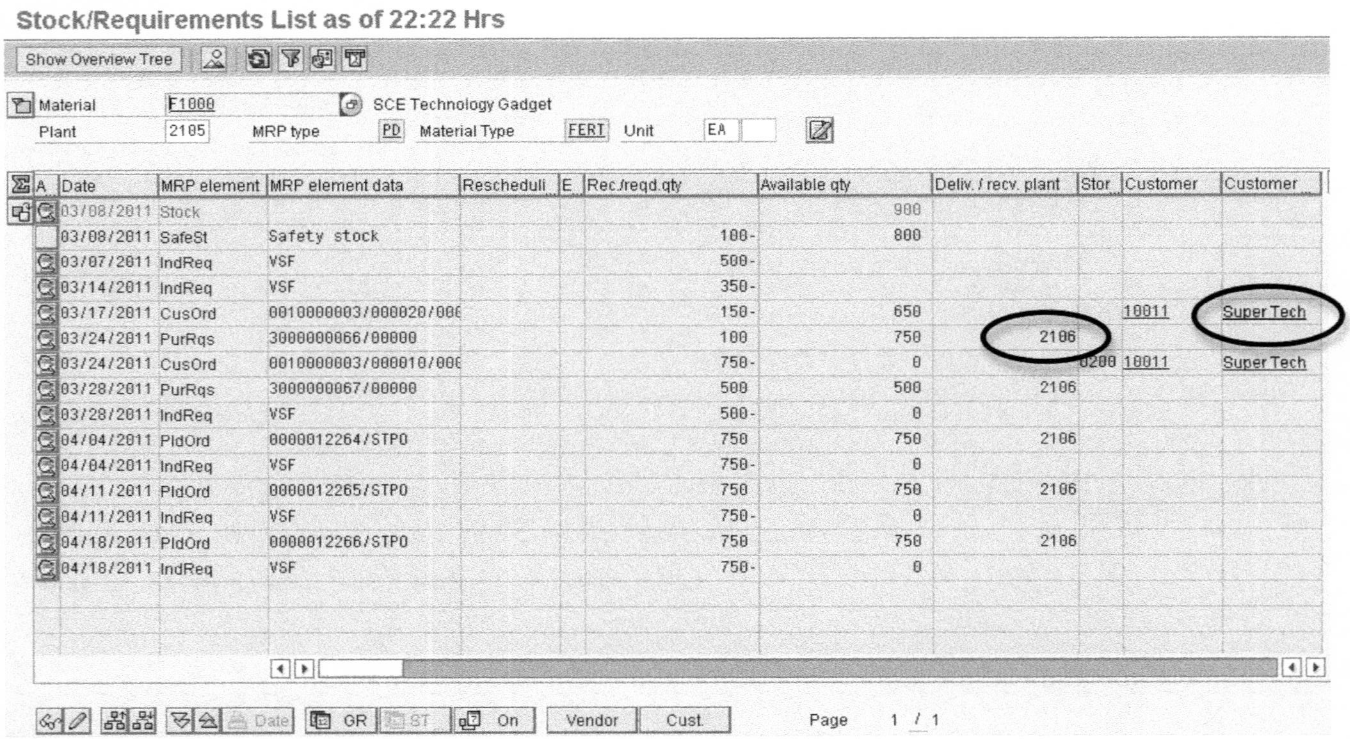

Stock/Requirements List as of 22:22 Hrs

Show Overview Tree						
Material	F1000	SCE Technology Gadget				
Plant	2105	MRP type	PD	Material Type	FERT	Unit	EA

A	Date	MRP element	MRP element data	Reschedul	E	Rec./reqd qty	Available qty	Deliv./recv. plant	Stor.	Customer	Customer
	03/08/2011	Stock					900				
	03/08/2011	SafeSt	Safety stock				100-				
	03/07/2011	IndReq	VSF				500-				
	03/14/2011	IndReq	VSF				350-				
	03/17/2011	CusOrd	0010000003/000020/0006			150-	650	2106		10011	Super Tech
	03/24/2011	PurRqs	3000000066/00000			100	750	0			
	03/24/2011	CusOrd	0010000003/000010/0006			750-	0	2106	0200	10011	Super Tech
	03/28/2011	PurRqs	3000000067/00000			500	500	2106			
	03/28/2011	IndReq	VSF			500-	0				
	04/04/2011	PldOrd	0000012264/STPO			750	750	2106			
	04/04/2011	IndReq	VSF			750-	0				
	04/11/2011	PldOrd	0000012265/STPO			750	750	2106			
	04/11/2011	IndReq	VSF			750-	0				
	04/18/2011	PldOrd	0000012266/STPO			750	750	2106			
	04/18/2011	IndReq	VSF			750-	0				

Vendor   Cust   Page   1 / 1

Figure 16-19. The planning time fence locks out automated changes during the production run.

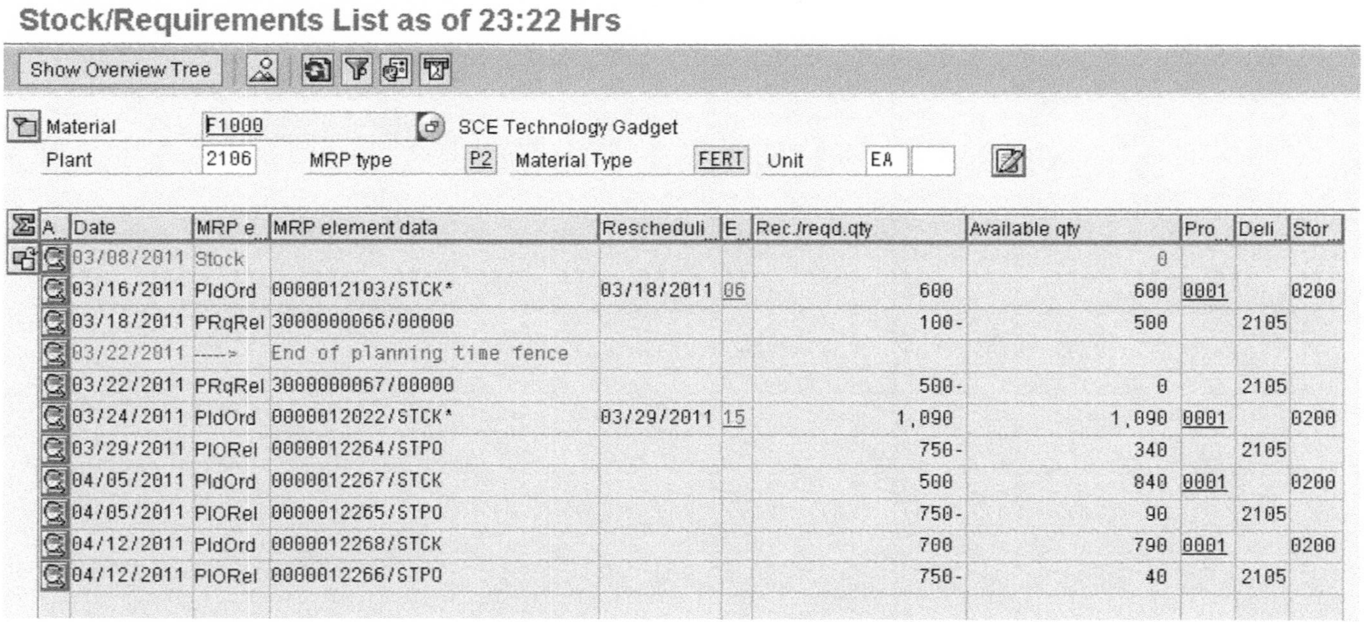

Stock/Requirements List as of 23:22 Hrs

| Show Overview Tree | | | | | | | | | |

| Material | F1000 | | | SCE Technology Gadget | | | | | |
| Plant | 2106 | MRP type | | P2 | Material Type | FERT | Unit | EA | |

Date	MRP e.	MRP element data	Rescheduli.	E.	Rec./reqd.qty	Available qty	Pro.	Deli.	Stor.
03/08/2011	Stock					0			
03/16/2011	PldOrd	0000012103/STCK*	03/18/2011	06	600	600	0001	0001	0200
03/18/2011	PRqRel	3000000066/00000			100-	500		2105	
03/22/2011	----->	End of planning time fence							
03/22/2011	PRqRel	3000000067/00000			500-	0		2105	
03/24/2011	PldOrd	0000012022/STCK*	03/29/2011	15	1,090	1,090	0001	0001	0200
03/29/2011	PlORel	0000012264/STPO			750-	340		2105	
04/05/2011	PldOrd	0000012267/STCK			500	500	0001	0001	0200
04/05/2011	PlORel	0000012265/STPO			750-	90		2105	
04/12/2011	PldOrd	0000012268/STCK			700	790	0001	0001	0200
04/12/2011	PlORel	0000012266/STPO			750-	40		2105	

Phase 4: Configure, Solution Test, Pilot, Refine, and Roll Out

▶ Moving the Needle on Performance

The typical elapsed time to get to this point of project implementation (steps 1 through 8 on the implementation checklist in Chapter 11) ranges from one to three months, depending on the process scope, complexity of the solution storyboard, and the priority of resources assigned. Fully implementing the solution (steps 9 through 13 on the checklist)—meaning rolling it out to all the intended supply chains—typically ranges from six to 12 months, based on the factors already mentioned. In between, there are four approval milestones or "gates": solution test, pilot one, refinement and pilot two, and solution rollout.

From an AcceleratedSAP point of view, this implementation phase aligns to the realization, final preparation, and go-live and support points of the roadmap. Tasks include:

- ◆ Review scope and design all development items
- ◆ Document and complete all functional configuration and programming work

- ◆ Baseline configuration
- ◆ Fine-tuning configuration

- ◆ Conduct system integration testing
    - ◆ Unit/functional testing
    - ◆ System integration testing
    - ◆ User acceptance testing
    - ◆ Load and stress testing

- ◆ Complete business acceptance and sign-off
- ◆ Prepare for production cutover
    - ◆ Transport configuration design from development to production system
    - ◆ Complete master data integrity check
    - ◆ Migrate necessary data from legacy systems
    - ◆ Complete final stability, availability, and performance checks

- ◆ Go-live
- ◆ Support operational stabilization
    - ◆ Setup and support process for end-user community
    - ◆ Fix bugs, and transport prioritized changes from development to production
    - ◆ Measure and respond to SAP performance metrics
    - ◆ Measure and respond to business performance metrics
    - ◆ Educate user community on standard reports and means to extract data
    - ◆ Manage documentation and training

Configuration (or Build)

With the process and system solution (business scenarios) approved, the system's functional experts can begin the process of configuring or building the system to perform the TO BE tasks. Relative to SAP functionality configuration, this involves selecting options that will refine how SAP transactions perform business requirements as defined in the storyboard.

The business team members of the project have other types of configuration tasks. First they must document all SCOR ENABLE process assumptions, policies, performance management, etc., for the process scope as defined. Second, they need to select and train "power users" in the Level 4 processes as well as in the detailed system transactions. Last, they need to publish or update standard operating procedures to accommodate the changes in process.

At Fowlers, the business team members had already built the master scheduling policy, and felt that it served as the basis for the ENABLE PLAN processes and could be refined during the pilot. They picked power-user candidates from the other regions to participate in the pilot as part of the learning process for rollout. They utilized their ISO Quality System change-management and document-control processes to update appropriate standard operation procedures. With an approved solution design (storyboard and SCOR Level 4 process), the SAP PP functional expert went to work. (See "Configuring SAP Functionality" on page 225 for details related to Fowlers' configuration of the tactical planning business process.)

Solution Test

Solution test involves setting up or using an existing system test environment or "sandbox." Essentially, this is a non-production system that has real data, part numbers, customers, suppliers, etc., and is intended to test configuration scripts. The sandbox can be used as early as building the storyboard and viewing TO BE scenarios for individual transactions. In fact, the earlier in the solution design process a sandbox can be used to demonstrate the TO BE, the faster the project team can gain consensus on changes.

For SAP solution test, there generally are four types. First, unit or functional testing validates each step of the storyboard and SCOR Level 4 process to ensure that each performs as expected. Second, integration testing involves walking through all the steps in the blueprint, using real data and business scenarios; the goal is to see if the entire process works together and the process operates effectively within the larger SCOR Level 3 blueprint. Relative to SAP functionality, common integrated test plans may focus on order-to-cash, procure-to-pay, or record to report.

Third, user acceptance testing is a detailed real-world test involving the power users. Ideally, the test scenarios are common and less-common business scenarios that occur on a daily, weekly, and monthly basis. And fourth, load or stress testing is required to ensure that the process is effective under a large volume of users doing their work of managing transactions. Database locking point and responsiveness are two key areas under scrutiny in this last testing phase.

The Fowlers team members felt that their use of the sandbox during solution design, and the results they could observe in the storyboard, met the expectations of the SAP unit test. Integration testing, on the other hand, proved to be more complicated than originally thought. For example, the team needed to ensure that the master scheduling process and transactions worked effectively with the production scheduling transaction. It had been configured as a Z transaction, meaning that it was customized to the plant away from the standard SAP transaction. The TO BE blueprint initially did not operate well with the scheduling transaction. User acceptance testing and load testing were carried out by the power users and functional expert team by the book.

Pilot One, Refine, and Pilot Two

With the testing and business acceptance complete, the next step is to pilot. The first step in a *solution pilot* involves selecting a very small scope on which to run the solution. Examples of a small scope could be one resource (production line) of one plant; one product to one customer; one product from one supplier; or one product family in one business. Next, the team needs to operate the process for at least four weeks; this ensures that the process is tested across a month-end reporting sequence. The third step is for the team to meet formally and conduct a detailed review of the SCOR Level 4 processes—assessing whether the process step was effective and if any changes need to be made to policy, process, system, RACI, etc. Last, a proposed change list is presented to the steering team and, as approved, is incorporated as refinements into the next pilot cycle.

In pilot two, the scope is expanded as appropriate, the processes are operated for another four weeks, and the review and refinement process is followed one more time.

Fowlers Pilot Results

Fowlers' pilot one process yielded some important discoveries that needed to be incorporated into pilot two. First, the team needed better data collection, analysis, and policy for schedule attainment as it related to what the master schedule expected. After the first week of the pilot, an analysis showed that the production line scoped for the pilot achieved 85 percent attainment on overall volume (actual production/scheduled production).

Underneath that number, however, the team discovered that 25 percent of the volume was for items that weren't scheduled. Moreover, another 10 percent of the volume was overproduction. After factoring unneeded volume out of the equation, the attainment was 55 percent (actual production of what was scheduled/needed production as reflected in the schedule).

Second, the team felt that the scope in pilot two needed to go to the entire plant, because one of the process steps was a shared resource among all production lines. It would be difficult to partially capacity-manage that resource. The processes were deemed sound and the SAP transactions worked effectively.

Rollout

At the completion of pilot two, the final step is to plan for and roll out the solution to the rest of the supply chains within the targeted scope.

The Fowlers project team members discussed a strategy that would go through the sequence of educate, pilot one, and pilot two with each of the remaining plants worldwide. They thought the super users from each region would develop a detailed plan, validate master data, translate documentation and standard operating procedures, and review specific regional configuration settings for potential issues.

The power users objected to this strategy for three reasons. First, based on a change-management standpoint, they suggested that the regional leaders needed to understand and buy into this change in the way they would manage plant capacity. Even though their boss was the sponsor, they did not understand the degree of effort and pain that would be needed to change some old habits. Second, the master data cleanup (and more important, maintenance) was too big for one person—whose primary job was to be an SAP transaction expert—to handle. Third, there was no performance baseline and, in fact, little understanding of how to measure the metrics as charted for the project.

The team achieved consensus that the rollout strategy would essentially go through the 13 implementation steps for each plant, with a local plant sponsor, steering team, project leader, and team. Where possible, deliverables could be modified based on previous work, but the plant team needed to address each deliverable for its own location. The kickoff meetings for the remaining plants would be staggered by two months, allowing for a plant to reach pilot two stage before the process was initiated at the next plant.

Configuring SAP Functionality

Trained and experienced professional users may customize SAP functionality to fit business requirements as defined in the SCOR Level 4 process diagram and the storyboard. Transaction SPRO (Figure 17-1) provides access to the *implementation management guide* (IMG), which contains all of the actions required to fully deploy the SAP functionality configurations. The software provides both IMG tracking and change management tools as part of its software solution.

One of the configuration challenges for Fowlers was the *formula* used to calculate capacity for production resources, which included both the actual *run time* (requirements) as well as the *changeover time* (setup). Working through the IMG main screen to production and to capacity planning, the team was able to get to a configuration transaction that allowed for a custom definition of available capacity.

To create the new formula (Figure 17-2), the following inputs were required:

- Unique formula key: Z006
- Description: Setup + Machine rqmts
- The actual formula: SAP_01 + SAP_02 $\star$ SAP_09 / SAP_08, which translates into Setup + Machine $\times$ Operation quantity / Base quantity (Figure 17-3)
- Then ensure the indicator for *Work Centers for Capacity Reqmts* is checked

The configuration activity is part of the realization phase of ASAP, and is a necessary activity to begin testing activity within modules as well as across modules.

Figure 17-1. The implementation management guide is the portal for customizing SAP functionality.

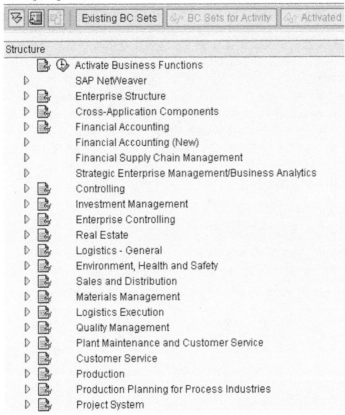

Figure 17-2. Fowlers requires a custom formula for capacity planning.

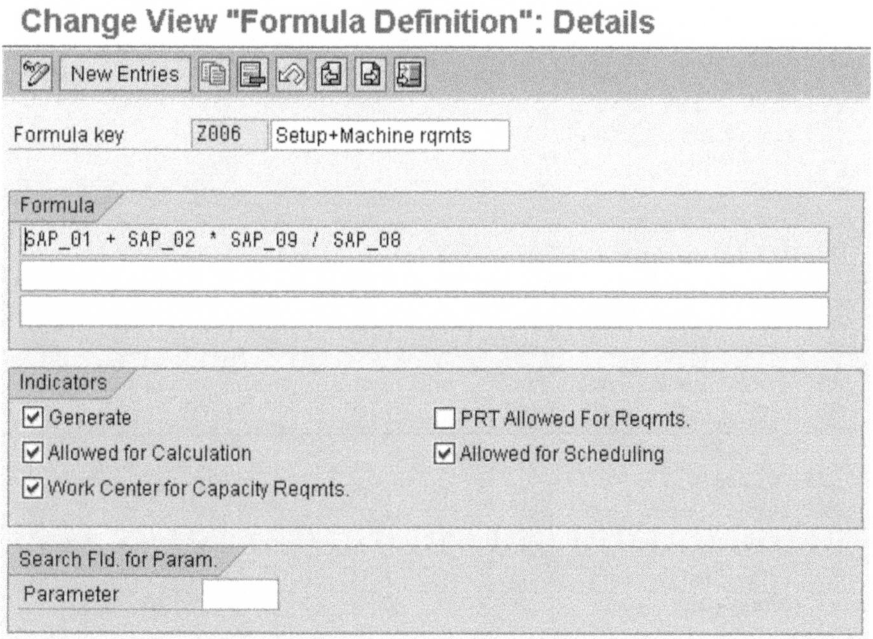

Change View "Formula Definition": Details

| ✐ | New Entries | 🗈 🗐 🖎 🗐 🗐 🗐 |

Formula key   Z006   Setup+Machine rqmts

Formula

SAP_01 + SAP_02 * SAP_09 / SAP_08

Indicators

☑ Generate   ☐ PRT Allowed For Reqmts.

☑ Allowed for Calculation   ☑ Allowed for Scheduling

☑ Work Center for Capacity Reqmts.

Search Fld. for Param.

Parameter

Figure 17-3. Fowlers' customized formula includes both run time and changeover time.

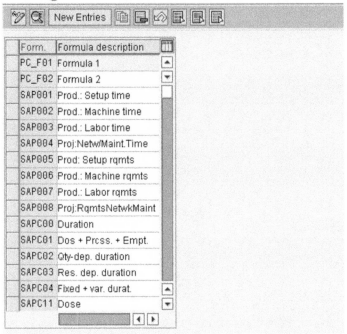

CHAPTER 18

Phase 4: Supply Chain Strategy

▶ **Supply Chain Excellence as a Way of Life**

In this third edition of *Supply Chain Excellence*, we've put to use the concept of "learning by doing." Based on 32 projects undertaken since we completed the second edition of the book in 2007, we have cut the time and resources required to develop the project list by 50 percent. We have eliminated "non-value-added" analysis by moving the material, work, and information flow analysis to the implementation phase, focusing only on those processes and SKUs that are in-scope for the project. We have changed the schedule and mode of meeting interface to accommodate global teams, for which regular travel is expensive and time-consuming, as well as small-business teams, in which a few people wear many hats and the amount of time available to devote to this type of endeavor is limited.

We filtered about 30 percent of the deliverables that, while good ideas in past editions, were not commonly utilized by project teams. And we integrated process and system efforts to minimize the lag time and rework between typical business process engineering and system implementation.

229

If restating the introduction seems like an odd way to begin the next-to-last chapter, here is the point: In the real world, if something doesn't get used, it atrophies. While most dictionaries start with the figurative definition of atrophy—a gradual decline in effectiveness or vigor due to underuse or neglect—I also like the biological version: to waste away. So in the business world, if we neglect or underuse the skill of Supply Chain Excellence, it will waste away.

How, then, can companies learn from their *Supply Chain Excellence* experience and maintain that continuous improvement mentality so that in five years they can look back and see how far they have progressed on their journey?

Of the five largest companies that have utilized the *Supply Chain Excellence* approach in varying applications since the first edition, all have been through major system implementations (some worldwide); all have global business challenges; each has been recognized by customers as a superior supplier; and though focused on different businesses in different industries, all would say that their supply chain is performing significantly better now than at the beginning of the journey, financially, with shareholders, and with customers. They would also say that with each new learning, they've discovered more opportunities to improve. Finally, they would likely state that they are not satisfied with aspects of their current performance and have plans to address those deficiencies in their supply chain strategy. Keep in mind that these statements are coming from companies that have achieved competitive advantage in their respective marketplaces and have continued to perform in superior fashion against their competitors.

What Is Supply Chain Strategy?

Table 18-1 is a matrix that provides a checklist of essential elements that make up a comprehensive supply chain strategy. The labels in these boxes have changed over the years, but the concept has not.

The theory behind these categories is founded in *Improving Performance: How to Manage the White Space on the Organization Chart*, 2nd ed., by G. A. Rummler and A. P. Brache (Jossey-Bass, 1995). Their theory supports the contention that there are three factors to effective supply chain strategy:

♦ Defining appropriate strategy and goals

♦ Utilizing effective design techniques to organize businesses, regions, functions, processes, etc.

♦ Managing performance measures

Theory supports the belief that there are five supply chain dimensions affected by these factors: (1) trading partners—customers and suppliers alike; (2) your company's organization as defined in the organization chart and business entities; (3) your company's processes relative to supply chain, including SCOR processes, other leading practices, and the physical network, both inbound and outbound; (4) your company's technology—most often fixed assets, but also including supply chain systems specifically; and (5) the job performers, referring to your company's individual contributors.

Table 18-1. Comprehensive supply chain strategy essential elements.

Elements of Effective Supply Chain Strategy	Strategy	Design	Management
Trading Partners	Define Segments, Requirements, and Capabilities	Relationships and Agreements	Joint Metrics
Organization	Supply Chain Competitive Priorities	Global Organizational Design	Balanced Scorecard
Process	Global Process Requirements	Process and Physical Network	Effective Process Measures
Technology	Technology Requirements	Technology Architecture	System Performance
Performers	Job Task Requirements	Job Design	Job Level KPIs

The rest of this chapter highlights key challenges in each dimension that have been addressed by the five large *Supply Chain Excellence* companies, and then summarizes an overall "to do" list for the Fowlers executive team as it begins to strategize for the 2012 fiscal year.

Trading Partner

The simple definition of a trading partner is illustrated on the SCOR model diagram (Figure 1-1), which includes the supplier, supplier's supplier, customer, and customer's customer. A more complex twist comes from Gartner Inc. and AMR Research; they have described the supply chain as a demand-driven value network (DDVN) in which your suppliers can be your customers and your customers can be your suppliers, all in search of the rhythm of the ultimate "pull system"; essentially, a consumer buying something off the shelf.

Trading Partner Dimensional Challenges

- Segment customers based on intended growth, profit, and cost to serve.
- Synchronize with customer and supplier supply chain capabilities.
- Develop, define, and manage effective collaborative relationships with targeted partners.
- Jointly define, measure, report, and manage supply chain metrics.
- Establish effective supplier portals.
- Make use of point-of-sale data in retail and inventory movements in distribution.

Organization

The academic definition of an organization is "a connected body of people with a particular purpose." Organizational theorists offer a more refined version: An organization contains the formal and informal relationships of inputs and outputs between defined groups of people (functions, regions, entities, etc.) who support the achievement of defined goals and strategy. Figure 18-1 illustrates the concept of supply chain execution roles within operating business units in a matrix relationship, with global process ownership at the corporate level. In this case, solid lines indicate primary reporting; dotted lines indicate secondary.

Organization Dimensional Challenges

♦ Aligning and prioritizing supply chain competitive requirements and cost-to-serve models with appropriate customer segments; getting away from the one-supply-chain-fits-all mentality.

♦ Defining appropriate accountabilities, roles, and responsibilities between business-unit supply chain personnel (who need to operate the supply chain on a daily basis) and supply chain process owners (who need to improve the effectiveness, efficiency, and standardization of the process) across the business units and perhaps across continents. This is the global supply chain organization chart.

♦ Defining, developing, and managing a global supply chain scorecard that looks, feels, and operates the same way in every corner of the company, and can be segmented by customers, suppliers, plants, products, and warehouses.

Processes

A business process is a series of steps that, when designed in a particular order, produces a product, service, transaction and/or information. In the case of SCOR, the processes are defined as PLAN, SOURCE, MAKE, DELIVER, RETURN, and ENABLE. In the case of Gartner/AMR, the processes are classified in three broad

Figure 18-1. Supply chain organization scenario with matrix reporting.

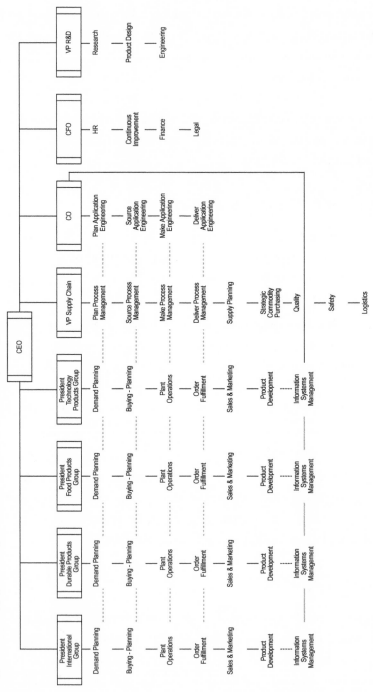

areas—Product, Demand, and Supply—with cross-area processes for Sense, Shape, and Respond.

Other leading practices that have been published also discuss the effective design of supply chain processes, including sales and operations planning, master scheduling, procurement, global sourcing, Lean Manufacturing, distribution requirements planning, demand management, sales forecasting, etc.

Process Dimensional Challenges

+ Translating competitive requirements into effective supply chain process strategy, configuration (MTO, MTS, ETO), and execution; this includes physical network, inventory and service requirements, collaboration requirements, internal processes, and associated transactions.

+ Building a supply chain process blueprint with the appropriate leading practices.

+ Conducting and implementing the conclusions of a physical network study.

+ Linking the global scorecard to process performance.

Technology

For this dimension, I would like to narrow the definition of technology to "supply chain information system technology." This encompasses hardware, software, data (warehouse), and the Internet, where interfaces have a direct impact on supply chain process. The most frequently used types of supply chain information system technology include Internet portals, Enterprise Resource Planning (ERP), advanced planning (AP), manufacturing execution (MES), forecasting, Electronic Data Interchange (EDI), point of sale (POS), warehouse management (WMS), radio frequency (RF), and a data warehouse.

Technology Dimensional Challenges

♦ Translating defined process requirements into a technology roadmap supporting the overall supply chain strategy and investment objectives.

♦ Effectively designing, configuring, testing, and rolling out integrated technology and process solutions.

♦ Linking aspects of system performance to process measures and managing them in the spirit of continuous improvement.

Performers

For this dimension, a performer is defined as someone who carries out his or her work in relation to a specified standard of expectation. I like this definition because in order to succeed, there are two requirements: (1) that the performer carries out the work and (2) that the work is defined in relation to a company standard. SCOR 10.0 contains a section on people. As stated in the manual, this section "introduces standards for managing talent in the supply chain. The key elements of the people section are *skills*, *experiences*, *aptitudes*, and *trainings*. This *skills* management framework within SCOR complements process reference, metrics reference, and practice reference components with an integrated view of supply chain skills in four areas:

1. Baseline skills necessary for the overall process area (e.g., Sourcing or Planning) and for the individual process.

2. Critical skills that differentiate leaders in a particular process area from those who only perform at a baseline level.

3. Performance measures through SCOR metrics that relate to continuous assessment of job performance in each process area.

4. Credentialing of supply chain skills, including training or certification programs, related to the specific process area that tend to indicate superior job performance."

Performer Dimensional Challenges

♦ Organizing job families and job ranges within the supply chain organization to facilitate movement within a process and between processes.

♦ Writing job descriptions that accurately represent the system, process, analytical, and experiential requirements for a supply chain role.

♦ Effectively setting goals, reviewing performance, and identifying growth opportunities.

Implications for Fowlers

The Fowlers executive team had already had an annual top-down strategic planning cycle. The process started in January with the corporate strategy; moved to the business units, which set macro sales and profit targets; and then transitioned into the annual budgeting process, moving in parallel to operations and product development.

The teams that had been involved in the process to this point assembled plans that included capital, labor, and materials. The last stop before the midyear review was finance. The midterm review in July compared the corporate top-down strategy to the business unit bottom-up strategy and annual plan, and worked through a gap-resolution process that, depending on the severity of the issues, could cycle in two to three months. The final piece of the annual budget and strategy review was to be completed in October.

To-Do List

Knowing they couldn't do everything, the team members decided to incorporate the Trading Partner and Organization Strategy, along with the elements of Organization Design, Organization Management, and Technology Requirements, into the executive strategic planning process scheduled to begin in January of the following year (2012).

This decision involved the following objectives:

♦ Task sales, marketing, and procurement to better define customer and supplier requirements, capabilities, and competitive landscape.

♦ Task human resources to understand the role of global process ownership with respect to the operation of supply chain in the business unit.

♦ Assign a designated global scorecard task team to define metrics and collect baselines for each of the business units.

- Task the CIO with summarizing the Fowlers current technology roadmap.
- Expect the business units to include baseline and projected performance levels from the global scorecard for the upcoming fiscal year (2012).
- Target Trading Partner Design and Management, Process Strategy and Design, and Performer Strategy for inclusion in the following year (2013) cycle.
- Expect that as part of the following-year (2013) cycle each business would have a portfolio that would relate to its projected performance levels.

CHAPTER 19

Extend to the Greater Value Chain

> ▶ Analyzing Barriers to Profitable Growth

Arvid Westergaard, president of the Fowlers Durable Products Group, was speechless after the midyear portfolio review. He had just seen the future leadership of the company collectively present an organized, customer-focused, financially sound review of *Supply Chain Excellence* portfolio projects that were driving real performance—"moving the needle," as a colleague put it. The presentation showed passion, conviction, and confidence. It was the first time he had seen anything like it at Fowlers.

The durable products group had a different set of challenges, and he wondered, "How do I take this approach further into my business?"

Arvid's group was developing a reputation for leaving money on the table. It had premium brands that commanded premium prices, but profits were average at best. Unlike any other operation in the company, its business model was primarily make-to-order and engineer-to-order. Although his business was routinely touted as the future growth driver for the company, Arvid lacked confidence in the team's ability to hit sales projections; there didn't seem to be any "science" behind the numbers.

Further, as sales, order fulfillment, manufacturing, sourcing, planning, and product design teams worked to get product introduced and out the door, they all had their own ways of getting the work done, and "exceptions" were the norm. In one plant tour he had received from a shift foreman, he counted 45 instances in which he was told, "It works like this except when those blankety blank engineers pull us in one direction, then the sales and customer service people yank us in another. How hard can this be?"

For a long time, the durable products group had been an early innovator in quick response and flexibility when faced with customer demands for new products, but the after-sale service business helped support "life cycle management" and showed the most potential for growth. It seemed like both parts of the business should use the same processes but, as the aftermarket business grew, walls were already begin established.

Arvid knew that competitors were catching up—and no one seemed to own the job of "taking it to the next level." Finally, he was under pressure from Jon Park, the chief financial officer, to commit to a plan to improve return on sales. Analysts were not being kind to Fowlers' stock price, and return on sales (ROS) in Arvid's group was a significant factor.

With all this on his mind, Arvid pulled the SCOR coach aside and shared his thoughts. The coach was planning to stay an extra day—so he could join the design team's scheduled celebration. The two agreed to use the full day before the final party to discuss how they might tweak the *Supply Chain Excellence* approach to include more pieces of *the value chain*. Fowlers COO Brian Dowell and David Able caught wind of the meeting and asked if they could join as well.

Value Chain Excellence

The concept of value chain is not new. Both Michael Porter and W. Edwards Deming had developed process frameworks that depicted the entire system of value creation.[1] Supply chain, the derivative of this work, was also not new when the Supply Chain Council released version 1.0 of SCOR in 1996. What was new was cross-industry process detail around common definitions, metrics, and practices, aimed toward the goal of companies using the framework to improve supply chain performance across industries and trading partners. As has been demonstrated, *Supply Chain Excellence* describes an approach for identifying a strategic project list to help drive sustainable improvement.

With the introduction of the CCOR 1.0 (Customer Chain Operations Reference) and DCOR 2.0 (Design Chain Operations Reference) processes, the Supply Chain Council (www.supply-chain.org) is again positioned to support value chain performance improvement through common process definition, metrics framework, and leading practices. The question is how to use these models in a project.

That's the question Arvid asked to start his meeting. The major phases of *Supply Chain Excellence* were adapted by inserting "value chain" as appropriate:

- Build organizational support
- Define value chain project scope
- Analyze performance
- Develop project portfolio
- Implement projects

The next challenge was to figure out how to adapt the major deliverables for each phase. Fresh off the *Supply Chain Excellence* project, the group members were familiar with the key deliverables. They wrote a list and then, for each supply chain deliverable, asked two questions:

- ◆ Is it necessary for a value chain assessment?
- ◆ What is the estimated degree of adaptation?

Figure 19-1 summarizes the team's descriptions of key value chain tasks by phase; the rest of this chapter summarizes the team's discussion, highlighting the adaptations for value chain.

Build Organizational Support

The team agreed to describe the deliverables from this phase as (1) identify value chain improvement roles, evangelists, active executive sponsor(s), core steering team, and design team; (2) assemble and deliver appropriate educational content; and (3) gain consensus for a pilot project.

Identify Value Chain Improvement Roles, Evangelists, Active Executive Sponsor(s), Core Steering Team, and Design Team

This task would use the same steps as used in Fowlers' supply chain project. As the discussion turned more philosophical, the coach described the concept of Learning Quotient (LQ)—an organization's ability to acquire knowledge and adapt behavior in response to changes in the business environment. A low organizational LQ (poor adaptability) is like a perpetual "Go to Jail" card in Monopoly. You never pass Go and are stuck watching the game from behind bars unless you get a lucky roll of the dice. The evangelist, active executive sponsor, core steering team, and design team are four key roles that will set the pace of the organization's LQ in relation to value chain improvement; all four roles must be in place to pass Go.

Assemble and Deliver Appropriate Educational Content and Gain Consensus for a Pilot Project

The team members reflected on how they progressed from knowing nothing about SCOR and *Supply Chain Excellence* to constituting

Figure 19-1. Key value chain tasks by phase.

Phase	Deliverable
Phase 0 **Build Organizational** **Support**	TBD
	Value Chain Excellence Overview
	SCOR, DCOR, CCOR Framework Workshop
	Executive Briefing--GO/NO GO
Phase 1 **Define Project Scope**	TBD
	Business Context Summary
	Value Chain Definition Matrix (with data)
	Project Charter
Phase 2 **Analyze Performance**	Kickoff
	Metric Definitions and Data Collection Plan
	Defect Data Collection Plan
	Defect Analysis
	Industry Comparison
	Competitive Requirements
	Benchmark Data
	Preliminary Scorecard
	Scorecard Gap Analysis
	OPTIONAL DEDICATED ON-SITE Staple Yourself to an Order Interviews
	OPTIONAL DEDICATED ON-SITE AS IS Process Diagram
Phase 3 **Develop Project** **Portfolio**	TBD
	AS IS Process Diagram
	Defect Analysis Part 2
	Brainstorm Event and Documentation
	Preliminary Project Portfolio
	Opportunity Analysis
	Assemble and Approve Implementation Project Charters
	Prioritize Implementation Projects
Phase 4 **Implement Projects**	TBD
	Kickoff Projects
	Develop Performance Baselines for Metrics
	Conduct Level 3 and 4 Process Gap Analysis
	Conduct Leading Practice Assessment
	Develop TO BE Process Blueprint
	Assemble Solution Storyboard
	Approve Solution Design
	Build and Test Solution
	Pilot and Verify Solution--Twice
	Define Process Control Measures
	Rollout to Project Scope
	Rollout to Enterprise

the final steering team in six months: light speed compared with other major initiatives. They defined three stages in their organizational learning and agreed that each must occur to move on to the next. They substituted the word "Value" for "Supply" and agreed that the durable products group would need to follow the same path.

Initial Exposure was the first stage; the objective was to investigate the *Value Chain Excellence* framework and the fit of the process models of SCOR, DCOR, and CCOR. The educational content of this phase would be characterized by the phrase "short and sweet." This is the stage at which evangelists and active executive sponsor(s) evaluate the fit of the method and the process frameworks with their business needs.

Learn How to Sell is the second stage; the objective of evangelists and active executive sponsor(s) is to sell core steering team members on the benefits of *Value Chain Excellence* and prepare them to sponsor a pilot project. The educational content of this phase takes the overview content style of the first phase and incorporates real company data in as many places as possible to give the leadership team members the best vision of a project in their own business language.

Implement a Pilot Project is the third stage; the object for the project team—including the evangelist, active executive sponsor(s), core steering team, and design team—is to develop the knowledge, skill, and motivation to successfully execute a project. The educational content in this phase is a mix of detailed "how to" templates and anecdotes that take theory to practice.

The amount of time spent in each phase depends on the organization's LQ. Companies with low LQ spend a lot of time in the first phase, often kicking tires until they're flat. High LQ companies can advance to the last phase in as little as three months; the typical duration is four to six months.

Define Value Chain Project Scope

In addition to the business context document, the team listed the other key deliverables from this second phase as follows: (1) calculate the number of value chains, (2) assemble high-level industry comparison, and (3) decide the scope of the pilot project and finalize the project charter.

Calculate the Number of Value Chains

Defining the number of company value chains requires the same technique as that of defining the number of supply chains (Chapter 3). Figure 19-2 illustrates the durable products group's adaptations. As in the supply chain, the rows represent lines of business or product families, and the lowest level of the row hierarchy is an item or stock keeping unit (SKU). The columns represent customers or customer segments, and the lowest level of the column hierarchy is a customer "ship to" location. The "X" indicates a product or service that is delivered to a customer; the number of X's provides a first draft of the number of company value chains. One adaptation includes growth rate (revenue, unit volume, and gross margin) data for each value chain.

Assemble High-Level Industry Comparison

The industry comparison is assembled using the same steps as for the supply chain, with five new data comparisons focused on the rate of growth from the prior period. These categories are revenue; sales, general, and administration expense; gross margin; operating income; and net income.

Decide on the Project Scope

The phrase "think big, act small, and scale fast" still works for value chain analysis. The value chain priority matrix is assembled in the

Figure 19-2. Durable products group value chains.

| Durable Products Group | | | U.S. Customer/Market Channels | | |
			Direct-to-Consumer	Home Delivery	OEM-Key Accounts
Lines of Business	Product Family A	Revenue	5.6%	X	X
		Unit	10.0%		
		Gross Margin	-2.5%		
	Product Family B	Revenue	X	X	
		Unit			
		Gross Margin			
	Product Family C	Revenue			X
		Unit			
		Gross Margin			
	Product Family D	Revenue	X	X	X
		Unit			
		Gross Margin			

same fashion as for supply chains. The team brainstormed other categories (columns), including revenue growth rate, percent of new product revenue, and return on sales.

Analyze Value Chain Performance and Project Portfolio Development

The team listed five deliverables for this phase: (1) identify appropriate value chain performance metrics, (2) assemble appropriate benchmark comparisons, (3) assess and prioritize competitive requirements, (4) perform metric defect analysis, and (5) develop a SCOR, DCOR, and CCOR process oriented project portfolio.

Identify Appropriate Value Chain Performance Metrics and Assemble Appropriate Benchmark Comparisons (Deliverables 1 and 2)

Although the previous scorecard provides a proven baseline to measure supply chain performance, it does not include measures for the other business processes. The coach suggested the team use a *Balanced Scorecard,*[2] an approach to strategic management developed in the early 1990s by Dr. Robert Kaplan and Dr. David Norton. The basic idea is that an organization should measure its performance from a balanced view against its goals as established in its vision and strategy. The Balanced Scorecard has four measurement categories: customer facing, internal process, financial, and individual employee.

The challenge for Arvid, Brian, and David was to pick the right metrics for each category. The coach discussed two methods to generate the list. The first starts with a blank sheet of paper; we've all been through that method. The second—which the team ultimately picked—is to identify relevant metrics from a pool of readily available benchmark sources. The coach suggested some of the same sources used in the supply chain project. They include the following: the Supply Chain Council (www.supply-chain.org), the Performance Measurement Group (www.pmgbenchmarking.com), Hoovers (www.hoovers.com), APQC—formerly the American Productivity & Quality Center (www.apqc.org), and Manufacturing Performance Institute (www.mpi-group.net). Figure 19-3 is the list that the team generated. Each metric was assigned to a Balanced Scorecard category; the team decided not to create employee metrics before brainstorming with a larger group. Figure 19-4 is a sample of some of the benchmark data available for select value chain metrics.

Figure 19-3. Value Chain Level 1 metrics and benchmark sources; SCOR metrics shaded.

Benchmark Source	Level One Value Chain Metrics	Customer Facing			Process				Financial		Employee	
		Reliability	Responsiveness	Flexibility	Supply Chain	Design Chain	Customer Chain	Aggregate	Profit	Growth	Performance	Development
APQC PMG	Perfect Order Fulfillment	X										
PMG	Warranty Fulfillment	X										
PMG	Service Order Fulfillment	X										
MPI APQC	Product Quality	X										
APQC PMG	Order Fulfillment Cycle Time		X									
APQC	New Product Development Cycle Time		X									
Data Gap	Selling Process Cycle Time		X									
APQC	Return Process Cycle Time		X									
PMG	Upside Supply Chain Flexibility			X								
PMG	Engineering Change Order Flexibility			X								
PMG	Design Reuse Flexibility			X								
APQC	Total Returns Management Cost						X					
Data Gap	Total Customer Chain Management Cost						X					
ALL	Days Sales Outstanding						X					
PMG APQC	Total Supply Chain Management Costs				X							
ALL	Inventory Days of Supply				X							
APQC PMG	Total Design Chain Management Cost					X						
APQC	Total Warranty Cost					X						
APQC PMG	New Product Revenue							X				
ALL	Cost of Goods Sold							X				
APQC PMG Hoovers	Sales, General, and Administrative Cost							X				
ALL	Cash-to-Cash Cycle Time							X				
PMG Hoovers	Asset Turns							X				
Hoovers	Return on Assets							X				
ALL	Gross Profit Margin								X			
ALL	Operating Margin								X			
Hoovers	Net Profit Margin								X			
Hoovers	Revenue Growth									X		
Hoovers	Gross Profit Growth									X		
Hoovers	Operating Margin Growth									X		

Assess and Prioritize Competitive Requirements

With respect to value chain competitive requirements, the team agreed that a broader framework was needed to assess overall business strategy. The coach suggested a modification of a Michael Porter concept,[3] which describes two basic strategies of competitive advantage: *low cost* or *differentiation*. These two strategies, when applied to a narrowly defined industry segment, create Porter's third

Figure 19-4. Sample benchmark data for select value chain metrics.

Process Model	Metric & Benchmark Source	Sample of Level One Value Chain Metrics	Value Chain Benchmark		
			Performance Versus Comparison Population		
			Parity 50th Percentile	Advantage 70th Percentile	Superior 90th Percentile
DCOR	APQC	New Product Development Cycle Time[1]	245 days	186 days	99 days
DCOR	APQC	Total R&D cost as a percentage of revenue (current reporting period)[1]	17.41%	10.00%	3.04%
DCOR	APQC	Total R&D cost as a percentage of revenue (three reporting periods ago)[1]	16.81%	7.99%	3.44%
DCOR	APQC	Design cycle time in days from start of design, build, and evaluate through completion of test market product/service for new product/service development projects[1]	720.0	437.4	334.5
DCOR	APQC	Total cost of the development cycle as a percentage of revenue[1]	13.00%	11.13%	4.13%
DCOR	APQC	Percentage of sales which is a result of products/services launched during the most recently completed 12 month reporting period[1]	16.50%	25.20%	50.00%
DCOR	PMG	Design Reuse Flexibility[2]	22%	37.15%	42.30%
DCOR	PMG	Total Design Chain Management Cost[2]	9.50%	8.49%	7.47%
DCOR	PMG	New Product Revenue[2]	22.50%	39.20%	55.90%
ALL	Hoovers	Sales, General, and Administrative Cost	19.45%	13.00%	9.06%
ALL	Hoovers	Revenue Growth	13.94%	18.99%	31.31%
ALL	Hoovers	Gross Profit Growth	18.01%	31.55%	39.66%
ALL	Hoovers	Operating Margin Growth	34.29%	63.55%	165.95%

© Copyright 2007 APQC. All Rights Reserved. Used with permission.

[1] APQC is reporting this data on the assumption that lower R&D costs, lower cycle time, lower product development costs, and higher sales due to recent product launches represent superior performance. APQC acknowledges that correlating these measures to various outcomes may support a different perspective. This is published with APQC's permission to present the perspective that best fits the needs of *Supply Chain Excellence*.

[2] Design Reuse Flexibility, Total Design Chain Management Cost (PLM Operating Cost), and New Product Revenue © Copyright 2003 The Performance Measurement Group, LLC, subsidiary of management consultants PRTM. All Rights Reserved. Used with permission.

generic strategy: *Focus*. Put another way, companies must answer two questions: "Will we focus on a broad industry or a narrowly defined segment?" and then, "Will we achieve competitive advantage through low cost or differentiation?" Porter describes companies that try to represent all strategies to all customers as being "stuck in the middle"—and they generally perform at or below parity in all dimensions.

The team also was enamored with the simple assembly and the large impact of the supply chain competitive requirements exercise.

The concept was easy to explain: A company must decide on a supply chain strategy to achieve superior and advantage positions in some metric categories, while maintaining at least parity in others.

So how can the concepts of Porter and SCOR be brought together? Figure 19-5 represents the team's best attempt to mock up an example using the durable products group. The left arrow represents performance in the "cost" strategy, and the right arrow represents performance in the "differentiation" strategy. Specifically, they related the left arrow with process measures and the right arrow with customer-facing measures. The base of the arrow is actual performance; the point of the arrow is target performance.

Arvid talked through one possible strategic scenario: By focusing on niche markets, the durable products group could adopt both cost *and* differentiation tactics to put itself into a better market position. The direction of the arrows suggests that durable products narrow its products and customer focus from "broad industry" to a narrow industry niche, and that it pursue superior cost performance within that niche, while customer-facing metrics operate at parity.

In value-chain metric terms, process measures need to move toward the 90th percentile, and the customer-facing measures need to move toward at least the 50th percentile. They all agreed this chart needed more work, but that the concepts made sense. They

Figure 19-5. Value Chain Competitive Requirements (superior, advantage, parity, below parity).

Competitive Performance	S	A	P	< P	P	A	S
Broad Industry	Low Cost			Stuck in the Middle		Differentiation	
Industry Segment	Focus: Low Cost					Focus: Differentiation	

recognized that if both arrows are in the shaded portion, action is required.

Perform Metric Defect Analysis

The team agreed that the disconnect analysis was critical to uncovering the issues related to performance. Although some templates would need to be created for the new metrics, the steps were identical to the supply chain project.

Develop a Project Portfolio

The team members agreed that this foundational supply chain deliverable would be necessary to help dissect the issues, build projects, and quantify the improvement. They thought the metrics and associated defect analysis would define the brainstorm categories and help the team associate "problems" with not just the supply chain but with the design and customer chains as well. The main conversation centered on determining the level of the process with which the team would associate the problems. All agreed that Level 3 was too detailed. All also agreed that the team needed to discern between Level 1 processes, i.e., Source vs. Research vs. Amend, etc. The main debate was whether to differentiate at Level 2. Did it help to identify problems at the level of make-to-order vs. make-to-stock vs. new product vs. refresh, etc? Their conclusion: Learn by doing.

Implementation Considerations

The team discussed four types of analytical tools that it thought were helpful in the *Supply Chain Excellence* implementation rollout and might also be useful in the value chain project implementation: (1) product-to-market map, (2) Level 2 process diagrams, (3) staple yourself interviews, and (4) TO BE Level 4 process diagrams with information system storyboards.

Product-to-Market Map

This analytical tool was the most difficult to adapt from the *Supply Chain Excellence* process. In the supply chain project, the geographic map was an easy concept to grasp. Although there are material movement aspects to value chains, the team discussed two other layers that needed to be considered as part of the analysis as well.

First, it would be necessary to understand sales by region, as the sales and marketing team views it. Figure 19-6 illustrates the three regions of U.S. sales for durable products. Layering the geographic map on top of the sales-by-region map was both intuitive and logical for the team.

The third layer was not as simple. In fact, a spreadsheet was a better tool than a picture. The concept the team was after was to understand the rate of growth in each sales region between new and existing products, and among new and existing customers. Figure

Figure 19-6. Durable product group's U.S. sales by region.

19-7 is a mock-up of the concept, which the team eventually labeled Value Chain Growth Analysis. The analysis attempts to calculate growth rates for revenue, gross margin, and unit volume for each cell in the matrix. With the use of predetermined criteria, a cell (product and customer) is graded positive (+), negative (−), or neutral (0). The results helped the team understand the issues behind growth. For example, Product Family B has growth issues across the board, whereas Product Family A has particular trouble building sales of existing products to new customers.

The benefit of this perspective is that the next set of "why" questions is not aimed just at supply. Marketing campaigns, pricing strategy, product quality, product life cycle management, sales incentives, and so forth are all in the mix of potential root causes and ultimate projects.

Figure 19-7. Durable product group's U.S. growth rate analysis.

Durable Products - U.S. Value Chain			Western US Sales Territory					
			New Customers			Existing Customers		
			Revenue	Gross Margin	Unit	Revenue	Gross Margin	Unit
North America Lines of Business	Product Family A	New Products	+	+	+	+	+	+
		Existing Products	-	-	-	+	+	+
	Product Family B	New Products	-	-	-	0	0	0
		Existing Products	-	-	-	-	-	-
	Product Family C	New Products	-	-	-	+	+	+
		Existing Products	-	-	-	-	-	+
	Product Family D	New Products	-	-	-	+	+	+
		Existing Products	+	+	+	-	-	-

Level 2 Process Diagrams

As in the supply chain project, the preparation required to create a Level 2 process diagram involved identifying the appropriate processes for each location. Figure 19-8 is a partial list of the choices for each location; one necessary adaptation is the small-letter designation in front of the Level 2 ID; "c" is CCOR, "d" is DCOR, and "s" is SCOR.

Figure 19-9 illustrates the team's work assembling a logical durable products flow. The dotted lines represent both information and product flow. As with any concept drawing, the team had a tough time differentiating the "should be" from "the AS IS." Arvid, David, and Brian also realized they would need to get signed up for DCOR and CCOR framework classes. They needed to affirm their intuitions about the difference between design classifications of "product refresh," "new product," and "new technology"—as well as between the customer classifications of sell to "intermediary," "grouped account," and "named account." For the mock-up, they used both *refreshed* and the traditional *new product* categories for design. For customer categories, they used *grouped account* (direct-to-consumer). Figure 19-10 is the first attempt at putting together a Level 2 process diagram relating the design chain (DCOR) for new products to the supply chain (SCOR) supporting the growing service business. The team decided that one of the necessary adaptations would be to create a set of primary and secondary connection rules among DCOR, CCOR, and SCOR Level 2 process elements.

Staple Yourself Interviews

The team decided that the steps in preparing and conducting the staple yourself interviews would be identical to that of the supply chain. The only necessary adaptation was to brainstorm major transactions for CCOR and DCOR. Here is the first draft list:

Figure 19-8. DCOR, CCOR, and SCOR Level 2 process categories.

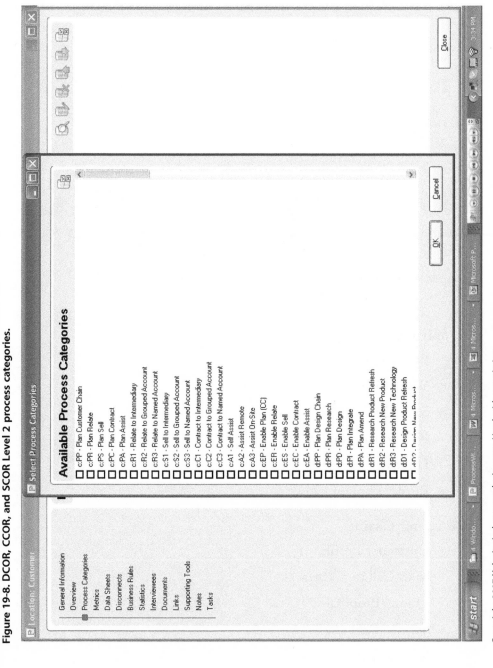

255

Figure 19-9. DCOR, CCOR, and SCOR Level 2 process categories by location.

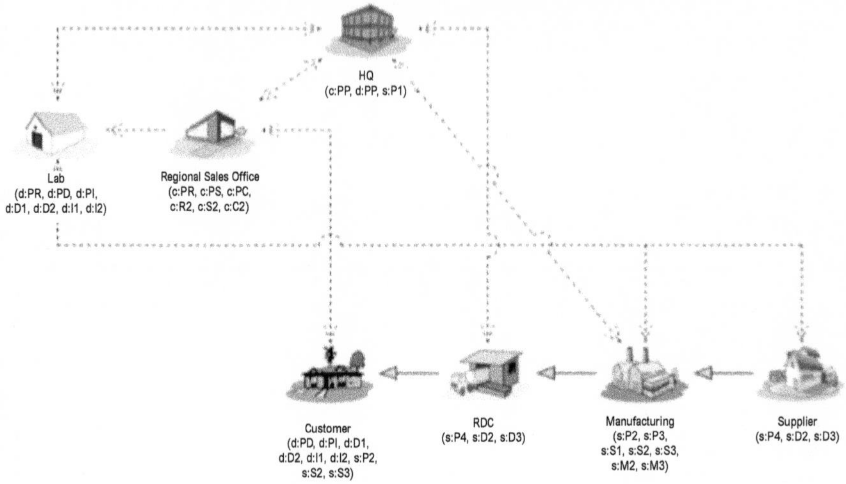

Supply Chain

- Purchase Order
- Work Order
- Sales Order
- Return Authorization
- Forecast
- Replenishment Order

Customer Chain

- Customer Profile
- Sales Call to Contract
- Quote/Proposal
- Service Request
- Sales $ Forecast
- Quota

Figure 19-10. Durable products group value chain Level 2 process diagram first draft.

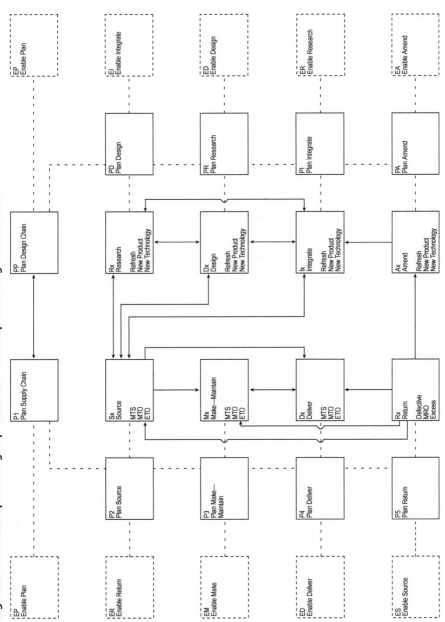

Design Chain

- Engineering Change Request
- Product Design Specification
- Manufacturing Qualification "Certificate"
- New Product Introduction Plan

TO BE Level 4 Process Diagrams with Information System Storyboards

Like a broken record, the team again found the steps to build Level 4 processes and educate team members through the information system storyboards were a direct application to value chain. No additional adaptations were deemed necessary.

Conclusion

The clock was pointing to 5:30 p.m., and the foursome sat around the conference table, exhausted. They were already a half-hour late leaving for the party that the supply chain design team was holding, but they had that satisfied, head-spinning feeling that a well-prepared college student gets at the end of final exams. Nobody seemed quite ready to move.

Surrounding them were three 12-foot whiteboards full of diagrams, notes, and numbers—each with a great big "SAVE" scribbled in the corner. In one day, they had outlined how to stretch the *Supply Chain Excellence* approach to cover the value chain requirements in Arvid's very different business. They were confident it would work—and just realistic enough to know that the method would have to be adjusted as they progressed.

David and Brian felt as though they'd just gotten two process improvements for the price of one. Arvid felt that great sense of being unburdened from the quiet troubles that had been building within his business.

"When can we get started?" Arvid asked.

Brian smiled and replied, "Can we wait until after the party?"

Notes

1. Michael Porter, *Competitive Advantage: Creating and Sustaining Superior Performance* (New York: The Free Press; 1985); W. Edwards Deming, *Out of the Crisis* (Cambridge, MA: Massachusetts Institute of Technology, Center for Advanced Engineering Study; 1986).

2. Balanced Scorecard Institute, Cary, NC, and Rockville, MD; www.balancedscorecard.org.

3. Michael Porter, *Competitive Advantage: Creating and Sustaining Superior Performance* (New York: The Free Press, 1998).

Fowlers Inc. *Supply Chain Excellence* Project Charter

Organizational Summary

Executive Sponsor:	Brian Dowell, COO
Business Sponsor:	Jovan Kojcic, President, Technology Products Group
Department:	Technology Products Group
Project Manager:	David Able, VP Operations—Technology Products
Start Date:	March 11, 2011, with executive GO Decision
Approval Date:	March 11, 2011
Revision Date:	April 18, 2011

I. Introduction

Purpose of the Project Charter

The project charter is created during the initiation phase of a project to ensure that a complete understanding of the project scope and objectives is established. The document allows confirmation of assumptions and expectations with the executive team; project sponsors; stakeholders; project managers; program manager; and project, validation, and resource team members. During the course of the project, change requests may be generated and approved that vary the scope, schedule, or cost of the project. These changes should be documented through the change management process and updates reflected through revisions of the project charter.

Project Charter Contents

The project charter documents the background and business need for the project as well as expectations for the project moving forward. The project overview provides the project scope, business and project objectives, and any assumptions. The project approach outlines the methodology to be used in completing the project along with the schedule, milestones, deliverables, and any project dependencies. A budget for the project is presented, and the organization of the project team is discussed. Project expectations, and the ways in which project success will be measured, are discussed. A plan for communication throughout the project also is presented.

Maintenance of the Project Charter

After initial approval by the project sponsor, the project charter is updated with approved change requests. Each update is noted with a revision date on the cover page.

II. Project Overview

Scope

Definition Matrix

Fowlers North America	Customer/Market Channels						
	Retail Markets	Distributor Markets	Direct-to-Consumer Markets	OEM and Key Accounts	Government	Home Delivery	International
Food Products	X	X			X		
Technology Products	X	X	Developing	X	X		X
Durable Products			X			X	X

In Scope

1. Technology products group including retail, distributor, OEM and key accounts, government, and international markets.

2. Business unit supply chain functions including materials planning, forecasting, purchasing, manufacturing, logistics, customer service, financial control; corporate functions including IT, sales, marketing, and finance.

3. SCOR metrics: perfect order fulfillment, order fulfillment cycle time, upside supply chain flexibility, supply chain management cost, cost of goods, and inventory days of supply.

4. SCOR processes: PLAN, SOURCE, MAKE, DELIVER, and RETURN; ENABLE as necessary.

5. SAP R/3® modules: Materials Management (MM), Production Planning (PP), and Sales and Distribution (SD).

6. All physical locations for the technology products group supply chains, including six regional distribution centers (two
   each in North America, Asia, and Europe); four manufacturing plants (United States, Netherlands, China, and India); raw
   material, component and packaging suppliers; and contract
   manufacturers.

Out of Scope

- The developing technology products direct-to-consumer
  market.
- Configuration changes to SAP Financial Accounting (FI),
  Controlling (CO), and Fixed Asset Management (AM).
- Food products and durable products groups.

Business Objectives

- Reduce inventory days of supply by 15 percent.
- Achieve parity level delivery performance.
- Add 10 percent of incremental operating margin.
- Standardize on a global supply chain operational blueprint.
- Improve utilization of SAP functionality.

Project Objectives

- Develop a global scorecard that is consistent worldwide and
  analytically repeatable on a frequent interval.
- Prioritize supply chain performance targets by region by
  market.
- Develop and prioritize a global supply chain project improvement portfolio that will help the technology products group
  rank comparably as one of the top 25 supply chains.

- Expose all of our global leaders to the process either as providing input, participating directly, and/or reviewing output.

- Develop internal Fowlers competence in implementing SCOR projects in the future.

III. Project Approach

Methodology

SCOR (Supply Chain Operations Reference) model Version 10.0 will be the basis for this project. The major work tasks will be organized using the discipline highlighted in the *Supply Chain Excellence* book and is summarized by the activities in Phase 0: Build Organizational Support; Phase 1: Define Project Scope; Phase 2: Analyze Performance; Phase 3: Develop Project Portfolio; and Phase 4: Implement Projects. *Supply Chain Excellence* uniquely combines the concepts of Business Process Engineering—Management, Project Management, and SCOR.

Project Schedule

Schedule for Global and Small Business Applications	Deliverable	Classroom Dates
Phase 0 Build Organizational Support	**February 1 to May 1, 2011**	
	Supply Chain Excellence Overview with wide audience	February 7, 2011
	SCOR Framework Workshop	Opportunity
	SCOR Implementation Workshop	Opportunity
	Organizational Briefings	As Needed
	Executive Briefing—GO/NO GO	March 11, 2011
Phase 1 Define Project Scope	**May 1 to July 1, 2011**	
	Business Context Summary	Remote Web-Based Meetings

	Supply Chain Definition Matrix (with data)	Meetings
	Project Charter	April 18
Phase 2 Analyze Performance	Kickoff	April 25
	Metric Definitions and Data Collection Plan	May 2 May 9
	Defect Data Collection Plan	May 16
	Defect Analysis	May 23
	Industry Comparison	May 30
	Competitive Requirements	June 6
	Benchmark Data	
	Preliminary Scorecard	
	Scorecard Gap Analysis	
	IDEALLY DEDICATED ON-SITE Staple Yourself to an Order Interviews	On-Site
	IDEALLY DEDICATED ON-SITE AS IS Process Diagram	June 13 to 17, 2011
Phase 3 Develop Project Portfolio	**July 11 to August 1, 2011**	
	AS IS Process Diagram	On-Site
	Defect Analysis Part 2	
	Brainstorm Event and Documentation	
	Preliminary Project Portfolio	
	Opportunity Analysis	July 11 to 15, 2011
	Assemble and Approve Implementation Project Charters	
	Prioritize Implementation Projects	
Phase 4 Implement Projects	**August 1, 2011, to July 31, 2012**	
	Identify and Approve Project Resource Plan	Combination On-
	Establish Project Schedule, Including Informal Kickoff Date	Site and Remote Management
	Review Project Charter, Background, and Expectations with Project Team	August 1, 2011, to July 31, 2012

Develop Baseline for Metrics Selected as In-Scope
Conduct AS IS Level 3 and 4 Process Gap Analysis
Develop Action Plans to Close "Quick Hit" Gaps
Assemble TO BE Level 3 and 4 Process Based on Leading Practice
Develop and Approve Solution-Design Storyboard
Build and Test Solution
Pilot and Verify Solution
Roll Out Solution to Project Scope and Evaluate Metric Impact
Define Process Control Measures
Scale Implementation to Targeted Supply Chains in the Definition Matrix

Steering Team Meetings

February 7   Introductory Session

March 11   GO/NO GO

May 16   Scorecard Review

June 17   Brainstorm Event Review

July 15   Preliminary Project Portfolio Review

August 1   Implementation Kickoff

Risks and Dependencies

♦ Active sponsorship

♦ A Fowlers financial analyst will be available for Phase 2: Analyze Performance

♦ Availability of Fowlers worldwide raw historical data to collect and calculate actual performance and associated defects

- Consistent availability of steering committee and design team members
- Desire and/or capability to accept the SAP "way of doing things"

Project Organization

Sponsors

Brian Dowell

Jovan Kojcic

Steering Team

Tadeo Morillo

Amanda Messenger

Timothy Ulrich

Girish Naagesh

Jon Park

VP Sales and Marketing—Technology Products Group

Finance Controller—Technology Products Group

Project Leader

David Able

Project Team

Director Applications

Director Customer Service

Director Logistics

Director of Purchasing

Plant Managers from the smallest two technology products group plants

Materials Managers from the largest two technology products group plants

Demand Manager Technology Products Group

Logistics Manager Technology Products Group

Supply Manager Technology Products Group

Finance Control Technology Products Group

Extended Team

SAP super users for MM, PP, and SD

Schedulers from each plant

Buyers from each plant

Production managers from each plant

Warehouse managers from each distribution center

Director Accounts Receivable

Director Accounts Payable

Director Supply Chain

Director Manufacturing

Roles and Responsibilities

Project Sponsor

+ Set strategic mission, vision, and direction as context for the project.

+ Review team progress against deliverables.

+ Provide resource support to project leader and design team.

+ Resolve escalated issues.

+ Approve budget and schedule.

+ Provide final approval for all changes within defined scope.

+ Attend steering team review meetings.

Steering Team

- ♦ Review and approve design team recommended changes.

- ♦ Ensure organizational and functional commitment.

- ♦ Resolve cross-functional issues.

- ♦ Provide resources to project team as needed.

- ♦ Lead change management cross-functionally.

- ♦ Initiate and champion projects.

- ♦ Attend steering team reviews.

Project Manager

- ♦ Recruit project team.

- ♦ Serve as liaison between project team and sponsors.

- ♦ Measure team progress against deliverables.

- ♦ Manage all external resources assigned to the project to contractual commitment.

- ♦ Manage all aspects of the project in a manner consistent with company business requirements, policies, project management methodology, and budget procedures.

- ♦ Define and plan the project. Responsible for establishing quality standards and acceptance criteria in the statement of work.

- ♦ Escalate the resolution of critical issues.

- ♦ Obtain necessary approvals.

Design Team

- ♦ Commit to class sessions and other blocks of time as required.

- ♦ Complete any assigned work (project deliverables) on time.

- ♦ Provide subject matter expertise as needed.

- ♦ Develop and validate deliverables as needed.

- Define, communicate, and facilitate necessary changes to policies and standards.

- Present results to the steering team.

- Identify extended team members.

Extended Team

- Expected to be available by appointment with advance notice.

- Participate in team meetings, as specified.

- Contribute to all activities of the design team as requested.

Coach

- Provide formal knowledge transfer to the project team regarding *Supply Chain Excellence*, SCOR, etc.

- Provide formal and informal direct knowledge transfer to project leader of all aspects of *Supply Chain Excellence*, project leadership, tools and techniques, and change management.

- Facilitate classroom sessions.

- Provide critique to deliverables.

- Modify instructional method as necessary.

- Ensure curriculum integrity.

Benefits and Measures of Success

Stakeholder Expectations

In addition to the project and business objectives, the following expectations are a summary of stakeholder interviews:

- Improve corporate inventory turns.

- Facilitate *global*, cross-functional process changes, ownership.

- Define a path to superior delivery.

- Increase purchased finished goods (merchandise) turns from 5 to 10.

- Improve transaction process with suppliers.

- Integrate metrics for each area of the supply chain.

- Clearly identify supply chain performance gaps.

- Drive 2011 and 2012 after-tax profit performance.

- Expand supply chain knowledge of the team.

- Develop a repeatable process for future SCOR initiatives in other business units in Fowlers.

- Use SAP functionality more effectively.

Benchmark Sources

- SCORmark™

- Performance Measurement Group

- Hoovers

- Manufacturing Performance Institute

- Warehouse Education Research Center

Benefit Analysis

TBD by July 15. In general, the average *Supply Chain Excellence* portfolio achieves a 3 percent operating income improvement with benefits falling into four areas: revenue growth, improved cash-to-cash, cost reduction, and productivity improvement.

Project Communication

A formal communication plan will be established for each group of stakeholders in this project including the steering team, project manager, design team, extended team and Fowlers at large.

Index